HOLLYWOOD BEDLAM

S0-BRV-704

HOLLYWOOD BEDLAM

CLASSIC SCREWBALL COMEDIES

by WILLIAM K. EVERSON

A CITADEL PRESS BOOK

Published by Carol Publishing Group

ACKNOWLEDGMENTS

I am particularly grateful to Howard and Ronald Mandelbaum of *Photofest* for their help in supplying many of the rarer stills in this volume. Grateful thanks are also extended to Alex Gordon, Tom Toth and Douglas Whitney for helping to fill in gaps.

Copyright © 1994 by William K. Everson

All rights reserved. No part of this book may be reproduced in any form, except by a newspaper or magazine reviewer who wishes to quote brief passages in connection with a review.

A Citadel Press Book
Published by Carol Publishing Group
Citadel Press is a registered trademark of Carol Communications, Inc.
Editorial Offices: 600 Madison Avenue, New York, N.Y. 10022
Sales and Distribution Offices: 120 Enterprise Avenue, Secaucus, N.J. 07094
In Canada: Canadian Manda Group, P.O. Box 920, Station U, Toronto, Ontario M8Z 5P9
Queries regarding rights and permissions should be addressed to Carol Publishing Group, 600 Madison Avenue, New York, N.Y. 10022
Carol Publishing Group books are available at special discounts for bulk purchases, sales promotions, fund-raising, or educational purposes. Special editions can be created to specifications. For details, contact Special Sales Department, Carol Publishing Group, 120 Enterprise Avenue, Secaucus, N.J. 07094

Designed by A. Christopher Simon

Manufactured in the United States of America

10 9 8 7 6 5 4 3 2 1

LIBRARY OF CONGRESS CATALOGING-IN-PUBLICATION DATA

Everson, William K.
    Hollywood bedlam : classic screwball comedies
by William K. Everson.
        p.   cm.
    "A Citadel Press book."
    ISBN 0-8065-1534-1
    1. Screwball comedy films—United States—History and criticism.
I. Title.
PN1995.9.C55E9   1994
791.43′617—dc20   94-19231
                                                            CIP

To my favorite wife,

KAREN

*With gratitude and the realization
that I have been a little but not
enough like Eugene Pallette*

CONTENTS

HOLLYWOOD BEDLAM

ONE

A DEFINITION AND A SURVEY

THE LADY EVE (1941)   Barbara Stanwyck has just tripped Henry Fonda, claiming it's *his* fault, the first of many Fonda pratfalls in the classic Preston Sturges comedy. Sturges regular Alan Bridge, as the waiter, lends a helping hand.

HIS MAJESTY THE AMERICAN (1919)   Douglas Fairbanks Sr. and Frank Campeau.

Screwball comedy, next to the great sight-gag classics of the twenties, is one of America's richest filmic heritages. Much as we may still enjoy it though for its overall "class" and elegance (it reached its peak, after all, at a time when Hollywood itself had a technical zenith), for the pleasure of watching Cary Grant, Carole Lombard, William Powell, and other sophisticates at *their* peak, and on a more academic level for the often fascinating study of such directors as Howard Hawks, William Wellman, and Gregory LaCava, the genre often doesn't seem as funny as it's supposed to be.

As a filmmaking school (it is not even technically a *genre*) film noir belonged primarily to the forties and early fifties, but it had its roots elsewhere, both domestically and internationally. Furthermore, it was a distorted, stylized reflection of its period, so much larger than life that, like the classic horror films of the early thirties, it had no "reality" to date. The

best of the film noirs still work superbly well, as well as having the added bonus of star personas and studio production values of a quality that we will never see again on a mass basis. Screwball comedy certainly benefits from these qualities, too; but unfortunately its effectiveness does depend, if not on reality, then on audience awareness of the realities it was reflecting, distorting, bypassing, or romanticizing.

Screwball comedy has never been clearly defined, least of all by the directors who specialized in it. Frank Capra frequently alluded to his *It Happened One Night* (1934) as being the first screwball comedy (he was never averse to making unsupported claims!), though it is far from being the first nor is it even genuinely or definitively screwball, being far too gentle even though it does contain many unquestionably screwball elements. Yet ironically, over time, certainly extending into the fifties, there were more remakes, rip-offs, and imitations of that film than of any other comedy, screwball or otherwise (*My Man Godfrey* [1936] a close second), and many of those copies *were* bona fide screwball.

Attempts by critics and historians to compile definitive lists of screwball comedy films do not necessarily fail, but invariably they contradict one another, leaving out titles that (arguably) should be in, and vice versa. Screwball comedy overlaps (primarily) into farce, but also into slapstick, sophisticated comedies of manners, and satire. No matter how expert the playing or how witty the writing, the screwball comedy is solidly locked into its era, and this is a major reason for its tendency to become dated. Audiences that saw the films on their original release invariably find them disappointing on a contemporary reviewing, while those encountering them for the first time often wonder what all the shouting was about. Hecht and MacArthur's four-times-filmed *The Front Page* provides a perfect example of the tenuous dividing lines between differing comedy styles all applied to the same basic script.

The first version, in 1931, slightly watered-down from the dynamic original Hecht-MacArthur play despite being a pre–Production Code film, and also coming well before a screwball comedy tradition had been established, lacked two basic qualifying ingredients. First, almost totally absent was a battle-of-the-sexes element, its plot revolving around the efforts of newspaper editor Walter Burns (Adolphe Menjou) to prevent ace reporter Hildy Johnson (Pat O'Brien) from resigning to marry his out-of-town sweetheart, played by Mary Brian. Second, and this is hardly a criticism, it took itself seriously as a film. If it was exposing yellow journalism and political corruption, it did so with energy and a bitter, hard-edged fervor, using humor and staccato wisecracking dialogue as a weapon, but not as an end in itself. Moreover, if it was rebelling against anything (a key element of traditional screwball, which will be breached later) it was a subliminal revolt against the static, ponderous, dialogue-laden theatricality of so many early talkies to that date. *The Front Page* was clearly influenced by Soviet technique in its editing (a technique that would not be familiar to or recognized by the bulk of audiences that saw *The Front Page*), creating remarkable rhythms and pacing in its combination of cuts and camera mobility. *Five Star Final,* another stage-to-screen newspaper melodrama of the same year, and certainly no contender for screwball comedy recognition, achieved a similar if more measured rhythm through its editing and low-angled compositions, but mainly through the brilliant performance of Edward G. Robinson, whose crescendo-building speeches toward the end of the film matched Menjou's and O'Brien's in their combination of speed and control.

With the same basic story line but one major change of sexual identity—the resigning Hildy Johnson was now played by Rosalind Russell, who had earlier been married to Cary Grant's Walter Burns—the first remake, *His Girl Friday* (1939) became one of the classics of its genre. Apart from the battle-of-the-sexes angle added by the recasting of the three leads (appropriately and at Columbia not surprisingly, Ralph Bellamy took over the Mary Brian role), the element of rebellion was far more prevalent. In screwball comedy this took many forms, but basically it was a thumbing of the nose at the polite and unreal conventions laid down by the Production Code, a key aspect of all screwball comedy that will be discussed at greater length later. One of the subthemes, or perhaps running gag might be a more appropriate description, of the original play and film of *The Front Page* was the political opportunism of blaming Communism and Red infiltration for every imaginable ill. During the thirties and early forties, Hollywood found Communism almost as useful a mass target and scapegoat in screwball comedies (such as *Red Salute* [1935] and *Public Deb No. 1* [1940]) as the American Indian was in westerns. In many cases of course, the anti-Communist stance was justified, but usually Hollywood's treatment was naive and ill-informed. *His Girl Friday* in a sense hit back at the irresponsibility of these films by reemphasizing the dialogue revolving around the Red scare—and coincidentally, made the film more

MY MAN GODFREY (1936)   Alice Brady asks Mischa Auer to do his ape impersonation.

14

topical and sardonically amusing during its re-issues during the McCarthy period.

The two subsequent versions of *The Front Page* were both disappointments, and neither qualify as screwball comedies. Despite Billy Wilder as director and a good costarring team in Jack Lemmon and Walter Matthau, the 1974 remake, which reverted to the original title, also reverted to the original characterizations, thus eliminating the all-important battle of the sexes. Too, the screen was now becoming more and more permissive: instead of rebelling against and satirizing Production Code rigidity, the film *exploited* its new freedom, resulting in too many tasteless and blatant homosexual gags, which in the original play and to a certain extent in the first film were limited to being gags of punctuation. The final (to date) remake, *Switching Channels* (1980), had interesting potential at first: it not only restored the sexual triangle of *His Girl Friday*, but also updated the venue to a television news station, burdened by even greater time pressure (and the need to keep news current, fast, and visual) than a newspaper. But somehow nothing seemed to work: Kathleen Turner, though her work lacked the zest of earlier performances, was so efficient and so clearly in her element as Hildy Johnson that there was obviously no question of her ultimate resignation. And Burt Reynolds (as her former husband/news editor) and Christopher Reeve (a much rewritten and now more attractive role initially to have been played by Michael Caine) were both so lacking in dynamic qualities (Reynolds's attempt to throw away lines, à la Cary Grant, failed totally) and both so undeserving of such a heroine, that one almost hoped that a little further rewriting would see her striking off solo at the end, leaving them both flat.

The film also tried rather pointlessly to inject "meaningful" social comment here and there—the man killed by the unfortunate murderer has now become a drug dealer—yet goes further over the top (especially in the person of Ned Beatty) in its political caricatures than any previous version. And far from least, all the wonderful supporting cameos from the first two versions—Gustav von Seyffertitz and then Edwin Maxwell as the alienists, Billy Gilbert as the man from the governor's office, the dieting reporter, his colleague who constantly shifts his chair to get a better view of the female legs passing in the street, and so many others—have been eliminated entirely. If the characters remain at all, they are purely functional, to deliver messages or information to keep the narrative in motion. Even in *His Girl Friday*, where the frenetic dialogue exchanges between Grant and Russell *could* have handled the comic content, one had hilarious scenes and lines generously handed out to Roscoe Karns, Gene Lockhart, Porter Hall, Clarence Kolb (immense as a blustering politician), Frank Jenks, Ernest Truex, Abner Biberman, Billy Gilbert, Frank Orth, and Cliff Edwards. Rather remarkably, considering the shifting approaches, all four versions maintained fairly consistent running times: the first was 103 minutes, and the last two 105 minutes. *His Girl Friday*, the funniest of the four and the only genuine screwball entry among them, was the shortest at a still substantial 93 minutes, and it's amazing that it ran *that* long considering its ultra-rapid-fire and overlapping dialogue, and the frenetically accelerated pace at which director Howard Hawks staged it all.

The screwball comedies emerged from essentially two launching pads: the Depression, and more especially Hollywood's self-censoring Production Code imposed at the end of 1933. Although 1934 was somewhat of a buffer year between the freewheeling pre-Code years and the inflexible restrictions that would soon be enforced, allowing for compromise while the shifting of gears took place, it already evidenced a move toward stifling respectability. Some directors, at least in comedic terms, were virtually stopped dead in their tracks. Raoul Walsh could never make "polite" conventional comedy, and the robustly ribald and even vulgar humor of such last-ditch pre-Code films as *The Bowery* and *Sailor's Luck* became as much a relic of the past as an unrestrained Mae West. Indeed, Walsh and Mae collaborated in 1936 on *Klondike Annie*. Not only were the restraints placed upon them obvious even then, making it her weakest film to date, but also adding

EVERY DAY'S A HOLIDAY
(1937) Fritz Krausmeyer
(Herman Bing) has just
bought the Brooklyn
Bridge from Peaches
O'Day (Mae West).

insult to injury, when it was reissued at the end of the forties, the then even more straitlaced Production Code insisted on cutting its one really strong scene! Apart from a brace of films Walsh made in England, his output in the balance of the thirties bore none of his signature irreverence and vigor, and only when certain aspects of the Code were unofficially relaxed in 1939, simultaneous with his joining Warner Bros., did he hit his former stride again.

Only sly and sophisticated Ernst Lubitsch was really able to cope with the Code, his "compromises" actually representing very real triumphs. Basically his *Desire* (1936) was virtually as amoral as his *Trouble in Paradise* (1932), but he got around it with a neat little fade-out that not only pacified the censors, but also at the same time made their nouveau puritanism look ridiculous. And in *Bluebeard's Eighth Wife* (1938)—an erotic comedy about would-be seduction and an unconsummated marriage— he legitimized the goings-on by having the two protagonists married fairly early in the proceedings.

The majority of the screwball comedies of its peak period hit back at the conventions and sexual restraints of the polite new comedies and portrayed individuals—usually women— challenging and rising above those conventions, sometimes by being tougher and more efficient than their male counterparts (Rosalind Russell vis-à-vis Cary Grant in *His Girl Friday*) or even without a sense of direct male competition. In *Theodora Goes Wild* (1936), Irene Dunne is an apparently respectable and prim small-town girl who shocks everybody by writing a sexy novel (the actual contents of which are never disclosed). In its day, *Theodora Goes Wild* seemed daring and audacious itself, its sharp bite tangy and welcome. Today, juxtaposed with contemporary and ultra-explicit comedies like *10* (1979), *S.O.B.* (1981), *Victor/ Victoria* (1982), and *Ghosts Can't Do It* (1990), even the more risqué of the old screwball com-

16

BLUEBEARD'S EIGHTH WIFE (1938) Millionaire Gary Cooper and male secretary David Niven discuss an antique French bathtub.

edies seem decorous in the extreme.

Since the Code comedies couldn't admit to the existence of sex, particularly among unmarried couples, exaggerated comic violence frequently took its place—as in *Nothing Sacred* (1937) wherein Fredric March slaps, buffets, and kicks Carole Lombard before knocking her out cold. In 1937, the violence (to say nothing of the constant irreverence toward practically everything in the rest of the film) was startling. But in *Death Becomes Her* (1992)—in different ways, both it and *Nothing Sacred* are comedies about death—its special-effects-enhanced violence renders the earlier film quite harmless in that respect, though leaving its reputation as a classic among screwball black comedies untarnished.

Vintage screwball comedies such as *Nothing Sacred* obviously work better if one has a fairly intimate knowledge of the period in which they were made, and this is one of the problems of film study today. On a casual, tele-vision-watching level, a surprising number of viewers simply refuse to watch anything in black and white, on the theory that anything *that* old can't be any good. But even at the university level, where audiences are naturally younger, there are problems. Happily, and thanks mainly to home video, much more is available today than ever before, and because one sees so many films from all periods juxta-posed, one tends to judge each film's success by the same yardstick. If it's a horror film, does it frighten? If it's a comedy, how much laughter does it produce? Such an approach isn't necessarily wrong, but it's unfair to judge any film by standards prevailing fifty years after it was made. One should at least *try* to see them through eyes refocusing on the past, its morals, mores, speech patterns, racial attitudes, and so forth. How many films of the late twenties and early thirties would be misunderstood without a knowledge of Prohibition and its results?

Certain elements are clearly crucial. Next to

17

HIS GIRL FRIDAY (1939)   Ralph Bellamy (raincoat and umbrella stressing his cautious nature) is mocked by
Cary Grant while Rosalind Russell sees through his scheme to wreck their announced marriage.

DEATH BECOMES HER (1992)   Black comedy ideas dwarfed by special effects; Bruce Willis and
Meryl Streep.

the literal and physical battle of the sexes, perhaps the most common denominator was disguise and masquerade—rich posing as poor, poor as rich, as the opposite sex, or on rare (and usually not too successful) occasions, adults as children. It's interesting that the words *bride* and *wedding* crop up with regularity in the titles of screwball comedies, just as the words *night, dark, fear,* and *city* dominated film noir titles. Screwball protagonists were often (though predictably only temporarily) divorced, and their lack of innocence coupled with frustration frequently led to both physical and mental mauling.

Screwball comedy, as with film noir, developed its own stock company of players: Claudette Colbert, Carole Lombard, Fredric March, Cary Grant, John Barrymore, and Irene Dunne, supported by such useful and instantly recognizable "types" as Eugene Pallette, Alice Brady, Mischa Auer, Clarence Kolb, Jean Dixon, and William Demarest. They were guided by directors (William Wellman, Howard Hawks, Mitchell Leisen, Gregory LaCava, Leo McCarey), writers (Norman Krasna, Preston Sturges, Joseph Mankiewicz, all of whom graduated into directing as well, and Eric Hatch), and even cameramen who specialized in a glossy yet brittle style, most notably Ted Tetzlaff, he, too, becoming a director in the same genre. This unofficial "stock company," spread over a great many years and varying fashions in comedy, did not have the same unity or near exclusivity as its noir parallel; Irene Dunne for example made but a handful of screwball comedies, as opposed to Claire Trevor, who was a noir icon from *Dead End* (1937) for almost thirty years, playing killers, victims, and femmes fatales with versatile impunity; in quantity, Wellman's screwball comedies couldn't match the noir output of Siodmak, Lang, or Anthony Mann; and cinematographer Tetzlaff certainly never had the chance to specialize as Elwood Bredell or John Seitz did in the noirs of the forties. Nor did any film-music composer carve out a comedic niche for himself as Miklos Rozsa was to do with film noir. Nevertheless, the best of the screwballs were made by a hard core of directors, writers, and players. A relative outsider

could invade film noir territory and often create a classic—as Jacques Tourneur did with *Out of the Past,* working with players and technicians already familiar with the conventions and stylistics of the school. Screwball comedy wasn't so easy a matter for the journeyman director to master: compare Carole Lombard's *20th Century* (Hawks), *My Man Godfrey* (LaCava), and *Nothing Sacred* (Wellman) with two films of almost equal potential that were decidedly not realized by their directors: *The Gay Bride* (Jack Conway) and *True Confession* (Wesley Ruggles).

While screwball comedy does basically owe its existence to the meeting of the Depression and the Production Code—a meeting that soon became a mating—in the early thirties, it still has some roots in the silent period. Although these (and other) silents will be discussed more fully later, one should at least mention a small handful in passing. *Sunshine Dad* (1916), a vehicle for stage performer De Wolf Hopper—slapstick, lions at large in a modern Hollywood hotel, and a murderous secret society—was a curious forerunner of the Beatles' *Help.* It even, in a perhaps far-fetched sense, contained the seeds of rebellion against conformity that are so present in the comedies of the Production Code period. In this case the conformity was the belief that fast visual and slapstick comedy belonged only in the two-reel format then being plied so successfully by Chaplin and Lloyd as performers, and Roach and Sennett as producers.

When feature comedies of five reels and more were filmed, they were supposed to be restrained and "polite" in the *Saturday Evening Post* tradition, more concerned with plot, characterization, and situations than sight gags. Quite a few of them were made, usually with noncomedy stars like Bryant Washburn. Most of them have been lost, and the few that have survived are not impressive—or very funny. Several of the modern pre-1920 Douglas Fairbanks comedies, and especially *When the Clouds Roll By* and *Down to Earth,* certainly qualify as screwball material, and from the twenties on, as the comedy boundaries open up, many more films should be considered, including several Constance Talmadge vehicles. *Open All Night* (1924) is a surprisingly modern comedy

BACHELOR MOTHER (1939) "I'd recognize my grandson anywhere!" Charles Coburn tells foster mother Ginger Rogers and innocently involved son David Niven.

about wife-swapping, and *The Cruise of the Jasper B* (1926)—made by one of the best Laurel and Hardy directors, James Horne—is a screwball comedy in every sense of the word, its climactic device being so similar to that in the talkie *Duck Soup* that one must assume that the Marx Brothers as well as director Leo McCarey had seen it.

However, the conditions were just not *there* for fostering a growth of screwball comedy in the silent period. Pre-1920, near-Victorian conditions prevailed in terms of movie morality and plot. For the most part, those conditions were approved of by the moviegoing public. And the movies, a new art and entertainment form, was having a tough enough time gaining respectability as it was. Nobody felt like rocking the boat by bucking what was not yet called "the establishment." In any case, there was no real need. With stars like Mary Pickford, Chaplin, William S. Hart, and Fairbanks at peak popularity, and directors like Griffith, Tourneur, Walsh, and DeMille constantly experimenting with new techniques and new styles of storytelling, there was none of the feeling of

FIRST LOVE (1939) Cinderella meets her Prince Charming at the ball; Deanna Durbin and Robert Stack.

PUBLIC DEB NO. 1 (1940)
Waiter George Murphy
meets madcap heiress
Brenda Joyce
accompanied by the
ubiquitous Ralph Bellamy,
who must sense that his
prospects as a bridegroom
are already doomed!

stagnation and restraint that hung over Hollywood in the Production Code years.

If there was rebellion in the twenties, it was
more artificial. The flaming-youth romances
and comedies of Clara Bow and Colleen
Moore promised a revolt against conformity,
but actually most of them merely confirmed
the advisability of maintaining the status quo.
There was Prohibition of course, but everybody rebelled against that anyway, thus soften-
ing the edge of some of the early W. C. Fields
films.

A lot of surrealism and insanity was already
in the sight-gag comedies, done with sophistication by Hal Roach (especially in the two-reel
comedies of Charley Chase directed by Leo
McCarey) and with imagination and vigor if
not much subtlety in the Mack Sennett two-
reelers. Yet, despite its name, screwball comedy
used insanity for punctuation rather than as a
driving comedic force. Having its roots in reality, it needed the subtlety of sound and the
ability to *underplay* dialogue for maximum effectiveness. (It's difficult, though not impossible, to underplay an intertitle.) Generally

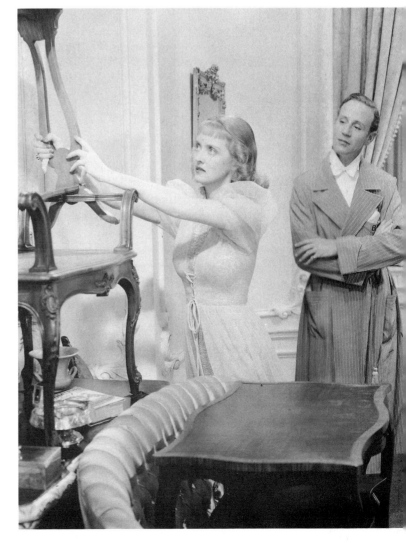

IT'S LOVE I'M AFTER (1937)   Bette Davis barricades herself in her
room, unaware that Leslie Howard has slipped in by another
door.

speaking, the screwball comedy is the most honest and the closest to a universal truth: hence *20th Century* and *His Girl Friday* are as good as they ever were.

Screwball comedies were not so much rebelling against the Production Code as they were attacking—and ridiculing—the dull, lifeless respectability that the Code insisted on for family viewing. Without a knowledge of the blunted, routine comedies of the period, the bite of screwball is often not very sharp. The desire to shock and create a reaction is at the heart of many films like *Theodora Goes Wild*.

The omnipresence of the Depression is also a major factor. Earlier, social films dealt realistically with the Depression, or, via films like Borzage's *Man's Castle* (1933), in a poetic/philosophic and comforting way reminiscent of D. W. Griffith, implying that so long as love was present, other problems would fade away or solve themselves—or at least become bearable. Another 1933 film, *Three-Cornered Moon,* was unique in being realistic about unemployment and a future without much hope, while at the same time being a bona fide "crazy family" screwball comedy.

When the Depression didn't go away, Hollywood made reassuring fun of it. Most of the Depression's screwball comedies are about *rich* people and the problems that money brings. (Although most of the poor heroines wound up with rich husbands, not knowing of course that the men were millionaires!)

The backgrounds of society elegance became a kind of gymnasium for physical comedy and comic punishment: Carole Lombard being dunked into a cold shower to wake her up and cure a hangover, or Mischa Auer hopping over furniture as he masquerades as an ape, both examples from *My Man Godfrey*, are typical. An unofficial companion piece to *My Man Godfrey,* Henry King's *One More Spring* (1935) is certainly a comedy and indeed a key Depression-era film. Like *My Man Godfrey* it is in many ways unreal. But it is whimsical and charming and only guardedly optimistic in its happy ending. *My Man Godfrey* is also a comedy (with William Powell in a casual parallel of Warner Baxter's role in the earlier film), but it

is lunatic rather than charming, and in addition to being unreal is totally dishonest. However, it *is* genuine screwball; *One More Spring* is not.

The screwball comedy often takes one of two directions: as in *My Man Godfrey* the theme is (or could be) intrinsically serious, and it is the treatment and the characters that introduce the craziness. Or as in 1939's delightful and underrated *Wife, Husband and Friend* (again with the ubiquitous Warner Baxter), the story is crazy, but the treatment is relatively sober and realistic. Worth noting, too, is that many "typical" Depression romances and comedies, decidedly *not* screwball, are easily converted into screwball material after a few years during which their formula has ripened into cliché. For example, there's *Palm Springs* (officially directed by Aubrey Scotto, but reportedly largely shot by Raoul Walsh), an extremely pleasant 1936 musical romance and one of the few Depression films in which the monetary problems are not solved at all and love is accepted as a perfectly satisfactory substitute. With Frances Langford and Sir Guy Standing foreshadowing Barbara Stanwyck and Charles Coburn, one has a rough blueprint for Preston Sturges's brilliant *The Lady Eve* of 1941. The major difference (apart from the lack of Sturges's magnificent dialogue!) was that in the original the romantic competition was between millionaire aristocrat David Niven and simple and penniless cowhand Smith Ballew, while Sturges conveniently—and convincingly—combined innocence and wealth into the single persona of Henry Fonda.

One of the most enjoyable offshoots of the screwball comedy is the lunatic family invariably presided over by Eugene Pallette, usually cast as the only member of the family with any common sense, and the one who ultimately rebels and turns on his own kin. Oddly enough, except for Preston Sturges's reviving of it in the early forties, this kind of zany family seemed to die out rather quickly in American comedy. Some of the *Godfrey* family and their lunatic traits were brought back in the 1939 Deanna Durbin vehicle *First Love*, but essentially that was a charming and sophisticated reworking of the Cinderella fairy tale rather than a screwball comedy—although Eugene Pallette's last-reel physical retribution on his scatterbrained wife, deceitful daughter, and shiftless son was a joy to behold. Undoubtedly the war had a great deal to do with the dissolution of the screwball family: with sons joining up and daughters giving blood to the Red Cross and working in war plants, there wasn't much room for them. Fortunately Preston Sturges was above such patriotic or topical considerations, and his *Palm Beach Story* blithely ignored the existence of the war and allowed *two* families to be as nutty, carefree, and self-centered as they wished! Curiously, and hopefully coincidentally, the screwball family was being reborn at the same time, six thousand miles away from Hollywood, in the French cinema of the Occupation period. Primarily in scripts by Cocteau and Prévert, and in such films as *Lumière D'Eté* and *L'Eternel Retour,* they were reincarnated in more sinister though often equally amusing form.

Just as film noir peaked (qualitatively and quantitatively, in Britain as well as in the United States) in 1947, so screwball comedy peaked in 1937. The best of the year's comedies was, almost inarguably, William Wellman's *Nothing Sacred,* from a biting, almost vicious Ben Hecht script. It was irreverent, black, and amazingly freewheeling for a film produced at the very height of the Production Code era, and its satire on yellow journalism seems more pointed and topical every year, as witness the press attention to the notorious Amy Fisher case in 1992, with no less than three *totally* different versions of the affair being presented in prime-time television specials. (Sadly and ironically, none of the networks involved had the wit to revive William Wellman's 1942 *Roxie Hart,* satirizing media exploitation of a parallel case.)

When it was reissued later, almost immediately after Carole Lombard's death, both *Nothing Sacred*'s black quality and its title seemed doubly ironic since Lombard's role was that of a small-town phony cashing in on big-city morbid interest in her apparently imminent death. The reissue may have been tasteless, not to say

tactless, in its timing, but it added another layer of irony to the film.

In the nineties, the film doesn't play as well (or as often) as it should. Television has taken over as *the* medium, and younger audiences don't understand the tremendous power of the press in the thirties, or the frequent abuse of that power. Likewise current younger (which means predominantly film-student) audiences don't always recognize the basic truth behind Hawks's *20th Century* (1934) because of the reduced stature of the theater today; they tend to see it as lampoon or burlesque rather than satire.

Just in the same *month* that *Nothing Sacred* was released, we also saw such other screwball comedies as *Stand In, The Perfect Specimen, The Awful Truth, Live, Love and Learn, Second Honeymoon,* and *It's Love I'm After.* The last (a comedy about battling theatrical costars, played by Bette Davis and Leslie Howard) rated reviews even superior to those accorded *Nothing Sacred* and was considered one of the year's top comedies. It has lost something of its reputation because it is now shown primarily on television, without the benefit of audience input and laughter. In that medium, it seems a trifle stolid and arch, but shown before an audience, it still works extremely well—not least because the Davis presence provides a kind of subliminal parallel to *All About Eve.* Like *The Rage of Paris* (1938), one of the most silken and sophisticated of all thirties comedies, it comes out of the Depression and deals with the extravagances of the rich. But it is not really *about* the Depression and comes just late enough in the Production Code period that it is no longer trying to hit back and shock. It settles for wit, charm, and elegance—qualities that never date, and in which *The Rage of Paris* (Douglas Fairbanks, Jr., and Danielle Darrieux under Henry Koster's direction) is particularly abundant.

Even apart from the impact of World War II, genuine screwball comedy seemed to be dying out in the early forties. If *Theodora Goes Wild* (1936) had deliberately called attention to its daring qualities and exploited them, then *Bachelor Mother* (1939)—a warm, witty gem of a comedy that was a remake of an earlier German film—used the now (unofficially) relaxed strictures of the Code to absorb its maturity almost as a matter of course. Even though there was a last-minute Code-ordered change of the film's final double-entendre line (it slipped through unnoticed in the script, but convulsed early preview audiences) *Bachelor Mother* was "grown-up" in a way that would not have been possible even a year earlier.

Just as the Depression spawned a specific style of screwball comedy (such as Michael Curtiz's *Jimmy the Gent,* the first of two comedies costarring James Cagney and Bette Davis), which contended that in hard times it was perfectly acceptable to be dishonest and unethical as long as one remained technically legal, so did World War II. Films like *San Diego, I Love You, The Major and the Minor, Rosie the Riveter,* and *The More the Merrier* poked lunatic fun at such domestic home-front problems as shortages in hotel accommodations and travel (especially railroad) difficulties. *Pubic Deb No. 1* exploited the general laxity afforded screwball comedy to make a decidedly intemperate political statement. (Like *Red Salute* in the mid thirties, it was hysterically anti-Communist without demonstrating that it understood what Communism was all about.) Films like *Hellzapoppin* and a tepid follow-up, *Hi Diddle Diddle* (really just old-fashioned bedroom farce repainted to give it a screwball look), introduced a genuinely crazy, surreal quality, including an element that survived to become a permanent part of the loose-limbed screen comedy: the actors breaking the barrier of the screen to talk to the audience, the director, or the projectionist. When this trick became commonplace, it was expanded by having recognizable screen icons (Crosby, Hope, Bogart) injected as unbilled guest stars to trade fairly obvious inside jokes with the official stars.

Even fairly orthodox slapstick or trick comedies, such as the Hal Roach duo *Turnabout* (1940) and *Road Show* (1941), reflected a new, if occasionally labored, craziness. Apart from Sturges, the only really interesting addition to the writer-producer ranks in the comedy field was the team of Michael Fessier and Ernest

Pagano, who made a handful of original comedies at Universal in the mid forties. They became repetitious and burned themselves out rather quickly, but their *San Diego, I Love You* was followed by the peculiar, often distasteful, but very entertaining *Frontier Gal* (in Europe: *The Bride Wasn't Willing*), which may have the distinction of being the leading contender for a screwball western categorization.

By the mid forties—the time of Fessier and Pagano—Hollywood had begun an aggressive attempt to create *deliberate* screwball comedy, to exploit traditions that had originally risen so spontaneously, and to justify their zaniness by welding them to newly fashionable and pseudo-Freudian dream imagery. *It Had to Be You* in 1947 (with an inept and graceless performance by Ginger Rogers, who had been so good in such earlier screwballs as *The Major and the Minor* and especially *Bachelor Mother*) was heavy, unfunny, full of overblown se-

quences, and typical of the sense of desperation that was creeping into so much Hollywood comedy at the time. Traditional screwball comedy really did finish with the first half of the forties, although directors like Garson Kanin and films like *Phffft!* kept its ghost agreeably alive from the fifties on.

For the most part, and certainly during the key years of the genre, screwball comedy was also very largely the almost exclusive province of Hollywood, the omnipresent Production Code of course being an important contributing factor. Germany has always tended to be rather heavy and to favor farce in its comic endeavors. The French have wit and certainly understand the mechanics of farce, which they practically invented, but they have never really understood the art of the sight gag, nor why there *should* be a battle between the sexes instead of instant repudiation or conquest.

The Swedes have also made intelligent and

JIMMY THE GENT (1934) Arthur Hohl (right) doesn't agree with James Cagney's plan to turn him over to the authorities; Allen Jenkins lends a restraining hand.

subtle satires, in both the silent and sound periods, but seem inhibited by a lack of confidence in their sense of humor, preferring to make their comedies so ambiguous that they can also be accepted for their straight narrative and/or dramatic values if the laughs don't come.

The British have always been repressed, and one would think that fields for screwball comedies of rebellion would be quite fertile. But they also find a comfortable kind of security in *being* repressed and regard rebellion as rather hopeless. When Princess Diana and Prince Charles were first headline news, the British theater put on a surprisingly biting (if goodnatured) satire on the royal family in general and the wedding in particular. Until that time, the royal family was absolutely sacrosanct, reference to it in theatrical ventures being rare and always respectful. When heads didn't roll at the Tower of London as a result of that play, one would have expected the movies to make commercial hay out of the new permissiveness,

THE RAGE OF PARIS (1938) Get-rich-quick schemers Helen Broderick and Mischa Auer find Danielle Darrieux (left) rather cool to the idea of fleecing a millionaire.

HELLZAPOPPIN (1941)   The opening scenes of the Olsen and Johnson extravaganza apparently take place in Hell—later revealed to be a movie studio set.

but they didn't, and it came into being only gradually and not in a screwball fashion.

Most British movie forays into screwball were more tied in to the comic traditions of the music hall, as in the various film versions of *Alf's Button,* the last and best of which, *Alf's Button Afloat* (1938, and starring the Crazy Gang), was a remarkable forerunner of the kind of humor that the Monty Python team were to unleash on television and then in theatrical movies decades later. The later anti-establishment satires such as *The Ruling Class* and *Britannia Hospital* certainly had elements of screwball, too, but not enough for them really to qualify.

Obviously, too, it follows that comedy, being

IT HAD TO BE YOU (1947)   A failed postwar attempt to return to screwball; Cornel Wilde and Ginger Rogers.

very much a matter of personal taste and personal experience, makes inconsistent demands on the viewer, and the very specialized kind of comedy that we refer to as screwball is even *more* personal, especially in the reactions it creates. For example, while I see Hawks's *Bringing Up Baby* regularly every few years, almost as a kind of penance, hoping each time to have its secret finally revealed, and am always surrounded by an audience howling with merriment, I always react as though watching a full, reconstituted version of Dreyer's *Le Passion de Jeanne d'Arc* and can rarely collect more than a few chuckles from it, those usually from the direction of Charlie Ruggles. Perhaps my resentment is centered in the fact that it is a screwball comedy that is not rebellious enough to take any chances. If only the dinosaur didn't collapse at the end as we all know it will . . . if only Cary Grant married the mousey little librarian who would have been much better for him than the abrasive, aggressive Katharine Hepburn. Interestingly, despite the growing popularity of Cary Grant, the film was a flop in 1938. The Howard Hawks cult had not yet developed, and possibly audiences sensed something labored, contrived, and basically unfunny about the film.

In a loose sense, screwball comedy is still with us today. But Mel Brooks, Woody Allen

MONTY PYTHON'S THE MEANING OF LIFE   Unemployed father Michael Palin tells his huge brood of children that he can no longer afford to feed and support them, and must sell them to be used for medical experimentation.

MONTY PYTHON'S THE MEANING OF LIFE (1983)   A classic of contemporary screwball comedy; John Cleese attempts to give a lecture on sex to bored schoolboys (from left) Eric Idle, Michael Palin, Graham Chapman, and Terry Jones.

27

S.O.B. (1981)   A funny though overdone satire on Hollywood; one of its running gags has Robert Preston frequently undergoing rejuvenating shots in the rear end, here enthusiastically administered by Jennifer Edwards.

ther charm or pep that a week after one saw it, one could hardly remember a single scene or player from it. Now, a decade later, one can't even conjure up an image of what it was like or what it was about. At that time, the highly touted new team of Cheech and Chong (now happily forgotten) announced a comic remake of Dumas's *The Corsican Brothers*. The mere thought (or *dread*) of it in 1983 made the recollection of the Ritz Brothers' highly enjoyable spoof of *The Three Musketeers* (1939) seem almost like a collaboration between Chaplin and Lubitsch.

Yet the basic *need* of and reason for good screwball comedy does still exist, and it is, occasionally, applied. One of the funniest skits of the eighties was John Cleese's hilarious satire of a sex education lecture in *Monty Python's The Meaning of Life*. Not only was it a devastatingly accurate parody of the manner of the pompous English schoolteacher, but also it was a reaction to the kind of comedy then becoming

KISS ME GOODBYE (1982)   An eminently forgettable eighties attempt with Jeff Bridges and Sally Field to reinvoke the screwball spirit of *Here Comes Mr. Jordan*.

(when he deigns, infrequently, to return to comedy), Gene Wilder, and the others have been producing it via a scattergun approach that takes in black comedy, satire of established if near extinct genres (*Young Frankenstein* was the most successful illustration of this), mechanically insane material, and sex farce, but usually lacking at least one of the basic ingredients, and above all lacking taste and sophistication.

In the early eighties there seemed to be a sudden onslaught of near-screwball renaissance: *The Toy*, the abysmal *Kiss Me Goodbye* (where the ineptitude of James Caan only reminded one of how effortlessly Cary Grant and David Niven used to do this kind of thing), and *Romantic Comedy*, so dull and devoid of ei-

commonplace on the screen, with nudity and sex a fait accompli. The skit reacts, in a directly inverse way from *Theodora Goes Wild,* by *not* trying to shock. It takes casually, and for granted, the kind of outrages that comedy was then laboring long and hard over and shows far less than it could easily have gotten away with. Moreover, it managed to suggest that what it was depicting was boring in the extreme, but just something we all had to go through. It's a marvelous piece of comedy, both on its own witty level and as a reaction against the leering kind of sex comedy that by then was becoming commonplace. On the other hand, it was made over a decade ago, and while John Cleese has probably emerged as the funniest performer on-screen, his obvious potential as a comic *creator* and, possibly, as the greatest hope for a reestablishment of the screwball tradition has not yet been realized.

TWO

THE SILENT YEARS

THE NUT (1921)   Douglas Fairbanks's last silent comedy, and one of his zaniest, has him and heroine
Marguerite de la Motte about to make a last-reel escape through the ventilation system.

WHEN THE CLOUDS ROLL BY (1920) Dr. Metz (Herbert Grimwood) tries to convince Douglas Fairbanks that he is going insane.

The probable reasons for the lack of a concentrated screwball comedy genre in the silent period (which in terms of feature-length films means from 1912 to 1928) were suggested in the previous chapter. However, even though supportive evidence is slight, one has to insist that at least the well-nourished *roots* of the genre can be found there. One also has to remember that it is from the silent period that most of the "lost" or at least missing films come, and that the further back one goes into that period, the higher is the percentage of missing titles. Pre-1920 the industry was less stabilized, far more producing and distributing companies existed, and with the length of the average feature film at only five or six reels, the quantity produced was much greater. Even the biggest stars—Mary Pickford and Douglas Fairbanks—made a minimum of between six and nine films each per year, as opposed to two (and often only one) a year in the twenties.

It would be absurd not to expect that among this huge mass of lost and probably permanently unavailable material there aren't several films that can reshape our thinking about the history of film comedy. It has happened too often in other fields. The relatively late discovery of Raoul Walsh's 1915 *Regeneration,* which anticipated both von Stroheim and Fellini, and showed that some of Griffith's lessons in editing had not only been copied but also surpassed, shook a lot of smug notions about the state of cinema prior to 1916 and *Intolerance.* Judging from the synopsis, though the film itself is tragically among the missing, Griffith's *Escape* would seem to qualify as a bona fide film noir feature, possibly the first, as early as 1914. Similar surprises almost certainly await us in the realm of comedy—*if* they can be found in time.

Since so much of silent screwball comedy has to be a matter for conjecture, the most reli-

31

able approach might be to establish its presence via films from the beginning and the end of the period, and then to go back to fill in the gaps in between.

Sunshine Dad, a five-reel release from early 1916, seems to exist today only via one or two prints, and it is unfortunately not a very funny comedy either on its own merits or as a showcase for the celebrated stage actor De Wolf Hopper, whose second film it was. Although it was made for Triangle, the group consisting of D. W. Griffith, Thomas Ince, and Mack Sennett, production was assigned to Griffith's Fine Arts arm of the company, indicating that what was wanted was a "respectable" comedy, not the speed and insanity of Sennett. Yet only two years earlier, Sennett had made the famous Marie Dressler stage farce *Tillie's Punctured Romance* a hugely successful feature film by thumbing his nose at respectability and adding the Keystone Kops, Chaplin, Mabel Normand, and most of his stable of comedians, along with much slapstick and a typical chase finale. *Sunshine Dad,* routinely directed by Edward Dillon, and with some of its bizarre and near-horrific plot situations probably attributable to Tod Browning, who was one of the scenarists, is notable mainly for its attempts to inject zaniness into what might have been a straightforward farce, and for the quite remarkable number of foreshadowings it contains of future screwball comedy. The stealing of jewels from a Hindu shrine, and the pursuit by a murderous secret society, anticipate both Peter Ustinov's British *Vice Versa* (1947) and the Beatles' *Help* (1965). The constant losing, finding, and hiding of the elusive jewels is of course one of the standard ingredients that kept many later screwball comedies on the move—Peter Bogdanovich used such a plot satirically in his *What's Up, Doc?* (1972)—while a lion on the loose in a Hollywood hotel also anticipates *Bringing Up Baby* (1938), though undoubtedly inspired by Sennett's successful comedic exploitation of lions, bears, and other wild animals in public places.

Griffith had little interest in comedy and his "supervision" of this film was undoubtedly far more limited than with the romances and melodramas with Mae Marsh and Lillian Gish that he was also producing for Fine Arts. Edward Dillon, both an actor and a director, likewise was hardly a specialist in comedy. It would be absurd to suggest that via *Sunshine Dad* an attempt was being made to establish a formula for a new, zany kind of comedy—yet in retrospect it *is* remarkable, if coincidental, how many of the standard screwball ingredients it contains. It might even have been funnier as a comedy with a personality more attractive than De Wolf Hopper. His role—as an out-of-work actor on the prowl for a rich widow—could easily have been adjusted to Johnny Hines, Roy Barnes, Adolphe Menjou, W. C. Fields, Bob Hope, or Groucho Marx in various periods of film history.

As a stage star of musical comedy and operetta—his range extended from Mr. Pickwick to Gilbert and Sullivan—Hopper was obviously at a disadvantage without his rich voice, and despite his energy and obvious willingness to give his all, he just did not project a likable comic sense. He was no longer young, of course, and showed it; moreover his wig and false eyebrows (he'd lost all his hair during an earlier attack of typhoid) were not treated too kindly by the merciless lighting and camera techniques of the period, which always added a few years to a player's age. To their credit, Triangle tried hard to sell him both as a prestige performer and as a popular comedian—*Sunshine Dad* had been preceded by *Don Quixote*—but Fairbanks and Barrymore apart, most of the stage-to-screen actors of that period were rapid casualties. Today, *Sunshine Dad* is interesting as an archaic blueprint for the screwball comedies to come—and for glimpses of contemporary fashions and of Hollywood exteriors that have long vanished.

Some ten years later, near the end of the silent era, Cecil B. DeMille's independent company, which he had formed after leaving Paramount, offered *The Cruise of the Jasper B* (1926). Curiously, it made quite an impression on critics, who then proceeded to remember it with considerable inaccuracy. One often found references to it as a crazy comedy about bootlegging. When it was finally rediscovered in the

THE GRAND DUCHESS AND THE WAITER (1926) Millionaire
Adolphe Menjou poses as a waiter to woo and win aristocrat
Florence Vidor, in another classic comedy of masquerade and
misunderstanding.

where, unbeknownst to her, it sticks to her wet
back, transferring its vital information to her
body. The old ploy of having secret plans or
other documents tattooed on the leading
lady's back dates to the much earlier silent
days, such as the 1914 British spy melodrama
Lieutenant Daring Captures a Spy. And of course
it would be used more than once in the sound
era, but most effectively in the early World War
II screwball spy spoof, *The Lady Has Plans,* in
which Paulette Goddard was the lady in question. This useful ploy allowed for farce, suspense, and sexual piquancy, which, because of
the outlandishness of the situation, sidestepped contemporary censorship strictures.

Hero and heroine are brought together accidentally; a note of black comedy is introduced

late sixties (though its recovery didn't result in
much exposure, and it remains a virtually unknown and unappreciated film), it proved to
have no connection with bootlegging whatsoever. But it is, if any film can make that claim,
the *definitive* silent screwball comedy, and a remarkable taste of things to come.

Without roots in the Depression, its story is
more scatterbrained than usual and consists of
nothing more than two minor story lines being
linked and sustained by surreal and frenzied
physical action.

Rod La Rocque plays Jerry Cleggett, whose
house, furnishings, and clothes are being sold
out from under him, and who in order to regain the family fortune—an inheritance from
pirate days—must marry aboard the old galleon *Jasper B.* A neighbor, Agatha (Mildred
Harris), is about to be cheated out of her inheritance by her crafty lawyer, played by the diminutive Snitz Edwards. Edwards has pur-
loined the real will leaving everything to
her—but a chance gust of wind blows it out of
his hands and through her bathroom window,

THE GRAND DUCHESS AND THE WAITER Raymond Griffith, a unique
comedian who welded the urbane manner of Menjou with the
elaborate sight gags of Keaton; although his films followed no set
pattern, the best of them, such as *Paths to Paradise* (1926), contained
many elements of genuine screwball.

THE CRUISE OF THE JASPER B
(1926)   Rod la Rocque and
Mildred Harris.

THE CRUISE OF THE JASPER B
The final shot: all that is
left of the *Jasper B*.
Incidentally the native
huts in the background
are quite inappropriate to
the film's setting,
suggesting that the
Catalina cove was also
being used as a South Seas
locale by another film
unit!

when they believe that they have accidentally killed the crooked lawyer and must dispose of his body (in a coffin that continues to turn up atop a taxicab or floating in a stream!) and the pace of melodrama quickens when they become involved with mail-truck thieves. The finale takes place aboard the dock-bound *Jasper B* (the "cruise" of the title is nonexistent) when a call for help involves naval, army, and air force personnel and results in a race to the rescue deliberately and obviously composed of spectacular stock-footage scenes, thus predating the climax of the Marx Brothers' *Duck Soup* (1933), where the war climax was zanier and more imaginative, but quite clearly drew its inspiration from *The Cruise of the Jasper B.*

Perhaps a trifle shapeless and undisciplined, the film is nevertheless unique among comedies of the mid twenties, and it's a pity that it tries to cover so much comedic ground. It is both satire and lampoon, spoofing Douglas Fairbanks as a performer, and kidding the chatty, informal intertitles of his earlier comedies. If the middle sections are too padded with rather childish comedy involving Snitz Edwards and Jack Ackroyd, then the inspiration of the opening and closing segments make up for it. Never a subtle actor, Rod La Rocque was a good pantomimist with a superb physique and a cavalier smile. In the opening reels, his clothes having been confiscated along with most of his other possessions, he appears clad only in a brief but well-tailored towel; when the plot—and the chase—take him outside, he is forced to turn to the only clothing available, an old buccaneer costume. Both outfits allow him to pose and prance in the best Fairbanksian manner with a sense of humor too few of his silents revealed.

Among the film's credits are few indications of the true source of its screwball quality. Its director, James Horne, directed some of the best Laurel and Hardy sound films including their genuinely classic feature *Way Out West.* But oddly enough, the only real evidence of his leanings toward screwball comedy was in some of his Columbia serials of the forties. As though knowing that they were too absurd to be taken seriously, he ridiculed them via sar-

castic end-of-chapter narrations (which were *supposed* to entice audiences back for the even greater thrills allegedly waiting for next week) and added distinctly screwball elements to liven up repetitious melodrama. One has especially fond memories of the villain's henchmen (Kit Guard, Anthony Warde, et al.) throwing a wild party and wearing ladies' hats in an episode of *The Spider's Web,* only to be embarrassed by the master criminal's eavesdropping on their activities via his super-television equipment—just one of many brief comic vignettes that could not possibly have been in the original script (if only because there was no need for them, and anything that ate up production money and time and did not add to narrative or action was automatically taboo in the economy-conscious serials at Columbia). Another name of note in the credits of *The Cruise of the Jasper B* was that of writer (and soon to be director) Tay Garnett.

Perhaps one shouldn't stretch analysis too far merely on conjecture, but nevertheless it's interesting that the very best of Garnett's later screwball comedies, *She Couldn't Take It* (1935) and *Slightly Honorable* (1940), shared major and uncommon traits with *The Cruise of the Jasper B*—total unpredictability, and the use of crime and murder (or apparent murder) to create sequences of decidedly black humor. Some totally unknown executive within the DeMille Corporation may also be responsible for a general undercurrent of subdued or tangential screwball quality in much of their twenties output, including *Bachelor Brides* (1926), *The Coming of Amos* (1925), either a melodrama out of control or a totally delightful spoof of melodramas, and *Chicago* (1927), an essentially straight version of the play later remade as an outstanding forties screwball, *Roxie Hart.* Phyllis Haver's vivacity and sense of fun helped to turn much of *Chicago* more in the direction of satire and semi-screwball-comedy than might otherwise have been the case; Robert Edeson as the opportunistic lawyer Billy Flynn showed none of the appreciation of absurdity that Adolphe Menjou later brought to the role.

Somewhere between *Sunshine Dad* and the end of the twenties lie an indeterminate number of near misses, misfires, and certainly many silent comedies that *do* qualify as screwball. Typical is *The Primitive Lover* (1922), a Constance Talmadge vehicle that starts out superbly with an overdone sequence of a trio of survivors—husband, wife, and would-be lover—on a raft, following a shipwreck. Just as the audience is beginning to feel that it is overdone, the scene dissolves to the same trio (Constance Talmadge as wife, Harrison Ford as husband, Kenneth Harlan the rather self-important hopeful lover) sitting comfortably at home. What we have just seen is the picturization of a chapter in Harlan's latest book. A romance-obsessed wife, bored with her husband, and seeking freedom so that she can marry the (in her eyes) far more romantic author, goes to Reno for a divorce. But the husband fakes a kidnapping of both wife and lover, forcing them to rough it in a mountain cabin with primitive cooking equipment, and apparently menaced by tough cowboys and renegade Indians. The lover of course is shown up as a big bluff, while the husband—with a little careful stage-managing—proves himself to be more rugged and romantic than his wife expected. The two are reconciled. The film, clearly a sort of blending of the motifs of *The Taming of the Shrew* and *My Favorite Wife,* is also one of the many near-screwballs of the twenties to revolve around divorce.

Although divorce in America carried far less of a stigma than in Britain, where it was regarded as something shameful at least up until the morality-modernizing influences of World War II, still it was something that, in Hollywood movies at least, was restricted to the affluent classes—so that it could be solved by money or a convenient rearrangement of leisure time. One or two films, such as *Dancing Mothers* (1926), did treat divorce realistically, if still on that upper social plateau, but most comedies, whether gentle and sophisticated (as in Mal St. Clair's *Are Parents People?* in 1925) or zany and physical, as *The Primitive Lover* certainly was, anticipated the thirties pattern of such classics as *The Awful Truth* and *His Girl Friday* of using divorce as a springboard for a battle-of-the-sexes conflict that would finally be solved by a happy reunion and remarriage.

While there is little in the way of traditional masquerade in the film, almost every character engages in some kind of role-playing, and the woman is subjected to threatened if not actual abuse. The hero, acting on advice from a friendly Indian that a squaw behaves better when she is beaten regularly with a stick, starves his former wife into submission and forces her to cook her food on a primitive, smoke-belching stove.

Constance Talmadge was such a delightful and animated performer, almost a female Fairbanks at times (a trait evident ever since 1916 with her mountain-girl portrayal in Griffith's *Intolerance*), that her personality alone was often all that was needed to hold together merely so-so material. In a way it is a pity that she was at her peak in youth and popularity before the era of sophisticated comedy really developed. Lubitsch, St. Clair, Monta Bell, William Seiter, and other comedy stylists could have joined forces with her and, giving her material more bite, transformed her into the silent equivalent of an Irene Dunne or Carole Lombard. As it was, her basic director was Sidney Franklin, whose talents veered more (in talkies) to the elegant sophistication of Molnar and Coward adaptations. But in *The Primitive Lover* they both demonstrated their adaptability to the broader, rougher kind of comedy, and doubtless in 1922 it must have seemed far more original and sparkling than it does today, after years of repetition. Although based on a play called *The Divorcée*, the Norma Shearer talkie of that name was not a remake. However, *The Primitive Lover was* remade as an early talkie, but by concentrating its thematics on the hero's proving himself to be a *real man* (via a protracted fight sequence), it lessened the elements of screwball comedy.

Constance Talmadge was to hover constantly on the fringe of the genre. Her *A Pair of Silk Stockings* (1918, directed by Walter Edwards) had too much plot for its tight five reels and was ultimately little more than a pleasing comedy of manners. Coincidentally, it costarred Talmadge with Harrison Ford (not today's star, of course) in what amounted to a dry run for their *The Primitive Lover* teaming, and it, too, was remade, somewhat more amusingly, at the

ORCHIDS AND ERMINE (1927)   Hedda Hopper (left), Colleen Moore, and Jack Mulhall.

end of the twenties as *Silk Stockings* with the charming Laura LaPlante—a logical successor to Talmadge—in the lead. One of the few other surviving Talmadge/Sidney Franklin vehicles is *The Duchess of Buffalo* (1926)—set in pre-Revolutionary Russia, with sumptuous sets designed by William Cameron Menzies. Unfortunately, in its original form it was both a stage vehicle *and* an operetta; removing the music and the (presumably) witty dialogue left it as a kind of pantomimic shell, needing to be diverted into physical screwball elements that could exploit rather than be defeated by its artifice. It was also not well served by the pantomimic acting of comic villain Edward Martindel, a good enough actor in normal circumstances, but here given far too much to grimaces, eye-flashing, and exaggerated reactions in a role needing the subtle underplaying of a Menjou.*

*The happy survival and rediscovery of *Her Sister From Paris*, (1925) should be noted. One of the best of the Talmadge/Franklin films, it is a risqué romantic farce rather than a screwball comedy, helped immeasurably by the surprising romantic/comic sophistication in the playing of Ronald Colman.

Like Talmadge, Colleen Moore had her own production unit. She was an enormously popular star, and her biggest hits were her comedies. Casual film history tends to regard her as an alternate to Clara Bow as a flapper heroine, and while there's some truth in that, it does a disservice to both players. They were good actresses and good comediennes. In particular, Moore's *Orchids and Ermine* (1927, directed by Alfred Santell, with gags and comedy construction by Mervyn LeRoy) is one of the cornerstones of twenties screwball. Few screwball comedies had more multiple masquerades. Colleen plays a small-town girl who emigrates to the big city (New York) and unexpectedly gets a job as a hotel receptionist because of her "sensible" good looks and lack of glamour. Enter Jack Mulhall and his valet, Sam Hardy. Jack is an Oklahoma oil millionaire sick of being chased by money-mad women. Valet Sam is girl crazy and would welcome such attentions. The two agree to swap identities while they are in New York—and of course attract a succession of role-playing gold diggers. Colleen falls, gen-

37

uinely, for the millionaire, thinking that he is only the valet—and almost loses him when she is persuaded, against her better judgment, to be a "hot mama" because that is what is expected in New York. Conversely, Mulhall, an innocent, has fallen for Moore and goes to his valet for "man of the world" instructions on how to woo and win her. After an amusing pantomimic courtship in which the valet plays the man and an embarrassed Mulhall the woman, the latter puts on *his* city-slicker act, totally alien to his real nature, and almost loses Colleen. Her mercenary girlfriend, Gwen Lee, in the meantime, is acting "classy" and "refined" to win the millionaire, who of course is actually the somewhat coarse valet. However, all of the masquerades are but the pegs on which the narrative is hung, and merely an excuse for a whole series of wonderful sight and situation gags, one of them involving six-

ORCHIDS AND ERMINE   A longer shot from the same sequence, giving some idea of the sumptuous art direction.

year-old Mickey Rooney playing an adult midget.

There is some delightful location work around New York's Plaza Hotel and uptown Fifth Avenue (especially a long sequence atop an open double-decker bus in a rainstorm), and for once the considerable physical mayhem is inflicted on the hapless hero rather than the heroine. Perhaps the biggest surprise is the effectiveness of the narrative and dia-

logue intertitles: they are short, snappy, pungent, cut beautifully in rhythm with the film, and most flavorsome in capturing the idiom of New York society, high life, and nightclub habitués. Too often what were once topical titles in a silent film date badly or throw the film off-balance. Here they work superbly well; it is like watching (and listening to) a snappy James Cagney–Joan Blondell talkie of five years later. While other Colleen Moore comedies of the twenties have both humor and charm, none of them have the bite and punch of this little gem, which one could well imagine being done at Paramount at the height of the screwball talkies with possibly Cary Grant and Carole Lombard in the leads.

The silent period was of course uncommonly rich in all kinds of visual comedy, and its star comedians—from Keaton to Raymond Griffith—all made at least one film (with Griffith it would probably be *Paths to Paradise* in 1924) that could quality as a screwball.

With Douglas Fairbanks, whose concentra-

THE GARDEN OF EDEN (1928)   Maude George shows the "menu" of her girls to roué Lowell Sherman.

39

THE GARDEN OF EDEN A bedroom marriage for the film's climax: Corninne Griffith, Charles Ray, Louise Dresser, and unbilled player.

tion on comedy came to an abrupt end in 1920 with *The Nut* and a wholesale switch to swashbucklers, the vital battle-of-the-sexes element was usually absent. Doug's independently wealthy, optimistic, and physically energetic heroes devoted much time to winning the heroines, but always suffered nobly when rebuffed and were much too gentlemanly ever to retaliate physically. But the element of deception and masquerade was frequently present. At least twice in 1917 alone, it was a key factor in his comedies. In *Wild and Woolly* a whole Western town (including the heroine) connives in a scheme to disguise itself and convince West-obsessed Doug that things haven't changed since the old frontier days. And in *Down to Earth* purely so that he can cure his high-living girlfriend of drinking and (especially) smoking, he buys an entire convalescent home and then contrives to have all of its patients believe that they are shipwrecked on a desert island, so that by hard work, exercise, and a total abstinence from liquor and tobacco, they can rebuild their health. (The desert island is actu-

ally a stretch of deserted coastline right off the main highway!)

When the Clouds Roll By (1919), arguably Doug's best and certainly his most ingenious comedy, satirizes the then current (and new) fad of psychiatry, with the doctor trying to cure Doug's alleged neurosis being an escaped lunatic himself. The narrative is frequently interrupted for elaborate visual set-pieces—such as an incredible dream/nightmare sequence in which all of the rich foods that Doug has eaten enjoy a kind of party in his stomach (a sequence reminiscent of early television commercials for stomach-acid and other products), which concludes with Doug's skipping and jumping around the walls and ceiling of a room in order to escape the now alive and pursuing collection of pies, rarebits, and vegetables! The refusal to stay within the "respectable" grounds laid down for normal feature-length comedies in the years 1916–20 also gives the Fairbanks films an innate sense of rebellion that links them with the genuine screwball entries of the thirties.

40

But perhaps it is in the two-reel comedies that Charley Chase made for Hal Roach in the twenties that one finds the closest links, and it is surely no coincidence that most of them were directed by Leo McCarey, who went on in the thirties to become one of the foremost

RITZY (1926)   Betty Bronson with James Hall.

Three "lost" screwball comedies from the twenties. Following her more sentimental chores as a James Barrie heroine in *Peter Pan* and *A Kiss for Cinderella*, Paramount switched Betty Bronson to decidedly modern comedies. It is especially sad that these are apparently lost today, since they all contain decided screwball elements of masquerade and deception, two are directed by screwball specialists (Gregory La Cava and William Wellman), and one even had the zany idea of giving one of the lead roles to a cat! (A fourth Bronson comedy, *Everybody's Acting*, combined elements of screwball with those of black comedy. While it's unlikely, it's not impossible that one of these will yet show up.)

PARADISE FOR TWO (1927)   A Gregory La Cava film with Bronson and Andre Beranger.

THE CAT'S PAJAMAS (1926)
William Wellman directs
Bronson and Ricardo Cortez.

practitioners of the screwball art with *Duck Soup, The Awful Truth, Ruggles of Red Gap,* and *My Favorite Wife,* to say nothing of such broader comedies as Mae West's, Eddie Cantor's *The Kid from Spain,* W. C. Fields's *Six of a Kind,* Harold Lloyd's *The Milky Way,* and the richly human and sophisticated *Love Affair,* which occasionally threatened to think about turning itself into a screwball comedy, but on this occasion wisely allowed the gentler tone to sustain itself throughout.

The Chase/McCarey comedies are rich, varied, and prolific, though despite McCarey's skill it is perhaps a mistake to split the credit evenly. McCarey in later years stated several times that he learned his comedy craft *from* Chase in those years. And Chase, apart from being a charming comedian, was also a gifted director and a creative gagman. Because normalcy was the keynote of his screen character—apart from a few early years with Sennett, he was never a clown—he was able to make the transition to sound films as easily as did Laurel and Hardy and maintained a remarkably high standard in his two-reel comedies, first for Roach and then for Columbia, until his death at far too early an age in the early 1940s. If normalcy was Chase's strength, it may also have proven a subliminal handicap. Because there was nothing particularly unique about his character, and because it did contain elements of the personas of Harold Lloyd and Reginald Denny, he never quite commanded the attention that his peers enjoyed nor made a transition from starring in shorts to starring in features. However, to movie audiences this was a blessing, giving them two uninterrupted decades of often outstanding and always engaging two-reel comedies.

Chase's forte was the comedy of embarrassment—of being totally innocent, yet becoming more and more meshed in apparent guilt as he tried to prove it. He was frequently a family man in his movies and happily so, so the battle of the sexes in the normal use of the term was not stressed. But occasionally he was up against a suspicious wife or a clinging earlier girlfriend. His films could be full of superb, often almost surreal, sight gags—or they could

withdraw to the purely situational. His brilliant *Innocent Husbands* (1925)—which begins with the destruction of a straw hat—might well hve been the inspiration for René Clair to make his classic *The Italian Straw Hat* the following year. (The stage farce was of course a French classic in its own right and did not derive in any way from the Chase comedy. But Clair was known to study the American comedies of Sennett and Roach, and it may not be coincidence that Clair's film followed so hot on the heels of Chase's, or that its star, Albert Prejean, normally a boulevardier of the Maurice Chevalier school, so closely resembled Chase in makeup and performance in this film.) *Innocent Husbands* starts beautifully with a gag in which Chase is quite innocently involved with a girl he encounters in a cab. For convoluted reasons, he needs to go to her hotel room. She asks him to wait a few minutes outside the hotel below an upstairs window, then whistle, at which time she will drop him her room key. Dutifully Chase waits, whistles, and is immediately buried in an avalanche of room keys! Later in the film he masquerades (in ingenious ways) as the ghosts of departed relatives, in order to convince his wife (a spiritualist) via unimpeachable endorsements from beyond the grave that his fidelity is beyond question.

Masquerades in Chase's films were frequent: posing as a madman in *Crazy Like a Fox* (1926) was straightforward enough; more complicated was another minor classic, *Fluttering Hearts* (1927)—distinguished also by the presence of Oliver Hardy as a lecherous waterfront tough—in which the girl's father is impressed by Chase, hires him to masquerade as a European count—whom his daughter is planning to marry—and in so doing thoroughly disillusions her about him. Needless to say, Chase *is* the count. The complications of that little plot took quite a lot of unraveling especially within the framework of a two-reeler. Best of all the "embarrassing" shorts was *Limousine Love* (1928), in which Chase, top-hatted, elegant, and driving to his wedding, innocently picks up a nude girl, Viola Richard, en route. (He has temporarily left his car to walk back for gas; she has lost her clothes in a roadside mis-

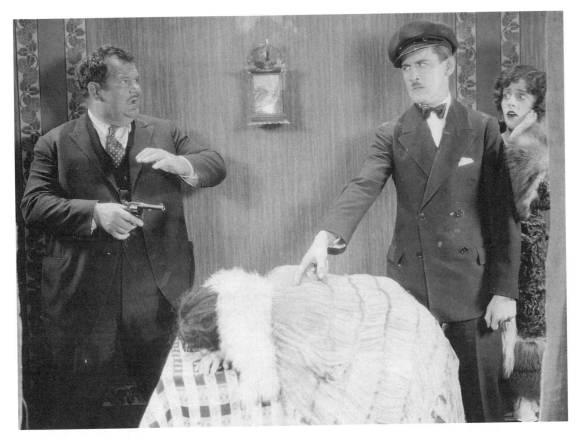

FLUTTERING HEARTS (1927) Oliver Hardy (left) as a comic villain, with Chase and Martha Sleeper.

Charley Chase's two-reel comedies for Hal Roach in the mid-twenties combined elements of sight-gag surrealism with frequently screwball plot lines; almost all of them were directed by Leo McCarey and were good training for his later sound comedy features.

MANY SCRAPPY RETURNS   Chase caught in a typically embarrassing moment with Bull Montana and his wife.

FLUTTERING HEARTS   Screwball stalwart-to-be Eugene Pallette (right) is roped into helping Chase and Martha Sleeper in a department store sale.

43

hap and taken refuge in the back of his empty car.) Returning with gas, Chase resumes his journey, and along the way picks up a hitchhiker—a fuming and jealous Edgar Kennedy, the girl's husband, who eventually settles down to man-of-the-world banter not knowing that his unclad wife is hidden in the back compartment. Chase's dilemma is to dispose of the husband and get the girl clad, without either the husband or his own fiancée catching on, which causes Chase to circle the church a dozen times, each time picking up a new contingent of well-groomed male wedding guests who have leaped aboard hoping to help stop the car in which the brakes have apparently failed. The comedy builds like a cascading downhill snowball, its solution fully living up to its potential.

His Wooden Wedding (1925), an almost Buñuel-like farce in the blackness of some of its humor, has Chase's best man trying (for reasons of his own) to sabotage the wedding by telling him that his bride has a wooden leg. The deception is helped along by the fact that she has just sprained her ankle and limps down the aisle, kneeling awkwardly as she faces the altar. Seeing Chase's consternation, the best man slips a walking stick alongside the bride's leg—and Chase, surreptitiously seeking confirmation of the dire news, gets it by picking up a splinter. In a marvelously bizarre flash-forward to ten years hence, all of Chase's offspring—including the latest infant arrival and even the family dog—hobble in on wooden legs. Horrified at the prospect, Chase calls off the wedding, but is soon remorseful, recalls what "a grand girl" she was, and seeks to make amends.

Best of all, and one of the highspots of both Chase's and McCarey's career, was *Mighty Like a Moose* (1926). Charley has "teeth like a walrus" and gets them fixed. His wife, Vivien Oakland, has an outsize nose, which, among other things, makes even a casual kiss a contortion. Both get their afflictions corrected at the same time, unbeknownst to the other; both meet, are mutually attracted (as would be natural since they *are* a devoted couple), begin a flirtation without recognizing the other (unlikely, but a conceit that is possible in the silent film without dialogue to give the game away), and finally, realizing that things are getting out of hand, confess to each other that they are married. Chase finds out the truth about the situation first and decides to give his wife a lesson, to pay her back for her potential infidelity. In a series of lightning-quick changes he poses as impassioned lover and outraged husband, and in the latter guise boots his rival from the house . . . just in time to get a comeuppance from his wife, who has now also discovered the truth.

It's a charming and civilized comedy, maintains a brisk pace despite a virtual lack of traditional sight gags, offers delightful and sophisticated side gags along the way, and basically works so well because of the inherent decency and affection of the couple involved. Many of the Hal Roach silents (notably a Max Davidson two-reeler, *Pass the Gravy*) have plot or behavioral patterns that entitle them to serious consideration as screwball entries, but perhaps only *Mighty Like a Moose* is entitled to stand in full equality with the later classics of the genre . . . no small accomplishment for a twenty-minute comedy.

STEPPING SISTERS (1931) A lost
Fox pioneer screwball effort?
Lost, certainly. With a plot
that somewhat foreshadows
Capra's *Lady for a Day* and a
high society/roughneck
contrast of characters that
begs for Preston Sturges's
attention (especially as Robert
Greig and Franklin Pangborn
are in the supporting cast),
one has high hopes. Yet the
combination of eight writers,
three songs, and a so-so
director (Seymour Felix)
makes one temper those
hopes. Will we ever find out?
Meanwhile, the teaming of
(from left) Louise Dresser,
Minna Gombell, and Jobyna
Howland *is* tantalizing.

The twin reasons for the major success
screwball comedy in the thirties—the Depr
sion and the Production Code—have alrea
been sufficiently discussed in chapter 1. Ho
ever, the virtual mass production of comedy
the thirties offers additional reasons for
sharp division between a handful of genui
classics and a prolific output of comedy (scr
ball and otherwise) running the gamut fro
the amiable to the competent to the alm
intolerable.

Before the government stepped in with "
vorcement" proceedings in the late forties
break up monopolies, most studios had the
own distribution arms and their own mov
houses. The distribution wings assessed h
best to merchandise the product; a weak A fil
could be salvaged at the box office by doul
billing with an above average programmer or
movie. Poor films could be guaranteed theat
cal exposure and at least a modest return
investment merely because the parent co
pany also owned the theaters. Comedies in t
thirties were popular; obviously, during t
Depression, audiences wanted to laugh if on
as a momentary escape. Moreover, unless si

STEPPING SISTERS Jobyna Howland (left) and Minna Gombe
flank Ferdinand Munier.

nificant amounts had to be spent for the acquisition of rights to hit plays or novels, comedies were relatively economical to make. Most of them had contemporary settings, so standing sets could be reused, shifted around, easily disguised. Key directors and players were obviously all-important, but under the old studio system, most of them were contracted for services over a period of years, rather than for individual films. If they were signed up for four films a year, then a quarter of that sum would be allocated to the budget of one specific film. Thus, at RKO Radio for example, popular but not yet major stars like Joel McCrea or Ginger Rogers could be moved around to add prestige and a certain amount of box-office insurance to fairly unprepossessing subjects that might have far less moneymaking potential with Norman Foster or Helen Mack.

If there was an assembly-line, mathematical-formula look to much of Hollywood comedy in the thirties, then it hardly mattered. Most audiences liked the formula and saw the films in ornate deluxe theaters (or cozy smaller neighborhood ones) where the shared experience of laughter was a key ingredient that often made the films seem funnier than they actually were. Many of the character comedians—Donald MacBride, Allen Jenkins, Erik Rhodes, Eric Blore—were by now regarded as old friends and had only to appear on-screen with a char-

Bert Wheeler (left) and Robert Woolsey were an enormously popular team in the early thirties. Today they are very much an acquired taste, but their vaudevillian routines still pay off, and some of their films, especially *Diplomaniacs* (1933), have a manic frenzy that entitle them to screwball representation.

TOPAZE (1933) There's often a thin line between screwball comedy and satire, yet *Topaze*, with Myrna Loy and John Barrymore, by far the best of many film versions of the classic French comedy, succeeded in both areas, although the elegance of playing and staging perhaps veered it more in the direction of sophistication.

47

TOPAZE Reginald Mason as the mineral water king out to exploit and cheat respectable Monsieur Topaze — who ultimately not only comes out on top financially, but also wins his boss's mistress (Loy) as his wife.

acteristic expression of bemusement to provoke instant laughter.

Surprisingly few of these comedies contain topical gags that are indecipherable to contemporary audiences. Occasionally those built around *specific* aspects of Prohibition are mystifying; gags about political parties usually signal their intent and their targets even if, again, the specifics aren't spelled out. But one rarely encounters the kind of frustration that cropped up in films like Fairbanks's preswashbuckler comedies of 1916–20, where he kidded about (via titles) events and personalities that were household topics in the days when newspapers were the only informational media, but that were no longer topical two years after the event, let along several decades.

The screwball comedies of the thirties that suffer most today are not so much those that did satirize current events or attitudes as those that were modest entertainment at best, depending on audience goodwill and participation in the confines of a movie theater. *We're Rich Again,* a 1934 comedy of a typically zany family trying to overcome Depression hard-

ships, had a solid director in William Seiter and an interesting cast headed by Reginald Denny, Billie Burke, Edna May Oliver, and (a somewhat unlikely immigrant to the screwball world) Buster Crabbe. What it didn't have was much in the way of laughs or originality, even though it came so early in the cycle. Even worse was one of the most catastrophic of all Depression screwball entries, *Down to Their Last Yacht.* Made the same year by the same company— RKO Radio—thus confirming the assembly-line origin of so much thirties comedy, its attractively zany title was the most appealing aspect of the whole enterprise. However, even second- and third-rate films like these, aiming at no more than providing time-killing diversion for an hour or so, usually succeeded in that modest aim at the time because of audience goodwill (or in some cases charitability). Today, when these films are seen at all, it is on television where they are fragmented for commercials, denied the necessary input of audience laughter, and deprived of even the technical quality that helped make them palatable in the thirties, for many of the lesser ones are

48

WE'RE RICH AGAIN (1934)
One of the first comedies about the adventures of a zany family in combatting the Depression. It provided a memorable teaming of two of screwball comedy's Grand Dames, Billie Burke and, seen here, Edna May Oliver. (Unbilled extra Dave O'Brien is at the wheel.)

"preserved" for television use only via lackluster 16mm dupe prints.

The assembly-line quality of so many thirties comedies can be observed in the way that clichés, once established, are rarely embellished or developed. If Claudette Colbert's runaway heiress in *It Happened One Night* (1934) can be considered the definitive such role, it is because it has some depth: she is in conflict with her millionaire father (Walter Connolly) and later with the reporter (Clark Gable) who befriends her; she is running *to* a marriage with a man she doesn't yet know is worthless, and en route she encounters the problems of ordinary people in the Depression and learns the value of money, humility, and loyalty. Something is constantly—and logically—happening to her during her flight to change and develop her character. In *Rhythm on the Range* (1936, and not a screwball comedy although it could easily have been turned into one) we first meet heiress Frances Farmer at a wedding rehearsal. She is so passive that she seems not to care whether she marries her fiancé, we never meet him or get to know him (as we did

in *It Happened One Night*), seeing only his photograph and gathering that he is something of a bore. For reasons never too clearly outlined, she follows the now time-honored pattern of running out on her wedding, stowing away aboard a westbound train on which cowboy and rodeo performer Bing Crosby is taking a newly acquired bull back to Arizona where he is a small-time rancher. After some bickering between heiress and cowboy, and some subplots to inflate the footage to A running time, at the halfway mark the heroine's red scarf causes the bull to break loose and escape as the train is in a siding. Heiress and cowpoke now team up to complete their journey on foot (and via a rattletrap of a car), providing a mild change of pace and a major reminder of the inspiration that *It Happened One Night* was to so many films. Heiress Frances confides to the hero's comic buddy (played by Bob Burns) that she has fallen in love with Bing; after more footage and a couple of songs, she melts into his arms for the fade-out. Nothing has really happened, dramatically or comedically, though there have been a few good songs. Ad-

49

THE GAY BRIDE (1934) Chester Morris (left), Carole Lombard, and gangster/bridegroom-to-be Nat Pendleton in an interesting forerunner to the much-later *Married to the Mob*, but a film that lost much of its potential through pulling its punches.

mittedly *Rhythm on the Range* was above average for an amazingly mediocre crop of Crosby vehicles of the thirties, and not until 1940 does one find him appearing in films commensurate with his talent and popularity.

The really sad aspect of so many thirties films like *Rhythm on the Range* is not that they were bad or routine, but that they could have been so much better with a little effort. But Paramount knew that Crosby musicals had a ready market and saw no need to try too hard; the casual lifting of the runaway-heiress motif from the screwball comedies for this story line underlines the lack of inspiration that was one of the curses of the old studio system (just as the concentration of creative talent from art directors, cinematographers, editors, and other crafts was one of its virtues).

The constant need for product in the thirties, when the double-bill system was at its peak, and when theaters had to be fed nonstop, meant that inevitably the screwball comedy found its way into the ranks of the B movie. On the whole, it didn't produce many surprises, let alone *really* worthwhile comedy. Like the musical, it needed specific writing and performing talents that were usually beyond the budgets of the B film, which was more easily

THE GAY BRIDE
Chester Morris, Carole
Lombard, Leo Carrillo,
and ZaSu Pitts.

THE GAY BRIDE   An interesting prerelease poster for *The Gay Bride* when it still had the more typically screwball title of *The Bride and the Best Man*.

able to come up with a "class" product in the realm of the western, the horror film, or the action melodrama, where the appeal was essentially visual and a good director (like Robert Florey) could work wonders with tired material.

Occasionally a good original story (the potential of which for a bigger production had gone unnoticed) or even an idea, or the right screen personality mated with an appropriate story (as with Lucille Ball's two scatterbrained comedies about a movie star, *The Affairs of Annabel* [1938] and *Annabel Takes a Tour* [1938]) could produce a miniature screwball comedy of some distinction. *Curtain Call* (1940) was such a film—a six-reel forerunner of *The Producers* (1968) and a much funnier, not to say less padded film, built around the idea of creating a deliberately bad play. But the 1940 date is significant: for a brief period between 1940 and 1943, B films had more importance and were used to train new directors (many of them refugees from the European war), with expanded running times and budgets, better casts and better scripts, brought into play. None of the emerging improved Bs could be considered classics—except, like 1942's *Buy Me That Town*, within the perimeters of the "B",

HANDS ACROSS THE TABLE (1935) More sophisticated than authentically screwball, but a charming film with Ralph Bellamy losing Carole Lombard to (an unseen) Fred MacMurray.

RHYTHM ON THE RANGE (1936) Runaway heiress Frances Farmer and cowboy Bing Crosby prepare to lift the "Walls of Jehrico" routine from *It Happened One Night*.

ONE RAINY AFTERNOON (1936) The presence of Hugh Herbert, Mischa Auer, Roland Young, Erik Rhodes, and Donald Meek assure this film a place in the thirties screwball pantheon, though actually it was its easygoing charm that was its major asset, a holdover from the French original (written by Emeric Pressburger) of which it was such a delightful remake. In this busy scene Erik Rhodes (as usual) tries to stake his claim on unwilling fianceé Ida Lupino over the objections of Francis Lederer.

ANNABEL TAKES A TOUR (1938) Ball and Oakie again in the second (and last) of the Annabel comedies.

THE AFFAIRS OF ANNABEL (1938) Lucille Ball as a temperamental star, and Jack Oakie as her over-enterprising press agent in a most entertaining "B bombshell."

53

BY CANDLELIGHT (1933)
Maid (Elissa Landi)
masquerading as Countess
falls in love with valet
(Paul Lukas)
masquerading as Count.

BY CANDLELIGHT   Adding to the confusion, genuine Count
Nils Asther poses as his own valet's butler.

but nevertheless there are enough of them for it to be unfair to shunt them aside with no more than casual acknowledgment. Since most of them do belong to the early forties, however, discussion must properly await the introduction to that decade. In the meantime there are individual films of the thirties to be recalled with affection and some less familiar ones to be introduced.

BY CANDLELIGHT

(UNIVERSAL, 1933)

Directed by James Whale; screenplay by Hans Kraly, F. Hugh Herbert, Karen de Wolf, and Ruth Cummings, from a play by Siegfried Geyer.

LEADING PLAYERS:
Paul Lukas, Elissa Landi, Nils Asther, Esther Ralston, Lawrence Grant, Warburton Gamble, Lois January.

There is a whole subgenre of the screwball comedy that perhaps deserves a book all to itself (there are certainly enough examples to fill such a book!)—namely the comedy of deception, or in most cases double deception. Since masquerade is a key plot element of most screwball comedy films, this subgenre is certainly sufficiently related to warrant more than a nod in passing. On the other hand, masquerade is virtually the only common denominator both kinds of comedy share. The comedy of deception was certainly not rebelling against anything or making pertinent social statements. True, one finds it at its peak in the early thirties—partly because the inherently risqué subject matter was easier to handle in pre–Production Code days, but perhaps mainly because the glamorous, often Riviera-based stories laid no claim to reality and were such ideal escapist entertainment during the Depression.

Moreover, many of these movies were based on hit plays—no small consideration in the early days of sound, when the art of original screenwriting, particularly insofar as dialogue was concerned, was relatively new. And most of them provided ideal vehicles for sophisticated, romantic stars such as Ronald Colman, Adolphe Menjou, Francis Lederer, Leslie Howard, and Herbert Marshall, all of them possessed of voices—soothing, dulcet, gay, enticing—that the new talkies could use to advantage. Nevertheless, the genre went well back into the silents, though reaching its peak then in the sophisticated mid to late twenties via such films as Raymond Griffith's classic *Paths to Paradise* (1925) in which brilliantly inventive sight gags tend to divert attention from the masquerade plot, or *The Garden of Eden* (1928) in which Corinne Griffith assumed Tallulah Bankhead's celebrated stage role in a Lewis Milestone–directed comedy of a dual masquerade at a Riviera hotel. In *The Gay Deception* (1935), smoothly directed by William Wyler, one had a near-definitive example of the genre as related though somewhat remotely to the financial woes of the Depression. Frances Dee played a working girl who had won five thousand dollars—virtually a fortune then—in a lottery, and came to a New York hotel, posing as a millionairess, to enjoy one uninhibited spree before returning to drab small-town life. In the same hotel was European prince Francis Lederer, masquerading as a commoner. There was no doubt about the ultimate outcome.

Since each of the parties in such films is out to impress the other, the battling of the sexes is usually absent; at best, there is disillusionment and argument near the end when the masquerade (of one or both parties) is revealed, leaving just enough time for a happy adjustment to reality and an all-around reconciliation. The films tend to be elegant, the pace leisurely, the dialogue witty and sophisticated rather than peppered with wisecracks. Even more than *The Gay Deception*, the relatively unfamiliar *By Candlelight* is arguably *the* definitive comedy of deception, perhaps the more so because it runs a mere sixty-nine minutes. While it constantly comes up with surprises, at the same time it compresses its masquerade/deception/revelation/reunion narrative so that the various complications never become tiresome or permit the audience to guess the plot, as so often happened in the much more overblown variations on the theme at MGM.

Betraying its stage origins, though not too obviously, *By Candlelight* opens with a first act in which the dressing-gown-clad, cigar-smoking Josef (Paul Lukas) preening in his Paris apartment, fights off the amorous advances of the maid (Lois January), presumably because he has another assignation. Surprise No. 1 arrives in the person of Prince Alfred (Nils Asther) with his latest paramour, a countess. Josef, it seems, is merely the butler—well-rehearsed in Alfred's seduction techniques, providing champagne at just the right moment, and appearing on cue with candles, when, thanks to his own ministrations, the lights have failed. But threat of an imminent exposure sends the countess packing, although clearly the affair has been proceeding nicely for some time. The prince admires Josef for his tact and efficiency in backing up his apparently nonstop career of seduction; Josef in turn is in awe of his boss's skill and smooth line. But things are getting too hot in Paris, and they decide to shift their operations to their Vienna house, Josef to go on ahead with the luggage.

En route, aboard the train, a well-dressed lady, Maria (Elissa Landi), is impressed by the family crest on the luggage, which she assumes to be Josef's. They strike up a friendship, which

55

ripens during a jolly peasant festival. Ensconced in the new villa, Josef starts his own campaign of seduction and entices the apparently reluctant but actually willing Maria to his quarters. Although obviously a lady of quality and wealth, she presumably feels that she can better herself by a liaison with nobility. Carefully duplicating all of the prince's bon mots, gestures, and tricks, Josef just doesn't have the assurance or experience to pull it off, and too many of the prince's surefire witticisms just don't work when Josef forgets a key word or mixes up an epigram. However, Maria is apparently succumbing to his spell. Then, at the critical moment, the prince himself arrives. Sizing up the situation at a glance, and being a good-natured fellow, he assumes the role of his own butler, treats Josef with deference as *his* boss, and even pulls the failing lights and candle routine. Josef is of course delighted.

When Maria gets home that night, she is met by an outraged countess. Maria is merely a maidservant who has been borrowing the countess's clothes. Moreover, the countess—elegantly played by Esther Ralston—is the prince's Viennese mistress and is looking forward to rekindling her romance with him, so long as she can allay the suspicions of her elderly husband, played by that expert at tyrannical curmudgeons Lawrence Grant. The complications are obvious and include some amusing byplay with a cigarette case that the prince always presented with great solemnity to his conquests, knowing that it would be rejected since, as married women, they would not want to be found with such evidence. (His name was engraved inside.) Josef has given the case to Maria, who, *not* being a married woman and being easily impressed by the phony history ascribed to it, accepted it eagerly. Needless to say it *is* discovered. In a hilarious (and genuinely suspenseful) sequence, the cuckolded count angrily confronts the prince and would, in a few minutes, discover his wife in the bedroom—were it not for the resourceful Josef's getting her to phone the count as if from their own apartment, then rushing her home before her husband can arrive. Yet there is no sense of contrivance to all these complications; light of touch, and often disposed of almost as soon as

they arise, they finally fit together like a well-ordered jigsaw.

Despite the fact that director James Whale's most celebrated films—*The Old Dark House, The Bride of Frankenstein,* and *Showboat*—come from earlier or later years, there seems little doubt that 1933 and 1934 represent the highlight period of his distinguished if brief career. Over those two years he made *The Invisible Man, The Kiss Before the Mirror, By Candlelight,* and *One More River*—a remarkable quartet of stylish, literate, tasteful, and above all cinematic works, despite their literary and theatrical origins. Lubitsch's *Trouble in Paradise* certainly established a high-water mark for sophisticated comedy, not just for 1932 but for decades thereafter as well, but *By Candlelight,* with Whale effectively in a Lubitsch mood for perhaps the only time in his career, isn't so far behind.

In many ways it is a more remarkable film than *Trouble in Paradise* (which had so much going for it in terms of script, cast, and budget) in that Whale squeezes (but gently, not forcefully) the sophistication out of not unduly promising material. Cinderella fables like this one were in generous supply in the early Depression years; the dialogue is bright but never devastatingly funny; Lukas and Asther are polished, but hardly in the same league as such Lubitsch perennials as Maurice Chevalier or Herbert Marshall; and yet everything works beautifully. It may be pseudo-Lubitsch in content, but the style is wholly Whale's own. The virtually nonstop musical score, which goes beyond Mickey-Mousing to include deliberate musical jokes, is a case in point. Not only does the sprightly music enhance and reinforce the action, but it constantly reminds one that this is unreal, a show, an entertainment never for one moment to be taken seriously. It even takes up the slack on those occasional necessary moments when, in order to change pace or location, nothing happens on the screen. At such moments one can be acutely aware of silence and thus of the mechanics of filmmaking. The score here gives one no time for such reflections.

One suspects, too, that Whale may have had a hand in the scoring, since it often reflects his mordant sense of humor. At one point when an irate husband arrives to trap an errant wife, the score switches to one of the old-fashioned mysterious themes familiar through use in horror films and thrillers of the period (the theme here had been prominent in the previous year's *White Zombie*) but never exposed to the light of day in such elegant comedic frolics as this. Whale also kids his own stock-in-trade by mock menace and low-key lighting in close-ups of his principals caught in embarrassing situations. Even Lukas's slight stiffness is put to work for the film's good in those scenes where, with superbly timed mistiming, he repeats so ineffectually the lines of purring intellectual superiority that succeeded so well for the more experienced Asther.

Despite being primarily an exercise in applied directorial style, the film does still work well with an audience on those rare occasions when it is shown. The original German play, Americanized by P. G. Wodehouse to modest success, was later turned into a musical, which flopped. The film *is* perhaps a period piece. The musical score seems excessive by standards of the nineties, but one has to recall that the full, original musical score only became a major and integral part of the new grammar of

sound films in 1933, and that Whale was experimenting with a new toy, not merely using it.

It's also pleasant to note that nobody gets hurt in the film . . . the cuckolded husband has his faith restored in his straying wife, the philandering prince goes on his merry seductive way, and the butler and the maidservant, their masquerades dissolved, settle down to happy wedded bliss. In pre-Code days, amorality was rarely punished if the protagonists were likable . . . as they certainly are here.

20TH CENTURY
(COLUMBIA, 1934)

Directed by Howard Hawks; screenplay by Ben Hecht and Charles MacArthur, based on their stage play, itself based on the play *Napoleon of Broadway* by Bruce Milholland.

LEADING PLAYERS:
John Barrymore, Carole Lombard, Walter Connolly, Roscoe Karns, Ralph Forbes, Charles Lane, Etienne Girardot, Herman Bing, Edgar Kennedy.

If any one film deserves the accolade "first" in introducing not only the basic but also in fact

20TH CENTURY (1934) John Barrymore as Oscar Jaffe and Carole Lombard as Lily Garland encounter Lily's agent "Once Max Mandelbaum and now Max Jacobs for some mysterious reason," as played by Charles Lane (formerly Charles Levine) aboard the titular train.

one of the finest finished products of screwball comedy to the screen, then it is probably *20th Century*. Oddly enough, it is the only one of the undisputed leaders of the genre—*It Happened One Night, My Man Godfrey, Nothing Sacred, The Awful Truth, The Front Page, Bachelor Mother, Ninotchka, Midnight, The Lady Eve, Ruggles of Red Gap, My Favorite Wife*—never to have been remade. One would like to think of that as a tribute to the original, an admission that the script and the work of its two stars and its inspired direction could never be topped; but that consideration never prevented attempts to "improve" *Midnight* and some of the other titles cited. The explanation is probably far more prosaic: the theater itself is no longer held in such awe today and satirization of it would seem anachronistic; too, stars, agents, and producers zip from coast to coast via planes rather than more leisurely and elegantly by train. Updating it to today's entertainment industry would probably give us television stars and directors commuting from Hollywood to New York by jet, thus dislocating the time frame and all the other complications that depend on the train as a background. As a Broadway play, it is of course occasionally revived, even as a musical.

John Barrymore is Oscar Jaffe, theatrical impresario, and Carole Lombard is Mildred Plotka, former chorus girl whom he develops into a star and rechristens Lily Garland. Her ego develops along with her stardom until it matches his. As his mistress, she clearly loves him; as his star, she wonders whether she hasn't become bigger than him and finally succumbs to the lure of Hollywood. Determined to prove that he doesn't need her, Jaffe creates new stars and new shows—all of them flops. When after a disastrous run of *Joan of Arc* in Chicago, he sneaks onto the 20th Century train to avoid his creditors, he finds that Lily, now the toast of Hollywood, is also aboard, en route to New York with her new swain, Ralph Forbes. In the balance of the film Jaffe easily achieves his aim of upsetting the new romance—by boasting of his technically illicit liaison with Lily in earlier years and by cajoling and tricking the initially hostile Lily into signing a new contract with

20TH CENTURY   One of the many Jaffe suicide attempts is foiled by Lily.

him. The riotous battle of the sexes between Barrymore and Lombard and a basically sound plot line would be quite enough to keep *20th Century* lively, but they provide only part of the fun.

Barrymore's incredible ability to switch moods within a scene, to be scheming one second, charming and apparently self-sacrificial the next, his remarkable use of his body (when he describes a camel's actions in a projected Mary Magdalene scene, he *becomes* that camel, both in gait and in mouth-chewing, eye-rolling facial expression), his conviction in comic masquerade (once as a Southern colonel), his willingness for self-parody, and above all his beautifully controlled displays of the loss of self-control make this not only his finest comedy performance but also one of the best acting performances in his entire film career. The rest may be essentially punctuation, but what wonderful punctuation it is: Walter Connolly and Roscoe Karns as Jaffe's long-suffering right-hand men, forever being fired, rehired, and sent out on impossible tasks, and equipped with some of Hecht and MacArthur's most barbed witticisms; Etienne Girardot as a religious zealot whose habit of slapping biblical messages all over the train and on passengers' backs is forgiven because he is also a millionaire who can finance a Jaffe comeback (of course his check turns out to be no good); and best of all, dear old Herman Bing, bearded this time, whose appearance on the train in biblical robes, explaining that he is a former passion player ("I am der Judas!") inspires Jaffe to produce a monumental passion play to star Lily as Mary Magdalene and with imported dervishes—the whirling kind—in support.

The pace never slackens; we had had faster films before, even with the Hawksian brand of overlapping dialogue, but never as well employed to comic effect as here. Many of the gags are especially neat combinations of sight and sound and assume that the audience is up

20TH CENTURY   Aides Roscoe Karnes (left) and Walter Connolly prevent yet another suicide attempt by Barrymore.

20TH CENTURY   Detective James Burke, assigned to arrest Barrymore, is fooled by his Southern Colonel disguise and accent.

on its film history. "Who does he think I am, Trilby?" Lombard shrieks at one point, whereupon there is an immediate cut to Barrymore, who had of course played Svengali in the 1931 classic, emerging silently, menacingly, out of the shadows in a readily identifiable Svengali pose.

The dreadful play in which Lily Garland makes her triumphant debut is clearly a parody of *Coquette*, the Southern melodrama that already seemed outdated when turned into a film in 1929, though it earned Mary Pickford a Best Acting Academy Award. The parody is so accurate, if cruel, that it could well have provided grounds for a lawsuit were *Coquette* not considered dead and buried by 1934. Some gags even take on added pungency over the years. Charles Levison, expert at playing stereotypical Jewish agents or shyster lawyers (or later, income-tax agents) and at one point dismissed by Barrymore as a Grey Rat "who came to me as Max Mandelbaum and is now Max Jacobs for some mysterious reason," later found it a good career move to change his

59

name to Charles Lane. Another line, referring to Barrymore in a despondent mood, says that he has hidden himself away under the name of Hemingway and plans to shoot himself—a line that became far more poignant in later years.

20th Century remains an absolute joy sixty years after it was made: for its acting, for its mastery and manipulation of the English language (what wit, sophistication, and brilliance flow, seemingly effortlessly, from the typewriters of Hecht and MacArthur, without the need—even once—to resort to off-color language), and above all for the sheer pleasure of watching John Barrymore, reportedly well past his peak, but apparently quite unaware of it.

As a postscript to *20th Century*, it is worth noting that in 1937 when Carole Lombard, now a major established star and a specialist in comedy, made Paramount's screwball *True Confession*, she insisted on Barrymore for a key supporting role. It was Barrymore's first of five years at Paramount, alas as a contract featured player, not as a star, but with at least two more screwball outings in the years ahead, the outstanding *Midnight* of 1939 and the at least enterprising *World Premiere* of 1941.

True Confession alas was a most unworthy follow-up to the earlier Barrymore/Lombard collaboration. Lombard and costar Fred MacMurray had earlier the same year made a felicitous team in *Swing High, Swing Low*, but in this, her farewell film for the studio, and certainly one full of potential, nothing really worked. There are those who call *True Confession* hilarious, but even allowing for normal differences of opinion, they just can't have seen it later. Lombard plays a scatterbrained but intensely loyal wife to lawyer MacMurray, who is down on his luck and needs a winning case. She confesses to a murder so that he can get her off on a self-defense plea and get himself the headline attention he needs. The ploy works—but not the film. Director Wesley Ruggles allows Lombard to mug and shriek without restraint; it's a most abrasive performance. MacMurray looks bemused, as well he might. Barrymore hams it up outrageously, but at least contributes a much-needed spark of inspiration. The lax morality that had added such pungency to the situa-

tions and relationships in *20th Century*—made in that "buffer" year of 1934 when the Production Code was still flexible—here had to be whitewashed and tidied up before the end. But disappointing as it was, worse was yet to come: *True Confession* was remade in 1946 as *Cross My Heart* as a vehicle for Betty Hutton, for whom no less than five songs were added. Sonny Tufts and Michael Chekhov replaced MacMurray and Barrymore. All of the bad qualities of the original were retained, including an insistence on noise and speed, and the new director—the talented but unsuitable John Berry—was as out of his depth as Ruggles had been.

JIMMY THE GENT
(WARNER BROS., 1934)

Directed by Michael Curtiz; screenplay by Bertram Milhauser, from a story by Laird Doyle and Ray Nazarro.

LEADING PLAYERS:
James Cagney, Bette Davis, Alice White, Allen Jenkins, Alan Dinehart, Mayo Methot, Arthur Hohl.

Jimmy the Gent was James Cagney's sixteenth film in less than five years. On first viewing it seems to be a rather tawdry comedy with a basically unattractive hero (and Cagney's extreme crew cut makes his brashness seem less breezy than usual) and a plot line that seems patterned on that of *Blonde Crazy* (1931), his seventh movie and first comedic starring vehicle. But if *Blonde Crazy* was a film that changed its mind, and its direction, too often and never settled into a screwball niche, then *Jimmy the Gent* is a one-direction film, and its curious atmosphere is obviously what it was striving for. In its brittle and casually morbid way, it is to the burgeoning screwball comedy field of the thirties what Polonsky's *Force of Evil* (1948) was to the crime films of the forties.

If one doesn't warm to it immediately, then it improves with repeat viewings, unlike the only other Cagney-Davis teaming, *The Bride Came C.O.D.* (1941), a screwball comedy that seems

JIMMY THE GENT (1934) James Cagney and Allen Jenkins, (white hat), try to persuade Bette Davis that her boss Alan Dinehart (right) is a bigger if smoother chiseler than they are.

more labored and unfunny the second time around. *Jimmy the Gent* opens with an amusingly overdone montage of disasters intercut with newspaper headlines—plane, train, and other crashes that result in the death of millionaires and the search for their heirs. Despite the violence, the absurdity of some of the disasters and the unlikely names spelled out in the headlines make this a dynamic opening.

Moreover, its frenetic pace is matched by the energy and tempo of the subsequent film, which crams all of its story into an extremely brisk six reels.

Cagney plays Jimmy Corrigan, who runs a seedy little business tracking down missing heirs for a large chunk of their fortune—or creating phony heirs where none seem to exist. His girlfriend, Joan (Bette Davis), works for

Charles J. Wallingham (Alan Dinehart), who is in exactly the same business, but is such a smoothie that Davis is convinced he is completely ethical. There's a running battle of the sexes between Cagney and Davis as he constantly outsmarts them, expresses regret, contritely seems to be handing over big fees to the victims/heirs, and is just as constantly being caught out in his deception. In one of the funniest sections, Cagney and his roughneck associate Louie (Allen Jenkins) try to "upgrade" Cagney's modus operandi to outdo that of his rival, serving tea to usually unwilling clients and oozing an unconvincing culture. Caught in the changeover from pre-Code to Code-dominated films, *Jimmy the Gent* might have been tougher and even funnier if made a year earlier, but is certainly one of the most raucous and near-the-knuckle comedies of 1934. Drug addicts and cold-blooded murderers are made to seem funny as witnesses in Cagney's cases, and manipulation of the loopholes of the law is given in such detailed fashion that one wonders whether a whole parade of spurious insurance claims followed its release!

Dubious dialogue is often presented in such a way that it must have only *just* scraped by the scrutiny of the Production Code. "I've always wanted to make you . . . ," Alan Dinehart purrs to secretary Davis, adding, "truly mine," only after a long enough pause to make his lecherous point obvious. And Alice White (Allen Jenkins's girlfriend, about to be asked if she'd agree to an in-name-only marriage to a client), questioned what she'd do for $500, pertly replies, "I'd do my best!"

The climax sees Dinehart revealed in his true colors and Davis about to be married to Cagney—but since he tries to pull another last-minute chisel, one suspects, and hopes, that the battle of the sexes will continue even after the wedding in this wonderful, zany, minor classic.

THE RICHEST GIRL IN THE WORLD
(RKO RADIO, 1934)

Directed by William A. Seiter; original story and screenplay by Norman Krasna.

LEADING PLAYERS:
Miriam Hopkins, Joel McCrea, Fay Wray, Reginald Denny, Henry Stephenson, Beryl Mercer.

WOMAN CHASES MAN
(SAMUEL GOLDWYN–UNITED ARTISTS, 1937)

Directed by John G. Blystone; screenplay by Joseph Anthony, Mannie Seff, and David Hertz, from a story by Lynn Root and Frank Fenton.

LEADING PLAYERS:
Miriam Hopkins, Joel McCrea, Charles Winninger, Erik Rhodes, Ella Logan, Broderick Crawford.

Although produced more than three years apart, these two high-society comedies are linked in a number of ways, principally with both costarring Miriam Hopkins (as the aggressor in the battle of the sexes) and Joel McCrea (as the passive and eventually willing victim), and perhaps more interestingly in that the films seem to have reversed their values over the years.

The Richest Girl in the World was considered a

THE RICHEST GIRL IN THE WORLD (1934) Miriam Hopkins and Joel McCrea in the first of their five costarring films over a four year period, only the first and the last of them being comedies.

THE RICHEST GIRL IN THE
WORLD   Joel McCrea (after a
dunking) with Miriam
Hopkins.

WOMAN CHASES MAN (1937)   Charles Winninger, Miriam Hopkins, and Joel McCrea.

major if surprise comedy hit in 1934, a year when the competition included *It Happened One Night* and *20th Century*. Most of the credit was given to Norman Krasna, an excellent comedy writer temporarily out of favor at MGM, although his best days as a writer, producer, and occasional director still lay ahead. His original story was considered literate and witty (if wordy), and the film was good enough to open at the Radio City Music Hall. But whatever appeal and style the film had, or seemed to have, in 1934 has certainly not survived the intervening years well. Its story line is its main problem. Miriam Hopkins plays a woman of incredible wealth who has such a passion for privacy, and such a fear of some young man whom she might fall in love with actually being interested only in her money, that she has never allowed a photograph of herself to be published. For public functions, she changes places with her secretary—played by Fay Wray—who is accepted by everyone as the heiress.

When Miriam and Joel McCrea meet and fall in love, it is genuine, and he of course believes *her* to be the secretary. But in order to test him fully, she has Fay Wray (likable and attractive herself) make a determined play for him. Joel clearly likes Fay (his romantic vis-à-vis from *The Most Dangerous Game* two years earlier) and—in one of the few really original touches in the film—decides that it's probably worth marrying her for her millions even though he really loves the apparent secretary. Usually in such comedies it is the girl who is the gold digger, but the originality stops at that point and the anticipated complications and misunderstandings end up with everybody happy: Hopkins convinced that she has at last found a man who loves her for herself alone, McCrea having finally sacrificed wealth for love and then finding that he has both. Perhaps too much repetition of the theme since has worked against *The Richest Girl in the World*, but it is doubly tiresome because it is not only rarely amusing but also entirely predictable, and the wait just doesn't seem justified for the few laughs generated. Hopkins comes across as shrewish and

64

WOMAN CHASES MAN Hopkins, Ella Logan, and Broderick Crawford (spread-eagled on floor) try to show McCrea a letter explaining why they have taken over his house.

conniving, making Fay Wray seem a much more desirable catch. William Seiter, normally an adroit and tasteful comedy director, seems unable to get it all together to create any kind of life, let alone sparks. Yet, its reputation survives unchallenged.

Conversely, the more ambitious *Woman Chases Man*, by far the best of Samuel Goldwyn's only sporadic ventures into screwball comedy (perhaps one should except Howard Hawks's *Ball of Fire* from the forties), seemed doomed to adverse criticism from the start.

Apparently it started life as a backstage comedy (written by Ben Hecht) and, as was not unusual at producer-dominated MGM (but was unusual for the independent Goldwyn), began an extended odyssey through several additional writers, many uncredited, eventually to undergo a total metamorphosis into a story quite unrelated to show business. Too many cooks and too much brewing invariably spell trouble, especially for a comedy, but in this case all the rewrites are seamless and the film emerges as a totally smooth, cohesive, and often original comedy. Even its "evidence" of production problems is purely circumstantial. At seventy-one minutes it seems far too short for a top-of-the bill A production. Yet Goldwyn was one of the few producers never to equate

WOMAN CHASES MAN Hopkins tries to get a willing McCrea drunk so that he'll sign a contract he'd never countenance while sober.

65

WOMAN CHASES MAN   The climax of the film finds Hopkins and McCrea — and other members of the cast — literally up a tree; one of screwball's more inspired sequences.

length with quality; in 1930 his Ronald Colman vehicle, *The Devil to Pay*, from a Lonsdale story, was quite possibly the most sophisticated and self-assured talkie made to that point, yet it ran for only a few minutes over an hour, maintaining a leisurely pace and a witty style without ever seeming rushed. Likewise *Woman Chases Man* tells its story admirably in the less than seven-reel length and shows no signs whatsoever of tampering, salvaging, or paste-work. In fact the only cause for suspicion at all is the credit to John Blystone as director. Essentially Blystone was a roughhouse director: he had done Cagney's *Great Guy* the year before and would follow *Woman Chases Man* with Laurel and Hardy's *Swiss Miss*. The elegance and sophistication of *Woman Chases Man*, so alien to

his normal style, led one to ponder that possibly he was the *last* director brought in and that his main function was to link and finish the work of others. If so, then he did his job well *and* had good prior material to work with.

Complaints that the film strained too hard for laughs and featured unsympathetic male protagonists in Joel McCrea as the millionaire and Charles Winninger as his conniving, skinflint father just don't hold water today. Without being a great comedy, it is still a very good one, and moreover it is the unstereotypical characterizations that keep it looking much fresher than many of its contemporaries, and especially *The Richest Girl in the World*.

Giving it added feminist topicality today, Miriam Hopkins plays an architect whose ambitions have been frustrated because of sex discrimination, and who ultimately sets her cap for McCrea, hoping to get him to finance her building scheme. (Curiously, her role is a sort of compression of the Colbert/McCrea roles in *The Palm Beach Story*, while McCrea can be seen as a slightly more colorful forerunner of Rudy Vallee in that later classic.) There are the usual masquerade complications, and McCrea, needless to say, has a fortune-hunting fiancée who is rapidly displaced by the energetic Hopkins. At a period when he had not yet had many opportunities to develop a comic persona, McCrea plays his dull, all-business hero with a neatly underplayed sense of humor, helped and punctuated by the occasional devastating one-liner from Dorothy Parker's contribution to the script. Presumably, too, it is to Ms. Parker that we must be grateful for the explanation of Charles Winninger's conservative mind that he was "born in Maine and weaned in Vermont." Winninger certainly isn't particularly endearing as the grasping father, but the role makes for a nice contrast to his cherubic face and

twinkling eyes, and he plays it well. In fact he repeated the role virtually verbatim in the 1947 Deanna Durbin comedy, *Something in the Wind*. Gruff, hearty, good-natured Eugene Pallette may have been a mere welcome permanent head of the screwball family, but Winninger made for a refreshing change of pace. One might also note the energetic, uncouth humors of Broderick Crawford in a supporting role (he was too little used at this early stage in his career, when his crudeness had more comic spontaneity) and Al Bridge, still essentially a B-western villain and here tapped as a bit process server, well before he joined Preston Sturges's stock company.

Completing its parallel with *The Richest Girl in the World*, The Goldwyn film also opened at the Radio City Music Hall—where critics obviously expected much better from it, but enjoyed it enough to at least class it as enjoyable lightweight late-Spring fun. Now, well over half a century later, it can be seen as one of the most enjoyable "sleepers" of the whole screwball cycle.

FOUR

ANCESTORS AND DESCENDANTS OF "IT HAPPENED ONE NIGHT"

IT HAPPENED ONE NIGHT (1934)   Clark Gable and Claudette Colbert in the hayrick scene.

FUGITIVE LOVERS (1934) Robert Montgomery and Madge Evans on the night bus that left before Capra's.

Whether or not *It Happened One Night* is a bona fide screwball comedy is, for the moment, unimportant. There can be no denying that it spawned a whole subgenre of cross-country chase/romances that *were*. But in any case, one has to grant pride of place to a film that preceded it, *Fugitive Lovers* (1933).

Even *it* was far from being the first of the cross-country comedy films. From the twenties on, as more roads were built and more cars made more places more accessible to more Americans, Hollywood exploited the East Coast to West automobile migration through such comedy shorts as Sennett's *Hoboken to Hollywood* and a large number of features. Among the Reginald Denny vehicle *California Straight Ahead* (1925), and probably the first feature to exploit the comic possibilities of a new industry, the auto camp, *Rubber Tires* (1927). But these were not even *potential* screwball comedies and were largely built around the sight-gag material of failed brakes on hillsides, lack of gasoline, and the hazards of nature and weather.

Fugitive Lovers was the film that set the pattern of boy meeting— and taming—girl in the course of a cross-country jaunt by bus. Its plot was less promising than its final outcome. Robert Montgomery played a convict who makes a bid for freedom in a mass jailbreak and winds up on a bus that is conveniently passing. The passengers include Madge Evans, a showgirl on the run from an amorous (but lethal) gangster, who, learning of her flight, has managed to be aboard, too. Montgomery and Evans pair off; a disastrous blizzard enables Montgomery to display his true heroic colors by sacrificing his chance at freedom in order to save others, and a pardon is fairly broadly guaranteed.

Fugitive Lovers beat Universal's *Cross Country Cruise* (a rather disjointed mixture of romance, comedy, and murder) into release by some two weeks, and *It Happened One Night* by a month, all three films getting in to movie houses in January and February of 1934. In fact, Robert Montgomery is said to have turned down *It Happened One Night* because he had already done the similar *Fugitive Lovers.* Production schedules don't make that claim entirely credible, and it is more likely that he was actively *preparing* to make the MGM film when the Capra offer came along. (On the other hand, MGM was notorious for postproduction "fussing" and delays, while economy-conscious Columbia was anxious to get its big ones into release as soon as possible to start recouping costs.)

Similarities between the two films are too strong to be entirely coincidental. One must suspect that the writers of *Lovers* had read the original story "Night Bus," on which *It Happened One Night* was based, and borrowed and reshaped, carefully keeping this side of plagiarism, which may well account for the sudden shifting of gears for the melodramatic climax. Since screwball comedy as a genre had not been fully shaped by 1933, *Lovers* veers from much genuine screwball material in the first half (involving both the bus passengers and the Runyonesque gangsters) to crime melodrama with romance and reformation thrown in. By today's standards, the climax seems somewhat of a cop-out, almost as though inspiration had run out before a logical ending could be reached. Thirties' thinking was rather different though: it is more likely that, even with a script by Frances Goodrich and Albert Hackett, it was felt that the original vein had been thoroughly mined, and action writer-director George B. Seitz was brought in to provide a bang-up, audience-satisfying finale.

It's a curious film all around. There's some magnificently obnoxious comedy from Ted Healy (who made coarse vulgarity something of a fine art) in the equivalent of Roscoe Karns's role in the Capra film, an odd role reversal in the use (and leadership) of the Three Stooges; some beautifully mordant humor from Nat Pendleton as the gangster; beauty and charm, as well as a good performance, from Madge Evans; plus some interesting location work and exciting action sequences that are played completely straight despite the basically comedic framework. Robert Montgomery, though usually at home in any kind of comedy role, has a rather ill-defined character

this time around. One is never too sure what crime landed him in jail or if in fact he was framed; the warden clearly loathes him because he is an intellectual and "read all those books"; and though Montgomery *is* sympathetic, his bust-out leads to a mass slaughter that is conveniently sidestepped when the question of his pardon comes up.

Director Richard Boleslavsky and cameraman Ted Tetzlaff pull off an interesting (and only occasionally obvious) stylistic experiment by ever-so-slightly undercranking most of the nondialogue scenes; this makes the film move faster *physically* than it normally would. It's essentially a subliminal effect, and only occasionally (as in reaction shots between faces) is one aware of the trick that is being pulled, but it does result in a stepped-up pace that certainly helps the film.

It Happened One Night* is surely too well-known (and described) to need a detailed recapitulation. Suffice it to say that Claudette Colbert, madcap heiress daughter of millionaire Walter Connolly, escapes from his yacht where she is being held a virtual prisoner to prevent her marriage to fortune hunter Jameson Thomas. With limited funds, she is forced to take a cross-country bus to make her wedding day. En route, and especially after circumstances force them to leave the bus together, she falls in with—and eventually in love with—reporter Clark Gable, who helps her first for the sake of a story, and then because he genuinely likes her. He humbles her, teaches her the value of money (an important element in the Depression), and finally marries her after a scatterbrained and aborted wedding ceremony at which original suitor King Westley (it's surprising how many rejected suitors in Depression-era films had the aristocratic Christian name of King!) arrives at her father's grounds in an autogiro.

By any standards, *It Happened One Night* was and is an excellent comedy, surprisingly

*(Columbia, 1934.)

Directed by Frank Capra; Screenplay by Robert Riskin from an original story by Samuel Hopkins Adams.
Leading players: Clark Gable, Claudette Colbert, Walter Connolly, Roscoe Karns, Jameson Thomas, Alan Hale, Ward Bond.

sprightly considering its two-hour running time. But apart from Colbert's madcap heiress, it had relatively few screwball ingredients. Gable and Colbert made superb sparring partners—it was one of the best vehicles either of them ever had—but their partnership never amounted to more than that. It was far less physical and violent than the Powell/Lombard and Lombard/March pairings that were to follow. Nor was the element of masquerade stressed; neither Gable nor Colbert were entirely what they seemed, but the only bona fide masquerade came when Gable posed as a tough kidnapper to scare off the too curious Roscoe Karns.

Two of the more blatant copies of *It Happened One Night* made their appearance the following year, in mid-1935. *Red Salute,* produced by Edward Small independently and directed by Sidney Lanfield, cast Barbara Stanwyck in a clone of the Colbert role. This time she's the daughter of an army general, Purnell Pratt, and while wealth is not stressed, it is made abundantly clear that she is of the capitalist class—and it thoroughly ashamed of it. She's in love with (or thinks she is) a Communist student and rabble-rouser played with even more nastiness than usual by Hardie Albright. Lectures on Americanism versus Communism having no effect, the general shanghais her aboard a plane and sends her to Mexico, to keep her from marrying Albright. There she falls in with a likable young soldier, Robert Young, and finally enlists his aid in rushing across country by car and caravan to join and marry her radical boyfriend. (A less political title, *Her Enlisted Man,* was dreamed up for a reissue, while in England the film was called *Arms and the Girl,* perhaps in the hope that it might suggest a subliminal connection with George Bernard Shaw.)

The inevitable happens, and though not weakening in her resolve to marry Albright, Stanwyck finds herself falling in love with Young—who on her behalf has become a deserter and committed enough illegalities to land himself in prison for life. The moment of truth comes when they attend a dance, and Young realizes that she can't be a Communist

because "deep thinkers are dodoes on the dance floor!" Father Pratt, like Connolly before him, backs Young, whom he sees as a prospective son-in-law and turns him loose at a student protest meeting that Albright has engineered. After his rousing speech on Americanism, Young uses his fists, too—and the FBI has agents waiting to pounce on the subsequently rioting students to deport them immediately! Even at that time, well before the McCarthy era, its hysterical stance on Communism was overwrought and left a bad taste; later years have made it no funnier though perhaps more interesting as an academic period piece. It's at its best when duplicating the quiet charm of *It Happened One Night*—as in scenes featuring Cliff Edwards and his pleasing, casual singing.

Columbia naturally tried to cash in on *It Happened One Night,* too, but to its credit its initial copy had a mind of its own. In *She Couldn't Take It* (rather oddly retitled *Woman Tamer* in Europe), Joan Bennett is the madcap heiress daughter in a screwball family whose antics, spending, and front-page publicity have reduced Dad (Walter Connolly again) to desperation. Nor is he helped by the almost equally dizzy attitude of his wife, played by Billie Burke. Facing business pressures and an income-tax-evasion charge, he happily goes off to prison leaving his family to fend for itself. There he encounters tough but likable gangster George Raft, and the two become firm friends. When Connolly has a heart attack, he calls Raft to his deathbed and charges the soon-to-be-released gangster with the financial control and behavioral reformation of his family.

For a while the film follows its expected taming-of-the-shrew path, until Bennett gets the bright idea of prying loose a big chunk of her inheritance by faking a kidnapping. Unfortunately she approaches Lloyd Nolan with the idea, not realizing that his casual exterior masks a cold and sadistic killer. Without losing its comic momentum, the film rings in some unexpected suspense and an especially chilling moment when Nolan cold-bloodedly murders the film's nominal comic relief (Wallace Ford). It may well have been this unexpected

RED SALUTE (1935)   Most
blatant of the many rip-offs.

RED SALUTE   Barbara Stanwyck, Robert Young, and some familiar hay.

mixing of styles—something of a trademark with director Tay Garnett—that caused the film to be extremely unpopular with the critics. It was still a little early for black comedy to be recognized as a natural complement to screwball.

The film came to a rousing climax with a spectacular semislapstick race to the rescue by hordes of police cars and motorcycle cops—a sequence that was to prove useful as stock footage in later Columbia films. (Buster Keaton appropriated virtually the entire climax for his two-reeler *So You Won't Squawk*). Still not a well-known film, *She Couldn't Take It* holds up ex-

tremely well today, perhaps because its almost callous mixing of comedy and murder seems to match the mood of so many nineties films.

The influence of *It Happened One Night* continued throughout the thirties, though mainly in B films and programmers like *Fifty Roads to Town* (1937), overlong for its thin narrative with Ann Sothern and Don Ameche as the mismatched travelers, and *Cross Country Romance*, 1940's farewell to the genre, with Gene Raymond coming to the aid of fleeing heiress Wendy Barrie. Heiresses had to take themselves a little more seriously in the forties; with the war upon us, the echoes of *It Happened One*

SHE COULDN'T TAKE IT (1935)   Columbia's own follow-up: reformed gangster
George Raft, madcap heiress Joan Bennett, scatterbrained wife Billie Burke.

73

SHE COULDN'T TAKE IT Gangsters (including Donald Meek, rear) play with trains and other toys while holding heiress Bennett for ransom.

Night lessened. In *Public Deb #1* (1940) it was heiress Brenda Joyce who was the Communist, and she wasn't rushing across country, being content to push her propaganda and chase an unsuitable husband within the boundaries of New York City. And in *The Palm Beach Story* spoiled heiress Mary Astor was too lazy and self-indulgent to rush anywhere, waiting instead for victims to fall into her comfortable Florida web. The second go-around for *It Happened One Night* had to await until 1945, when Ann Miller reduced its essentials to provide the framework for a B musical, *Eve Knew Her Apples* (not an official remake, but a legal one since it was also a Columbia film), and then until 1956, when an official, color remake entitled *You Can't Run Away From It* not only proved unsuccessful, but also showed that June Allyson (who later played the Carole Lombard role in a remake of *My Man Godfrey*) just did not belong in screwball comedy.

IF YOU COULD ONLY COOK
(COLUMBIA, 1935)

Directed by William Seiter; screenplay by Howard Green and Gertrude Purcell, from an original story by F. Hugh Hubert.

LEADING PLAYERS:
Herbert Marshall, Jean Arthur, Leo Carrillo, Lionel Stander, Frieda Inescort.

Engaging and entertaining, *If You Could Only Cook* is also included in this survey as a representative of all those honorable if nonmemorable seven-reel programmers that were turned out so regularly in the thirties while the screw-

74

ball era was at its height. Columbia probably made more of them than any other studio. Without their own theater chain to absorb automatically whatever product they had, Columbia made a lot of the seventy-minute comedies, which, with a decent star or two, could fill single-bill, top-of-the-bill, or bottom-of-the-bill requirements, depending on the geographic location and the clientele. Moreover, throughout the thirties, though not always all at the same time, Columbia had under contract any number of players—Melvyn Douglas, George Murphy, Ann Sothern, Rosalind Russell, Joan Blondell, Cary Grant, Jean Arthur, Virginia Bruce, and others—who fitted so effortlessly into the screwball cycle. Melvyn Douglas seemed quite the most overworked actor in this genre, backed up of course by the ubiquitous Ralph Bellamy, who probably retained his sanity by balancing his dunderheaded Other Men roles in comedies with virile hero roles in detective B mysteries and actioners like *Eight Bells.*

If You Could Only Cook achieved fairly rapid notoriety within the trade, and belated notoriety with the public, when Harry Cohn, head of Columbia, decided to release it in England initially, and then the rest of Europe, as a Frank Capra production—an unusually shoddy piece of fraudulent opportunism. Capra makes much of the incident in his book *The Name Above the Title,* although as with everything else in that readable but unreliable autobiography, it is fictionalized (quite unnecessarily) beyond belief. Ostensibly he heard about the deception when exhibitors referred to his *second* Jean Arthur film. (This was well before he had made his first with the actress, *Mr. Deeds Goes to Town.*) He also claimed that he was in Europe for the openings of *Lost Horizon* (a 1937 film!) and that while he was there he tried to contact Eisenstein in Russia and found him to be both in political disgrace and physical hiding. The former didn't happen until the forties, and the latter never happened. So much for Capra as a historian! Capra's anger at Cohn, and his subsequent lawsuit, were both understandable and justified, yet his wrath is so mingled with ego that nowhere is there any gesture of sympathy toward the director (William Seiter) who had made a movie good enough to be sold as a Capra film and yet in Europe was being deprived of the satisfaction of seeing his name on his work.

Despite the popularity of *It Happened One Night,* Capra's name at the box office in Europe was not all that big in 1935. Audiences in England readily accepted *If You Could Only Cook* as a smaller, more intimate Capra comedy, just as they would welcome *Wagonmaster* in 1950 as John Ford's smaller, more personal western follow-up to his 1949 spectacular *She Wore a Yellow Ribbon.*

One of Columbia's major assets in screwball comedy was Jean Arthur. A variable actress in straight roles (and especially in the soap operas to which the studio often consigned her in the early years), she had the happy knack (perhaps a *potential* knack that was recognized and developed by key directors) of pacing herself to the characteristics of her costars. In Columbia screwball comedies she appeared opposite Edward G. Robinson, Melvyn Douglas, Herbert Marshall, Gary Cooper, Cary Grant, Joel McCrea, and Ronald Colman, and at other studios opposite John Wayne, Ray Milland, Robert Cummings, James Stewart, and William Powell. Those stars all retained their specific personas while appearing opposite her. She, in turn, retained her trademark husky voice, making relatively few concessions to her costars, switching emphasis from hard-boiled self-assurance to baby-faced innocence when her roles switched from tough reporter to enterprising underdog, but basically projecting the same beguiling mixture of ruthlessness and sweetness. It was a style eminently suited to the screwball comedies of the thirties and may explain why her *least* appealing performance was in a straight role opposite Cary Grant in Howard Hawks's *Only Angels Have Wings.* But in comedy, and despite the extreme disparity in acting styles and personalities of the aforementioned actors, the chemistry of teaming *always* worked. This is no minor achievement, and not always easy to perfect.

Compare for example the perfect teaming of Arthur with William Powell in *The Ex-Mrs. Bradford,* a first-rate *Thin Man* clone, with that of

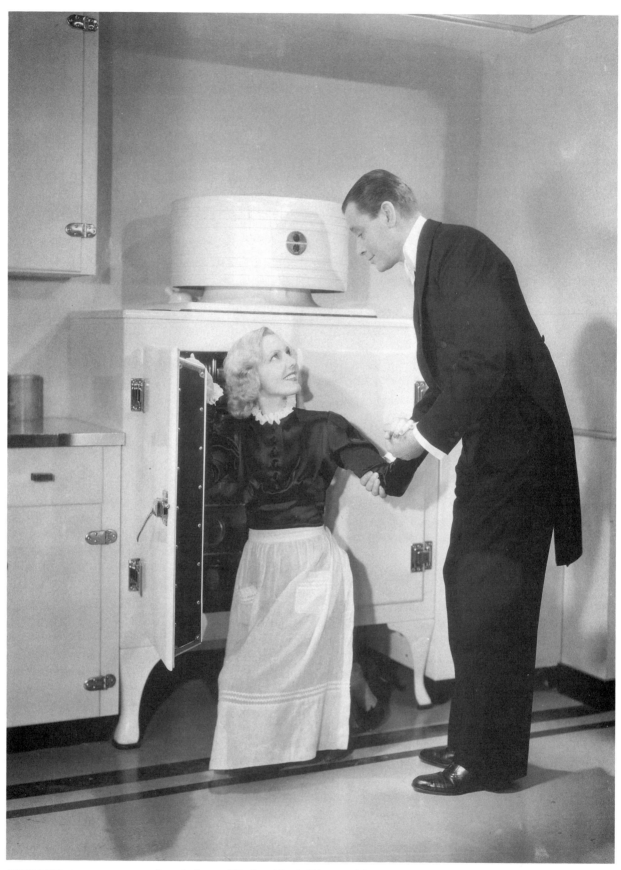

IF YOU COULD ONLY COOK (1935) Jean Arthur and Herbert Marshall in one of the many thirties masquerades.

Ginger Rogers and Powell in *Star of Midnight*. Powell was exactly the same in both films, as urbane and polished as ever. Both films were almost identical in content and audience appeal. Yet somehow Rogers was totally unable to connect with Powell; there was no teamwork, merely two performers playing individually, and the film suffered. Still, in *Bachelor Mother* (1939) the Rogers teamwork with David Niven was superb, and their chemistry perfect. Factors other than script and sympathetic direction may of course be involved. Rogers has always had something of an ego problem, and it's possible that in 1935 in *Star of Midnight* she may have been on the defensive, aware that she was neither as polished a performer nor as big a box-office name as Powell, and thus unable to relax in the role. With *Bachelor Mother*, however, she had already begun to establish herself both as a straight actress and comedienne separate from her popularity in the Astaire/Rogers musicals. Moreover, there was no doubt that she was a bigger name than the still up-and-coming David Niven. If that is what allowed her to relax more in her role, all well and good; it emerged as one of the best of all screwball comedies and offered one of the best Rogers performances, in comedy or otherwise.

It would seem that *If You Could Only Cook* has basically served as a launching pad for discussion of other aspects of screwball comedy— but that is entirely consistent with the film's history. When it was first released, audiences enjoyed it, remembered it for its unique title and for the smoothness of Marshall's performance, but recalled little of its specifics or any particular highlights. Seen again, years later, it had much the same effect: instant and thorough enjoyment, and a fairly quick retreat into pleasant nostalgic memory. Still, it's a fate eminently to be preferred to that of many mediocre comedies of the thirties where one recalls highlights vividly—because they were the *only* memorable aspects of films which totally deserved their oblivion.

For the record, *If You Could Only Cook* teamed Herbert Marshall as a millionaire automobile tycoon (but also a creative one, since he was an engineer/inventor, too) with Jean Arthur, pen-

niless and homeless. For complicated reasons that doubtless seemed reasonable enough in the Depression, they masquerade as a husband-and-wife, valet-and-maid team, enabling them to move into the mansion of mobster Leo Carrillo, whose henchman is the gravel-voiced, wisecracking Lionel Stander. (In this period, Carrillo rather surprisingly fluctuated between playing genuine gangsters or ruthless bandits, as in *Viva Villa*, and burlesque versions of the same roles, as here and in *The Gay Desperado*.) An added complication is that the gangster is a gourmet—and Arthur is no cook, although she has to pretend to be one in order to keep her job and possibly her life. Without any special highlights, it was smooth, bubbly, and a pleasing time-killer for the winter of 1935, when it was released, another reminder of what a good all-round comedy director (*In Person, Sons of the Desert, Rafter Romance, Professional Sweetheart*) William Seiter usually was in the midthirties, despite the occasional *Richest Girl in the World* misfire.

THE WHOLE TOWN'S TALKING
(COLUMBIA, 1935)

Directed by John Ford; screenplay by Jo Swerling and Robert Riskin, from a story by W. R. Burnett.

LEADING PLAYERS:
Edward G. Robinson, Jean Arthur, Wallace Ford, Arthur Byron, Etienne Girardot, Donald Meek.

The idea of a Milquetoast having an exact double who is a killer or a gangster is a fairly familiar one in film, especially for stars seeking a change of pace with a dual role. Just the year before this film was made, Buster Keaton did this in an interesting French comedy, *King of the Champs-Elysées*, and in the fifties France repeated it with Fernandel in the abysmally labored and unfunny *Public Enemy #1*. The intervening years saw many variations on the theme. Here, Edward G. Robinson plays Killer Manion and a meek little clerk whose identi-

THE WHOLE TOWN'S
TALKING (1935)   Jean
Arthur points out to
Edward G. Robinson as
Jones, the mild-mannered
advertising agency clerk,
how much he resembles
the escaped convict Killer
Mannion.

THE WHOLE TOWN'S TALKING   Press and police make life miserable for Jones.

THE WHOLE TOWN'S TALKING
Testing out his resemblance,
Jones pulls "tough" gangster
faces over lunch—to the
consternation of fellow diner
Donald Meek.

ties become mixed up when the gangster seeks to kill off his look-alike and thus literally bury his past. Jean Arthur's tough, self-reliant guardian-angel role predates the similar parts she would play opposite Gary Cooper and James Stewart in later Frank Capra films at Columbia.

The Whole Town's Talking (released in England as *Passport to Fame*) is an extremely good film; perhaps a trifle overlong, but efficient, looking far more expensive than it probably was, well cast, and unusually well-handled in its many action and crowd scenes. However, it does come off rather better as a *film* than as a screwball comedy, though in the latter regard, it had few precedents for comparison. John Ford, then working primarily for Fox and RKO Radio, made it on loan-out, sandwiched in between the more typical Fordian vehicles *Judge Priest* and *The Informer.* Comedy, except as

punctuation within another genre, was never Ford's strongest area and, too, Robinson and writer W. R. Burnett—the old *Little Caesar* team—seem too much of a powerhouse for him to handle. Robinson had shown in *Little Giant* that he could be a facile comedian, but his best comic work—most notably *A Slight Case of Murder*—was still in the future. In any event, despite a Preston Sturges–like emphasis on speed, chaos, and noise, with police sirens never absent for long, the story seems to take precedence over its comic possibilities. Much of the lighting and camerawork (Joseph August, who was also to shoot *The Informer*) is also so much in the accepted tradition of then current gangster cycle that the balance is further shifted.

Establishing Robinson as a cold-blooded murderer in one scene was probably deemed necessary in order to lose audience sympathy

THE WHOLE TOWN'S TALKING   The inevitable confrontation between clerk and killer; the film employed some of the best trick split-screen photography to that time.

THE WHOLE TOWN'S TALKING   A striped shirt and expensive suit help identify the "bad" Robinson to Jean Arthur.

for him prior to his own sticky end, but up to that point he has been quite a likable rogue, and the change is disturbing. Bogart, in the later *It All Came True,* managed to remain sympathetic despite being established as a killer; here it doesn't work as well. However, it is easy to make these criticisms so long after the event when we are more familiar both with Ford's whole body of work and the cynical satires of the thirties. In 1935, the year of *G-Men,* the gangster cycle had undergone some changes in emphasis but was still in full swing; story values counted far more than satiric ones. And, too, while the dual-role gimmick wasn't new, it wasn't commonplace either, and with Robinson in the two leads the extremely well photographed trick role still had novelty value.

THE WHOLE TOWN'S TALKING   With Mannion wiped out, Jones, a hero, is finally able to declare his long repressed love.

The film was a solid if not spectacular success at the time, but could have done with more purely comedy scenes (such as the one where the "mild" Robinson tries to convince himself that he looks like his killer double and pulls tough, menacing faces in a mirror—to the consternation of Donald Meek, sitting nearby) and fewer harrowing dramatic sequences, such as the one where the innocent Robinson is driven to near insanity by the intensity of a police third-degree.

Curiously, in Europe, some reviews credited the film to Walter Lang, suggesting that Lang may have been the director originally planned and named in advance publicity. (In the mass production methods of the day, erroneous credits were often released.) More than one critic complained of lack of cohesion in the plot and queried whether the film (already in excess of ninety minutes) might not have been too heavily edited prior to release. Certainly the casual way we are asked to accept Robinson's apparently hopeless infatuation with Jean Arthur, and the skimpy appearances of an aunt (after much talk about her), suggest that a lot more footage was shot than was used, although that would be unusual for Ford. On the whole, though, despite its uneven qualities, the film stands up well and is a pleasing companion piece to Columbia's other crime/screwball entry of the same period, *She Couldn't Take It*. Its casual similarity to some of Preston Sturges's later work is curious, too, since the one time that Ford returned to all-out comedy, with *When Willie Comes Marching Home* (1950), it was for a film much in the tradition of Sturges's *Hail the Conquering Hero* (1944).

POINTS OF NOTE: most of the big-scale prison scenes are stock footage from Howard Hawks's *The Criminal Code*. And in certain circles there is a persistent (but erroneous) belief that the film is a remake of the 1931 *Ex-Bad Boy*, also with Jean Arthur—probably prompted by the fact that *that* was a remake of the Universal silent *The Whole Town's Talking*. The fact that Jean Arthur later costarred in Columbia's *Talk of the Town* merely adds to the confusion—as does the fact that Frank Capra in his autobiography credits the success of his (1937) *Lost Hori-zon* with John Ford's being given the freedom to make this (1935) movie!

REMEMBER LAST NIGHT?
(UNIVERSAL, 1935)

Directed by James Whale; screenplay by Doris Malloy, Harry Clork, and Louise Henry, from the novel *The Hangover Murders* by Adam Hobhouse.

LEADING PLAYERS:
Robert Young, Constance Cummings, Edward Arnold, Sally Eilers, Reginald Denny, Robert Armstrong, Jack LaRue, Gregory Ratoff, Arthur Treacher, Edward Brophy, E. E. Clive, Louise Henry, Gustav von Seyffertitz, Monroe Owsley.

Equally as influential as *My Man Godfrey* and *It Happened One Night* in the number of imitations it engendered, *The Thin Man* (1934) was at least salutary in its *effect*. It produced more high-class variations on a theme than outright imitations. Recognizing that the basic appeal of *The Thin Man* lay in the delightful collaboration between William Powell and Myrna Loy as the husband-and-wife team of amateur sleuths, and in the escapist milieu of "civilized" murder and crime in high-society circles and usually "among friends," the many follow-ups made no attempt to duplicate incidents or an overall plot line. It was enough to adapt the many available crime stories to a like plateau of society, and to tailor them to the specific personalities of the stars involved.

Some of the best came from Britain, most especially *Seven Sinners* (1936) with Edmund Lowe and Constance Cummings, who turned up with some regularity and effectiveness as a substitute for Myrna Loy, and *This Man Is News* (1938) with Barry K. Barnes and Valerie Hobson. In that film, and a James Bond–like espionage thriller *Q Planes* of the following year, the poised, sophisticated, and beautiful Valerie Hobson showed that she could easily have been Britain's own unique Myrna Loy in a whole series of screwball comedies. But that kind of comedy was not Britain's forte, and while her career was a notable one, her talent for comedy was sadly wasted. Apart from their romantic sleuthing duos, these post–*Thin Man* comedies all shared two common characteristics: a sensible reliance on directors of taste (Stephen Roberts, Albert de Courville, David MacDonald) and an exaggerated emphasis on the pleasures of social drinking. In American films, this was a reaction to the long period of Prohibition when on-screen drinking had to be curtailed and done as much as possible via suggestion; in British films the alcoholic element was there primarily because it was chic to copy so integral a part of the Hollywood equivalent.

But with the possible exception of *Seven Sinners* (itself a much-changed remake of a silent and influenced as much by *The 39 Steps* as by *The Thin Man!*) only one of the follow-ups at-

tempted to expand the screwball framework of *The Thin Man.* The film was *Remember Last Night?* with Robert Young and Constance Cummings as the incessantly imbibing Tony and Carlotta Milburn. The film opens with one of the wildest and most surreal of all Post-Code Hollywood parties, with the art deco design of the Milburns' home including a huge bar shaped like a galleon. In this opening sequence, a cannon is fired at a yacht moored nearby in Long Island Sound—which up-anchors and steams away in a speeded-up trick shot. The wild pace slackens a little the next morning when the body of a murdered guest is found, and everybody is suffering from such extreme hangovers that alibis and recollections make little sense.

Remember Last Night? then becomes a murder

REMEMBER LAST NIGHT? (1935) A bar to put to shame anything Nick and Norah ever offered! (From left) Sally Eilers, Reginald Denny, George Meeker, Louise Henry and Monroe Owsley (seated), Arthur Treacher, Constance Cummings, and Robert Young. Within a few drunken hours, one of these characters will have been murdered by one of the others.

REMEMBER LAST NIGHT? Constance Cummings and Robert Young make an especially engaging if not always sober sleuthing couple.

mystery almost as complicated as Howard Hawks's *The Big Sleep,* with so many characters (including a contingent outside of the house party) that it needs two or three viewings for all of the ramifications to be fully understood. However, the element of wacky comedy remains: Edward Arnold as the city detective called in to investigate plays it straight, but his subordinate is chubby Edward Brophy, who maintains a steady stream of black-humor wisecracks. The corpses pile up, and unbilled E. E. Clive (a Whale regular) has some choice scenes as a dignified mortuary photographer, striving "to do our best" amid all the chaos, and to "retain the artistic touch" in his photographs of the bodies.

There are in-joke references to Whale's *Bride of Frankenstein* of the same year, and to *Dracula's Daughter* (which he was scheduled to direct in 1936, though it subsequently went to Lambert Hillyer), and at one point Whale kids his own stylized lighting design in a sequence wherein hypnotist Gustav von Seyffertitz uses bizarre equipment to mesmerize all of the suspects. Unfortunately, in so doing he discovers the killer's identity and becomes his next victim. Actually, veteran whodunit fans familiar with Hollywood typecasting will have no difficulty in spotting the killer almost as soon as he appears, despite the maze of suspects, clues, and red herrings. But knowing who still doesn't tell us how or why, and interest and suspense are well maintained until we find out. And there are moments of tension and near-terror when the veneer of crazy fun is abandoned too quickly for comfort, and murder suddenly becomes the serious matter that it should be.

Remember Last Night? is a wonderful illustration of what skilled playing and direction can do for basically commonplace material. Richard Thorpe, Sam Wood, or Paul Sloane could have taken this material and at best it would provide eighty-five harmless time-killing minutes today. James Whale, aided especially by his art director, Charles D. Hall (who worked with him in 1932 in a more serious gothic vein on *The Old Dark House*), has made it an object lesson in how personal style can bring a film to life. Striking clocks never seem

to be so imbued with a life of their own as in a Whale film, and when his gliding cameras move, they do so with a vengeance—through hallways, across rooms, up stairs, sometimes all in one sweeping shot. But Whale knows when *not* to use a mobile camera, too, to concentrate instead on lighting or close-ups. In *Remember Last Night?* a lot of elegant sets and camera technique are there purely for their own sake, but in a piece of froth such as this, why not? It may not be a classic screwball comedy or an outstanding mystery film—but it's one of the best-looking combinations of those two genres, and curiously, because of legal complications over story rights that now keep it out of circulation, one of the least known.

MY MAN GODFREY
(UNIVERSAL, 1936)

Directed by Gregory LaCava; screenplay by Morne Ryskind and Eric Hatch, from Hatch's novel.

LEADING PLAYERS:
William Powell, Carole Lombard, Alice Brady, Gail Patrick, Eugene Pallette, Mischa Auer, Alan Mowbray, Jean Dixon, Franklin Pangborn, Grady Sutton.

1936 was a banner year both for screwball comedy and for William Powell's contributions to the genre. All four of his films that year fell into that category, and since two were for his home studio (MGM) and two on loan-out to other studios, the quartet offered considerable variety in content if an agreeable familiarity in his performances. For MGM he made the second and best of the *Thin Man* films, *After the Thin Man*—almost a double bill in itself since the first half of the nearly two-hour film was devoted to loose-limbed comedy, the second half to zeroing in on the murder story—and *Libeled Lady.* Apart from being a fine comedy, this latter film boasted a powerhouse cast headed by Powell, Myrna Loy, Spencer Tracy, and Jean Harlow—with the ubiquitous Walter Connolly in support—that acknowledged the

William
POWELL · **LOMBARD**
Carole

My Man Godfrey

ALICE
BRADY
GAIL
PATRICK
JEAN
DIXON

EUGENE PALETTE · ALAN MOWBRAY

MISCHA AUER · JOHN LIGHT · PAT FLAHERTY · ROBERT PERRY · FRANKLIN PANGBORN

CHAS. R. ROGERS

Based on the novel by Eric Hatch
Screenplay by Morrie Ryskind and Eric Hatch
Directed by Gregory La Cava
A UNIVERSAL PICTURE

MY MAN GODFREY (1936)
Carole Lombard, William
Powell, and Gail Patrick:
two spoiled heiresses and
a millionaire posing as a
butler.

MY MAN GODFREY   To amuse a bored Carole Lombard, mother Alice Brady
(center) persuades leeching live-in guest Mischa Auer to do his ape pantomime;
father Eugene Pallette (left) is, as always, bored by all the nonsense.

MY MAN GODFREY
Franklin Pangborn
presides over the
scavenger hunt to which
Carole Lombard brings
"forgotten man" William
Powell to claim her prize
(Mischa Auer and Alice
Brady are to the left of
Powell).

box-office importance now given to this kind
of comedy. For RKO Radio, partnered with
Jean Arthur and under the expert direction of
the now nearly forgotten Stephen Roberts
(whose early death may be responsible for the
oversight), Powell did *The Ex-Mrs. Bradford,* not
only one of the best of the *Thin Man* imitations, but also boasting a really good and involving murder mystery to back up its comic
byplay. And of course for Universal he made
the most famous (though not necessarily the
best) of all screwball comedies, *My Man Godfrey.*

The following year was as good and prolific
a one for crazy comedy, although Powell wisely
reduced his output in that area. Of his three
1937 films, only *Double Wedding,* a *Taming of the
Shrew* comedy originally written by Molnar and
transferred to an American milieu, qualified,
and that somewhat halfheartedly. However,
with Powell reunited with Myrna Loy, audiences certainly had no cause for complaint.

My Man Godfrey sets its tone with a magnificent set of main titles, designed as neon lights
on a Manhattan skyline. (The device was frequently copied, not least by Wesley Ruggles for

his British supermusical *London Town* in 1946.
There, in Technicolor, the titles were so splashy
and spectacular that they quite eclipsed the
big-scale but routine film that followed!) Main
titles, incidentally, were of particular importance to both romantic comedies (*Love Affair*)
and screwball comedies (*The Rage of Paris*) in
the thirties. They immediately established a
mood of elegance and luxury, contrasting with
the Depression world in which they were
shown, and by simple motifs—rolls of silk being unfurled to stress the world of fashion, or
"invitational" credits revealed as layers of tissue paper are removed from them. Comedies
involving themselves with high-society wed-
dings, as of course most of them did, not only
established the kind of direction the subsequent stories were about to take, but also put
audiences in exactly the right frame of mind
for such escapism. Woody Allen, in several of
his films from the eighties, recognized the sub-
liminally important function that these titles
had performed and studied the originals carefully, reproducing them in such films as *The
Purple Rose of Cairo.*

87

The basic plot of *My Man Godfrey* must be too familiar to need detailed repetition. Irene (Carole Lombard), most scatterbrained member of the self-centered and minimally crazy Bullock family, goes out on a "scavenger hunt" to find and bring back a "forgotten man." The Depression term was already a cliché by 1936 and had of course formed the basis of a grim production number by Busby Berkeley in *Gold Diggers of 1933*. At the city dump Irene finds hobo Godfrey (William Powell) and persuades him to come back with her so that she can claim her prize. Initially indignant and resentful, Godfrey changes his mind out of casual curiosity—and after being "ticked off" the list by party master of ceremonies Franklin Pangborn as just another oddity, gives the assemblage a piece of his mind. Irene, despite her ditziness, is impressed by this man, who is clearly no ordinary hobo, and decides to "reclaim" him as a kind of worthwhile social project. She gives him a job as butler, and his courtliness and intelligence make him a huge success at the job. Ultimately of course it turns out that he was a Harvard man, disillusioned by business reverses and a bad marriage, who had found "real values" in a life as a hobo. He straightens out the assorted Bullock malfunctions—which range from dishonesty to sheer idiocy—saves them from financial disaster, puts himself back on his feet, discovers a way of salvaging other forgotten men—and of course marries Irene, though strictly through her machinations.

My Man Godfrey is one of those awkward films that seems to fluctuate in values over the years. Probably overrated at the time, when it certainly had more bite than most of its contemporaries (*Libeled Lady*, for example, though pleasingly unpredictable, was a typically "polite" MGM film) and when most of the imitations it spawned seemed inferior if for no other reason than that they couldn't match its inspired casting, it seemed to fall a little flat when seen again in the forties. By then the Depression was recent history, and the shams and evasions of *My Man Godfrey* seemed all too apparent, especially when contrasted with the trenchant, wittier, and generally more honest comedies with which Preston Sturges was then

regaling us. Yet thirty years later, it appeared in another light: films of the thirties (and not just Hollywood comedies) told us as much about the Depression and attitudes toward it by their evasions as by their truths. Thus we no longer needed to be too critical of its artificial characters, none of whom were *really* affected by the Depression (Godfrey's oblivion was largely self-sought), or by the ludicrous cure-all climax.

Another twenty-year leap into the nineties sees its status unchanged in that respect—although television and home video have taken over from theatrical exposure, so that denied the backup of shared audience laughter, it may from this point on seem less funny to those discovering it for the first time. With a theatrical audience, the genuinely funny sequences seemed hilarious, and the mildly funny lines

MY MAN GODFREY   Powell is put to work as a butler and attracts the attentions of Gail Patrick.

MY MAN GODFREY Godfrey/
Powell brings an early morning
antidote to dissolve the pixies
bothering Mrs. Bullock (Alice
Brady).

MY MAN GODFREY A happy (if not very convincing) ending sees
fortunes restored all around, and Powell happily wed to heiress
Lombard.

provoked reactions greater than they probably deserved, all of which of course is good film-making and good comedy construction.

While one tends to recall *My Man Godfrey* not as a classic entity (which *Nothing Sacred* and *20th Century* certainly were) but rather as a collection of elements and highlights, those qualities are almost enough. One remembers most of all the dazzlingly bright look of the film, the result of a collaboration between art director Charles Hall and cameraman Ted Tetzlaff. As a director, Gregory LaCava was famed for being unconventional and for his occasional disregard of script and schedules. *My Man Godfrey* is certainly the best possible vehicle to both exploit those characteristics, *and* to keep them well-hidden. William Powell is William Powell, which is all that is needed: whether he is momentarily serious, soothing as he prepares Alice Brady's pixie-removing hangover antidote, or treacherously but smoothly reassuring as he leads an equally hungover Carole Lombard to the trap of an ice-cold shower, he never mistimes a line or places a foot wrong. Lombard occasionally goes a little over the top in her shrieking and nonsensical stream-of-consciousness ramblings, but it's as much director LaCava's fault as hers for not exerting more discipline. When controlled by tougher directors in other screwball films—Howard Hawks in *20th Century*, William Wellman in *Nothing Sacred*, Lubitsch in *To Be or Not to Be*—she was superb.

Gail Patrick, too, often merely the other woman, pulls off the difficult trick of being a semivillainess, yet remaining appealing and ultimately convincingly contrite. Mischa Auer's pantomime of an ambling gorilla remains one of the glories and highlights of all screwball comedy. As always, Alice Brady was used as the convenient symbol of all that was wrong with the thoughtless rich: stupid, tactless, abrasive. She could be such a warm, human actress when given the right role that it's a pity her position in the screwball family as the brainless wife was so one-dimensional. (When her role was copied virtually verbatim in the 1939 Deanna Durbin comedy *First Love*, director Henry Koster and actress Leatrice Joy managed to give it enough humanity that it wasn't an immediate audience turnoff.) Eugene Pallette's role as the head of the screwball family was equally standardized in its own way, but he was funnier, warmer, and more deserving of audience sympathy. Although the breadwinner, he was taken for granted, ignored, and abused by his family. When the scripts allowed him to raise himself from his defeatist lethargy and exact revenge—as *First Love* did—then the results were a joy to behold!

While *My Man Godfrey* was of direct influence on a number of clones, most obviously *Merrily We Live* for Hal Roach the next year, its indirect impact on other films was perhaps of greater importance. We have already mentioned the bodily transfer of its screwball family to Deanna Durbin's *First Love*, a charming and literal updating of the Cinderella fairy story that is discussed in detail in the 1979 Citadel book *Love in the Film*. But it also impacted on an earlier (1937) Durbin film, *One Hundred Men and a Girl*, a (proportionately) more realistic view of the Depression. Again, a party-giving family (headed by a slightly toned-down Alice Brady and Eugene Pallette) with their wasting of money on luxuries and expensive food is contrasted with the plight of a group of starving, unemployed musicians. Led by Adolphe Menjou, normally as sartorially elegant as William Powell, he is here appropriately seedy and run-down. Durbin, as Menjou's daughter, invades the party to return a bag—which though stuffed with money has never been missed—and her honesty is a way of bringing the two disparate levels of society together and paving the way for an optimistic ending.

Because of its unassailable reputation, the personas of its stars, and certainly its streamlined slickness and infectious gaiety, *My Man Godfrey* will probably always be a trifle overrated. But it will also probably remain a permanent and useful reminder of Hollywood's most extravagant tribute to the Depression's "forgotten man."

NOTHING SACRED

(SELZNICK–UNITED ARTISTS, 1937)

Directed by William Wellman; screenplay by Ben Hecht, from a story by James A. Street.

LEADING PLAYERS:
Carole Lombard, Fredric March, Walter Connolly, Charles Winninger, Frank Fay, Sig Rumann, Maxie Rosenbloom, John Qualen, Monty Woolley.

If one had the thankless (and pointless) task of trying to pinpoint the best screwball comedy of the thirties, it might well turn out to be *Nothing Sacred*. That it has all the elements—a bat-

NOTHING SACRED (1937)
Janitor Troy Brown whose
pose as the Sultan of
Mazapan in a phony publicity
stunt causes trouble for
Fredric March as the reporter
responsible, Wally Cook.

tle of the sexes that at one point becomes literally that and very physical, a masquerade as a
plot launching pad, a wonderful cast of character players, not all of them even comic types
but superbly deployed to comic ends—is only
one of the reasons for its success. It also has
vitality, energy, a constant change of venue
even though New York City is its basic backdrop, and most of all it manages to be funny
without apparently trying to. Enormously enjoyable though *My Man Godfrey* is, it must strain
for its effects and introduce elements of inspired but still forced lunacy. But keynoted by
Fredric March's performance—much underrated, and one of his best—*Nothing Sacred*
seems to offer a kind of sincerity beneath it all,
underplaying opportunities for major comic/
dramatic highspots, and yet eventually revealing that underlying sincerity to be phony, too.
In that respect March's performance is beautifully complemented by Ben Hecht's script and
dazzling (but often thrown away) dialogue,
which provide far more bite than was to be
found in James Street's original story.

That story is of course fairly familiar by now,

due no little to its having been turned into a
Broadway musical as *Hazel Flagg,* which itself
was transferred into a movie remake with Jerry
Lewis (*Living It Up*). It concerns one Hazel
Flagg, a small-town girl thought to be dying of
radium poisoning. When a major New York
tabloid sends its star reporter to bring her to
Manhattan to brighten her last days (and incidentally provide circulation-building copy),
she jumps at the chance—even though the in-
vitation arrives within an hour of her discovering that she is in fact perfectly healthy and the
victim of a mistaken diagnosis. With her doctor in tow, as would be normal if she *were* criti-
cally ill, but also to provide guidance as to how
to keep up the illusion of being a dying girl,
she takes off for New York. Believing in her
absolutely, her reporter/champion eventually
falls in love with her. Already the victim
(and perpetrator) of some earlier newspaper
hoaxes, he is stunned when he eventually finds
out that she is a fake, but loves her too much to
care. The rest of the film, in which the tempo
increases to include a number of comic suspense sequences in which her deception seems

NOTHING SACRED   In his first visit to Vermont, March meets New England reticence in the person of Margaret Hamilton.

sure to be revealed, deals with his attempts to help her carry on the masquerade and find a way out of the dilemma—finally solved with a farewell note of thanks to the world, saying that she is going to disappear and die alone, "like an elephant."

The really great comedies of 1932 through 1937—from *Trouble in Paradise* through *Blessed Event, 20th Century,* and *Bombshell* up to *Nothing Sacred*—might have varied in their proportions of elegance and degrees of lunacy, but they all had two key qualities in common. First, they were all satires, and contemporary satires to boot; and second, they had no inhibitions whatsoever, caring little whom they offended or what sacred cows they ridiculed.

Today's "adult, mature" movies fall all over themselves to prove how grown-up (and unentertaining they are) by using once virtually taboo words like *rape* and *pregnant* and by overuse of four-letter expletives. Yet at the same time they shy away from lines or situations that might offend minority (and even some major-

ity) groups. *Nothing Sacred* isn't a great comedy because at one point Fredric March refers to a Negro janitor as "Old Black Joe," any more than *20th Century* depended for its humor on John Barrymore's frequent references to a Negro stagehand as "Uncle Remus." But it's difficult to be offended when the same film presents lines of dialogue or situations designed to deflate the president, the governor of New York, Communists, Girl Scouts, wrestlers, German doctors in particular and the medical profession at large, newspapermen in general and especially editors, small-town mentalities (with New England a particular target), Swedes, and God—not necessarily in that order. The movies of the twenties and thirties had a wonderful capacity for laughing not only at themselves, but also at everybody and everything, whether the issue at hand was politics, religion, race, or sex.

Perhaps because death is an issue that is always topical (even though the yellow journalism of the thirties is little remembered or un-

92

derstood today), *Nothing Sacred* remains one of the best and most pungent films of its genre. It gets off to a magnificent start with a mock poetic foreword by Ben Hecht that makes New York sound funny, absurd, and somehow lovable all at the same time. Its use of the new three-color Technicolor system—doubly new in a purely contemporary, dramatic, big-city context (though Selznick used it the same year for *A Star Is Born*)—provided the unique blend of glamour and artificiality that the story demanded. Ben Hecht's often deliberate pretentiousness is, on this occasion, admirably suited to the story, and few of his scripts have had more bite.

Audiences seem to remember best the episode in which the reporter tries to work up a sweat in Hazel by engaging in comic fisticuffs with her and finally knocking her out, so that she has presumably collapsed with fever. But the funniest elements of the film are those of subtle satire: March's initial encounters with the taciturn New Englanders (Olin Howland, Margaret Hamilton) or the fiasco of the newspaper's tribute to a visiting African potentate and religious guru who is revealed as a local bootblack when his wife and family rush in to the ceremony. The film is peppered with hilarious dialogue, but few of the lines would seem funny repeated out of context. Charles Winninger, as the small-town doctor, expresses his opinion of newspapermen as "the hand of God, reaching down into the mire, couldn't

NOTHING SACRED   Editor Oliver Stone (Walter Connolly, right) uses Maxie Rosenbloom's muscle to keep March in line.

NOTHING SACRED
Typical physical
violence between
Fredric March and
Carole Lombard.

raise one of them to the depths of degradation!" It is a funny usage of language on its own—but in context, prefaced by Winninger's explanation of why he dislikes the press, accompanied by eloquent bodily pantomime (he is partially drunk, and anger is mixed with instability), and then followed by March's mock-serious partial agreement, it forms the backbone of a hilarious *sequence*. Likewise, as their plane flies over lower New York, Carole Lombard's Hazel, all gaiety and excitement, yet remembering the pose she must maintain, tells March that she's going to have a wonderful time in New York, and not worry about anything until her hair and teeth start to fall out. Then, turning to her doctor—Charles Winninger—hunched in his seat, already filled with foreboding about possible exposure, she asks him if that is indeed when she should start worrying. "It's as good a time as any," he agrees—certainly not a funny line in itself, but again, in context, a perfect wrap-up for the sequence.

Throughout, the best lines are almost straight, made funny by their placement and delivery. The cast could hardly be bettered. March, especially in the earlier sequences, employs for comic effect the kind of fake sincerity that Glenn Ford was later to use as his basic stock-in-trade. In a nightclub revue, "Heroines of History," Frank Fay captures perfectly the nauseating yet somehow engaging sham of the bleeding-heart performer. Walter Connolly, such a tower of strength in so many comedies of the thirties, was literally immense as the newspaper editor who has a certain amount of compassion but (not in on the hoax that he finally discovers and describes as "the greatest betrayal since Judas Iscariot") mingles it with a realistic hope that if Hazel does away with herself, she'll do it at a time convenient to the upcoming edition.

Carole Lombard, as the pivot around which the comedy revolves, has surprisingly little opportunity to be funny, but underplays some choice lines with superb abandon and manages throughout to retain the sympathy of the audience, which knows she's a phony. Moreover, although the film rarely takes itself seriously, Lombard manages to make Hazel's growing love for the reporter, Wally, quite poignant, especially as she realizes that her masquerade may wreck his career. Well-controlled and directed (as she was not in *My Man Godfrey*) as she is here by William Wellman, Lombard had a wonderful facility for shifting gears and changing moods within a scene. Had she not died when she did, she might have made a wonderful addition to Preston Sturges's stock company, since he was a director who possessed that same unique quality. *The Miracle of Morgan's Creek* and *The Palm Beach Story* are comic masterpieces as they are and might not have been better had she played the female leads. But they would certainly have been different, and just thinking about the possibilities is mouthwatering.

In these days of marathon-length movies (comedies included) what joy to see again a film like *Nothing Sacred* that zips and crackles along with no letup in the pace and is still needling manipulated sentiment even in its last wrap-up sequence aboard ship as Hazel and Wally sail for oblivion and happiness. And occasionally it fools you delightfully: romantic music, a lyrical shot of March and Lombard skimming across the sea in a small yacht, a misleadingly conventional line of dialogue, and you feel that an unavoidable if excusable lapse into cliché romantics is at hand. But no—March returns Lombard's straight line with a little speech about the dangers of elderly waitresses, and we're off again!

THE AWFUL TRUTH

(COLUMBIA, 1937)

Directed by Leo McCarey; screenplay by Vina Delmar and Dwight Taylor, from the play by Arthur Richman.

LEADING PLAYERS:
Irene Dunne, Cary Grant, Ralph Bellamy, Alexander D'Arcy, Molly Lamont, Robert Warwick, Asta the Dog.

The Awful Truth poses something of an enigma. When it was first presented, it was greeted amiably as little more than an expert reshaping of

94

THE AWFUL TRUTH (1937) Cary Grant and Irene Dunne as the divorcing couple, discuss the situation with Esther Dale as the mother of perennially hopeful husband-to-be Ralph Bellamy.

old-fashioned farce. (In truth, it originated as a play in the early twenties and was made into a silent film in 1925, with Agnes Ayres, Warner Baxter, and Phillips Smalley in the leads.) Although it followed the release of such genuine screwball comedies as *It's Love I'm After* (by a week or so) and *My Man Godfrey* (from the previous year), it was not then suggested that it was a part of a major and relatively new lunatic screen-comedy tradition.

Yet today one finds it being hailed as "hilarious"—which was neither its intent nor its result—and the equal of *My Man Godfrey* as a cornerstone in screwball comedy. One can only assume that its underlying story and its directing/starring combination of Leo McCarey, Irene Dunne, and Cary Grant (who would reunite for a more orthodox screwball with *My Favorite Wife* in 1940) gave it a kind of auteurship in retrospect. With those ingredients, it supposedly *had* to be a screwball classic. (Possibly its removal from theatrical exhibition after the early fifties meant that writers were basing opinions on private or television screenings and were thus denied the proof, via

THE AWFUL TRUTH Asta the Dog, cast as "Mr. Smith," helps Dunne to hide a hat from suspicious Grant.

an audience, that the film really generates few laughs.

It's very much a cinematic case of the emperor's new clothes. *The Awful Truth,* standing there naked, still generates so much warmth and entertainment that it creates the illusion of being clothed. But they are not the garments of screwball comedy.

In essence, and this applies to all three versions (there was a 1953 musical remake, *Let's Do It Again,* with Jane Wyman, Ray Milland, and Aldo Ray), the story boils down to a once happily married couple having decided on divorce. After the papers are filed, both parties, but the husband especially, scheme against the other—even though both have decided, somewhat unenthusiastically, on remarriage to new mates. Still quite in love, husband and wife are reunited in a deserted mountain cabin minutes before their marriage is legally supposed to end.

In this film, the traditional battling between the sexes is reduced to a kind of maneuvering in which each party, still loving the other, tries to outguess and outwit the opposing partner. In a sense it reminds one of those precise, mathematical battles that Laurel and Hardy had with their foes (usually Jimmy Finlayson or Charles Hall) in both their silent and sound comedies—the silent ones often having been supervised by McCarey—in which the chaos and destruction were disciplined, and each side waited patiently for the other to retaliate. If Laurel and Hardy had ever devoted an entire subject to such a battle against each other (which they never did), one might have a kind of broad and more physical forerunner to *The Awful Truth.* Devoid of the battling, *The Awful Truth* is almost a gentle film, especially as the outcome is readily foreseeable. The dialogue isn't particularly witty, and the development is essentially along visual lines; in fact a closer parallel than Laurel and Hardy would be the silent Charley Chase two-reel 1926 classic, *Mighty Like a Moose,* discussed earlier, and not coincidentally also directed by Leo McCarey.

These notes, seemingly trying to disqualify *The Awful Truth* as a screwball contender (without minimizing its values as a romantic com-

THE AWFUL TRUTH   The last-second reconciliation: Dunne and Grant.

edy) basically lead up to this problem: if *The Awful Truth,* which lacks so many of the ingredients essential to screwball comedy, is still considered a cornerstone of the genre, then where does it leave such marginal films as these?

Blessed Event (1932), the most savage of the several Walter Winchell satires. Its frenzied pace, irreverence, and black-comedy highlight sequences (such as Lee Tracy's long and hilarious description of an electrocution) overcome *its* lack of screwball ingredients and place it almost on the same level as *His Girl Friday.*

96

its plot is rife with deception. It's the best and most sophisticated of all of Stan and Ollie's films. Had the same script been filmed just six years later, with Adolphe Menjou and John Hubbard replacing Laurel and Hardy, and with Mary Astor and Verree Teasdale as the wives, we'd have had a neat (and identically cast) companion piece to *Turnabout,* and none would have questioned its classification.

The point here is not to plead for those three films (and dozens like them) or against *The Awful Truth,* but merely to suggest that a new perspective is due on that film, and that its main value—in terms of film history—may be to stress the almost undefinable boundaries of screwball comedy.

EASY LIVING
(PARAMOUNT, 1937)

Directed by Mitchell Leisen; screenplay by Preston Sturges.

LEADING PLAYERS:
Jean Arthur, Ray Milland, Edward Arnold, Luis Alberni, Mary Nash, William Demarest.

MIDNIGHT
(PARAMOUNT, 1939)

Directed by Mitchell Leisen; screenplay by Charles Brackett and Billy Wilder, from an original story by Edwin Justus Mayer and Charles Shultz.

LEADING PLAYERS:
Claudette Colbert, Don Ameche, John Barrymore, Francis Lederer, Elaine Barrie, Mary Astor, Hedda Hopper.

These films are discussed jointly since they share common virtues and perhaps a common flaw, though in view of the skill presented and the entertainment values offered, the word *flaw* is possibly a trifle harsh. Perhaps not coincidentally, both are also Arthur Hornblow, Jr.,

The Good Fairy (1935), a sparkling, sophisticated romantic comedy, in every way (except that of later influence) superior to *The Awful Truth.* Its theme of masquerade and misunderstandings would certainly qualify it as at least fringe screwball; yet William Wyler's elegance as director, and its source material (a Ferenc Molnar play) would seem to remove it from the running, despite Preston Sturges's somewhat frenzied rewriting of dialogue and acceleration of pace.

Sons of the Desert (1934), a Laurel and Hardy feature as a screwball comedy? Yet its seven reels are nonstop battle of the sexes (first psychological, then decidedly physical) and

productions and share a production elegance common to his work, though admittedly often taken for granted in the comedy field.

Both films were directed by Mitchell Leisen, a former art director and costume designer who had made the switch to full-time director earlier in the thirties. He was a good director, but not yet a major one, nor as imaginative in comedy as he might be. Unsurprisingly, given his background, visual flair remained a dominating characteristic in his work. Later in the forties, when a visual flair was essential to the script—as it was in *Kitty*—some truly outstanding work resulted, but even then there were too many films like *Frenchman's Creek* and *Lady in the Dark* in which images (often in color) submerged dramatics.

Leisen's main handicap, if one could call it that, was that at this stage he was as good as his scripts but no better. In one sense that was enough, as he was getting some very good scripts. In another, it meant that that little extra something that could take a script a step forward instead of just literally translating it was lacking. This is what caused Preston Sturges to complain to Paramount executives and led to his being allowed to direct his own scripts. Ironically, the last Sturges script to be directed by Leisen—*Remember the Night* (1940)—emerged as an utter charmer, a blending of the unique talents of the two men, seamlessly mixing the satiric wit of Sturges with the warmth of Leisen.

Neither *Easy Living* nor *Midnight* could really miss: with those scripts and casts they were virtually foolproof, and no really valid criticism of the Leisen films emerged. Except . . . how much greater they might have been had Sturges directed *Easy Living* and Billy Wilder *Midnight*.

Almost everyone remembers *Easy Living* for its startlingly original opening sequence in which a mink coat, falling from a penthouse window, lands in the lap of Jean Arthur as she rides a bus to work. European audiences also remember particularly a slapstick sequence in a Horn and Hardart cafeteria; cafeterias were of course no novelty in Europe, but the H&H variety, with their little cubicles of food, certainly were. The heroine is right away assumed

EASY LIVING (1937) Jean Arthur in the well-remembered Automat sequence.

EASY LIVING   Millionaire Edward Arnold and flunky Luis Alberni almost swamped by typical Mitchell Leisen décor.

to be a millionaire's mistress—a stock masquerade-in-reverse of many comedies of the period—and ultimately fulfills Cinderella's destiny by marrying the son (Ray Milland) of business magnate Edward Arnold.

The character names—the autocratic Nora Cecil as Miss Swerf, William Demarest as Wallace Whistling—immediately suggest the whimsical nature of Sturges's writing. Many of the players in this particular comedy (Demarest, Andrew Tombes, Arthur Hoyt, Franklin Pangborn) and in other earlier Sturges scripts were to become Sturges regulars in his

own films—suggesting that he was either rewarding them for such understanding interpretation of his comic cameos, or, equally likely, that he was creating those roles with certain actors in mind, and that his suggestions were wisely followed.

Midnight was a fond, affectionate farewell to a Paris that, at the time of the film's release in early 1939, was enjoying its last days of living up to its worldwide reputation for fun and gaiety, knowing that war was inevitable. Some six months later, when war came, it put an end to the kind of comedy that Lubitsch especially—

99

in films like *One Hour With You, Desire, Bluebeard's Eighth Wife,* and *Angel*—had made almost a Paramount monopoly.

With such a stellar cast, *Midnight* is still a showcase for the scintillating comedy talents of Claudette Colbert, playing a penniless American stranded in Paris who exploits a Middle European émigré cabdriver (Don Ameche, surprisingly funny and effective in an offbeat role for him) into supplying free transportation. He ultimately backs her up in a masquerade that eventually becomes a kind of triple masquerade since he agrees to pose as her aristocratic husband, and she extends the deception by "revealing" that he is insane! Augmenting their unorthodox romantic adventure is the equally crazy but finally rather touching subplot of John Barrymore and Mary Astor, whose marriage is on the rocks but is eventually happily salvaged. Barrymore, on occasion, would seem to be taking enjoyable (and worthwhile) liberties with his script, adding expressions and witticisms that look wholly his own, but fortunately not in a self-mocking manner. His last *serious* acting, in Garson Kanin's *The Great Man Votes,* released just a month or two earlier, was well received and seemed to have revitalized him. While his acting renaissance was not supported by the opportunities pro-

MIDNIGHT (1939)   Claudette Colbert arrives in Paris in a glamorous evening gown, and not a penny to her name . . . a typical start to a madcap screwball frolic.

MIDNIGHT   John Barrymore as the inevitable millionaire and Don Ameche as a struggling cab-driver, both of whom champion the stranded Colbert.

MIDNIGHT   Francis Lederer, Claudette Colbert, and John Barrymore.

vided in his two remaining screwball comedies, *The Great Profile* and *World Premiere*, it did
provide him with the impetus to make this
graceful semifarewell in *Midnight*, itself a wonderfully appropriate goodbye to a wacky world
of Parisian luxury that probably didn't totally
exist outside of Paramount's glossy imagination.

THERE GOES MY HEART
(HAL ROACH–UNITED ARTISTS, 1938)

Directed by Norman Z. McLeod; screenplay by
Eddie Moran and Jack Jevne, from an original
story by Ed Sullivan.

LEADING PLAYERS:
Fredric March, Virginia Bruce, Patsy Kelly, Alan
Mowbray, Nancy Carroll, Eugene Pallette, Claude
Gillingwater, Arthur Lake.

By rights, *There Goes My Heart* properly belongs
in the chapter on *It Happened One Night* and its
many descendants, but somehow the sheer gall
of its cloning, the ingenious way its stock characters are shunted around by stock players,
and the genuinely entertaining film that is the
upshot of it all somehow earn the film an individual entry.

Earlier the same year, the same director/pro-
ducer combination had come forth with *Merrily We Live*, spawned by *My Man Godfrey*. Apparently emboldened by its success, producer
Hal Roach seemed to drop all effort at camouflage, and despite an "original story" credit to
columnist Ed Sullivan (who was contributing a
number of story ideas and personal appearances to movies in the thirties), *There Goes My
Heart* is virtually a remake of *It Happened One
Night*. It even starts out the same way, with heir-

101

THERE GOES MY HEART (1938)   Taming an heiress and introducing her to the simple pleasures enjoyed by the "other half": Virginia Bruce and Fredric March coming home from a Coney Island day via subway . . .

. . . and at a skating rink.

ess Virginia Bruce making her escape from grandfather Claude Gillingwater's yacht. A minor change en route—presumably dictated more by budget than by originality—had the young lady, quite unused to hard work, going into hiding by getting a job in a department store and being befriended by Patsy Kelly. The newspaper reporter this time is Fredric March, replaying his *Nothing Sacred* role from the year before, and doubtless hoping that audiences won't notice too much that the script gives him far fewer opportunities to shine in bits of individual comedy than Clark Gable got in *his* script.

THERE GOES MY HEART   Reporter March gets pointers from salesman Hal Dawson on how to take a picture of heiress Bruce without her knowing it.

Claude Gillingwater—an inveterate father, grandfather, or substitute parent figure to Mary Pickford and Jackie Coogan in silents and Shirley Temple in talkies, his irascibility designed to be melted by the final reel—takes over from Walter Connolly. A fairly imaginative bit of against-type casting gives us Eugene Pallette, deposed as head of a screwball family, and *also* taking over the Connolly of *Nothing Sacred* as March's editor. It is he of course who breaks the story that a now love-smitten March has torn up, leading to the inevitable last-minute boy-loses-girl complication and its equally inevitable and speedy resolution. One other quite unnecessary complication is the addition of a girlfriend for Kelly, who turns out to be both unreasonable and unsympathetic. Since the role is played by the always delightful Nancy Carroll, in one of her final screen ap-

THERE GOES MY HEART   No sign of a letup in the imitations! Reporter Fredric March gets instructions from boss Eugene Pallette.

pearances, there's a certain amount of audience resentment in seeing an old favorite so shabbily treated.

The cost of borrowing Fredric March and Virginia Bruce from their respective studios must have cut into the budget considerably, and the film is far less glossy than *Merrily We Live* or even some of the more elaborate Laurel and Hardy features such as *Our Relations*. The sets are serviceable and no more, one outdoor "island" location looking particularly threadbare, and neither cameraman Norbert Brodine nor art director Charles Hall have too much opportunity to shine. The back projection screen gets a good workout, too.

But, Capra rip-off or not, it manages to be good fun—though screwball more in its rigorous adherence to screwball traditions rather than in any inspired comedic insanity. Perhaps

THERE GOES MY HEART   On the loose in the big city, runaway heiress Virginia
Bruce learns the facts of cafeteria life from busboy Ernie Adams.

THERE GOES MY HEART
Final confrontation and
explanations. Left,
grandfather Claude
Gillingwater (always a
reliable substitute for
Walter Connolly), Virginia
Bruce, and Fredric
March. In the
background: Etienne
Girardot, Irving Pichel,
and Arthur Lake.

104

because one knows exactly what is going to happen, one can just relax with it and enjoy its few surprises. Department-store comedies are usually amusing, and this one is no exception, with Patsy Kelly's energetic demonstration of a piece of massage and reducing equipment a comic highlight. (Not a new comedy device— the same gag was worked in the silent *Love 'Em and Leave 'Em*—but it works better with a chubby Patsy Kelly being slapped around by the mechanism!) A skating-rink sequence was hardly new either: over the previous two years we had seen skating-rink highlights in at least three movies (*Wife Versus Secretary, The Joy of Living,* and *One Rainy Afternoon*), but they were essentially lighthearted sequences designed to move the romantic narratives forward. Here at least the emphasis was on comedy, and physical comedy at that, involving Fredric March on skates and a persistent drunk. Other surprises in the film included a brief, winsome, and utterly charming appearance by onetime comedy great Harry Langdon (now primarily a Roach writer) as a minister.

If *There Goes My Heart*'s lack of originality seems disturbing today, one must remember that under the old studio system of the thirties, so much product was made that a good deal of it was automatically derivative or even plagiaristic. At worst the lack of originality could result in a dull, lifeless, unentertaining film. But when they worked, one could forgive a lot. And without being memorable in any way, *There Goes My Heart* did work in 1938—and again when it was reissued in the forties, and still later on television and home video.

A SLIGHT CASE OF MURDER

(WARNER BROS., 1938)

Directed by Lloyd Bacon; screenplay by Earl Baldwin and Joseph Schrank, from a play of Damon Runyon and Howard Lindsay.

LEADING PLAYERS:
Edward G. Robinson, Ruth Donnelly, Jane Bryan, Allen Jenkins, Bobby Jordan, Edward Brophy, Harold Huber, Willard Parker, Margaret Hamilton.

Far more so than with James Cagney, Warners sought to cash in on and expand Edward G. Robinson's gangster persona by periodically presenting him with the dilemma of going straight. In *Little Giant* (1933) he had been Bugs Ahearn, trying to break into high society when the impending end of Prohibition signals an end to his racketeering days. Later, in *Larceny Inc.* (1942) he was Pressure Maxwell, just released from Sing Sing and determined to go straight—but needing to knock over just *one* bank first to finance his life of respectability. But best of all, rather surprisingly in that it came from one of the movies' worst years and a Production Code–dominated year to boot, was *A Slight Case of Murder.* (Curiously, Warners never tried to have Humphrey Bogart intentionally reform for comedic purposes; when reformation came, as in the wartime *All Through the Night,* it was *thrust* upon him.)

In *A Slight Case of Murder* Robinson played— and to the hilt, in his best comedy performance ever—Remy Marco, gangster-era beer baron who likewise has reformation imposed on him. He has a number of problems. First and foremost is that he has to make a huge payment due on his brewery or he'll lose it— and only now does he realize that his beer is so bad that, with legalization, nobody will buy it. A second and not inconsiderable problem is that four hoodlums involved in a half-million-dollar heist have been shot and their bodies left in the country home where he plans to weekend. Apart from making Remy look bad in the eyes of the law, the situation obviously isn't going to enhance his reputation in the eyes of his daughter, Jane Bryan, whose policeman fiancé, Willard Parker, and his high-toned society parents will also be visiting over the weekend. Nor will the school board be impressed: they have loaned Remy its toughest kid (Douglas Fairbanks Rosenbloom, played by Bobby Jordan of the Dead End Kids) for a few days on the theory that exposure to a better environment will help to mend his ways.

The first step is to dispose of the bodies, which is managed with relative ease. But then Remy's assistants—the flavorsome trio of Allen

A SLIGHT CASE OF MURDER
(1938) Reformed
bootleggers going
straight; Harold Huber
(left), Allen Jenkins, and
Edward G. Robinson.

A SLIGHT CASE OF MURDER Robinson pushes reluctant state trooper
Willard Parker into a "showdown" with an already dead mobster
propped up in a closet.

Jenkins, Edward Brophy, and Harold Huber—
hear that there's a reward out for the crooks,
dead or alive, and rationalizing that the reward
money will pay off the boss's debts, they sneak
the bodies back into the house while his weekend party is in full swing.

The film is missing many of the "required"
elements of the screwball comedy, not least a
total absence of the battle-of-the-sexes element.
Ruth Donnelly is quite wonderful as Remy's
tough, somewhat scatterbrained, but totally
loyal wife. But thanks to the pacing, the ma-
chine-gun-fast dialogue, the absurd yet somehow logical complications, and the curiously
tasteful if raucous manner in which corpses
are used for running gags, the overall effect *is*
of vintage screwball. A slight disclaimer should
be made to the effect that it is a terrific audience picture; seen in a theater, the film automatically gets and builds laughs at an increasingly rapid tempo. Seen on television—or on
home video, which is unfortunately the only
way it seems to be shown these days—it automatically loses the essential aspect of audience
reaction and input and may seem something

less of a classic. But even under such disadvantages, its highlights are magnificent.

Best of all is the sequence where Robinson and company discover the bodies of No-Nose Cohen and his three cohorts, and their dismay turns to glee as they figure out how to dispose of the bodies to the best advantage, by dumping them on the doorsteps of old enemies. And there's a curiously touching episode at the height of the party when Remy and his friends decide to call a pal, seriously ill in hospital, and cheer him up with a nostalgic song over the phone. The poor fellow dies during the serenade, the nurses cover the body, put the phone back on the receiver—and Remy, thinking his friend has hung up on him, just goes on with the party. It's Robinson's show all the way and came as a welcome (and needed) booster shot after Warners loaned him to MGM, which had put him into *The Last Gangster* the year before, a slow, sentimental, and unsuccessful contribution to that year's uncertain rebirth of the gangster genre.

In another sense, too, *A Slight Case of Murder* must be adjudged a major success. Most attempts to put Damon Runyon on the screen—and there were many in the thirties and forties when his short stories enjoyed their zenith of popularity—failed rather badly. Runyon's strange kind of whimsy, which made him a sort of James Barrie of the underworld, was as elusive as Barrie's. Adaptations of his work tended to shift gears into excessive sentiment (*The Big Street*) or heavy-handed lampoon (*Butch Minds the Baby*), and most damaging of all, his tightly constructed short stories, often climaxed by a twist that could be encompassed in a single sentence, were padded to stretch them to feature length. Oddly enough, *A Slight Case of Murder* succeeds where Runyon himself failed; he wasn't able to adapt his style to the theater, and as a play this story was neither very successful nor especially funny. Transformed into film, it is a substantial improvement and possibly the definitive screen Runyon. (Curiously, those thirties films that had the most "authentic" Runyon feel to them—*Blood Money* and *Broadway Thru a Keyhole*—were not based on Runyon stories, nor of course did they pretend to be.)

To its credit, *A Slight Case of Murder* bypasses all of the obvious chances for laughs; it plays everything straight, underplays its best lines, and in so doing, as a black comedy achieves much of the subtlety that *Arsenic and Old Lace* (which incidentally was produced on stage by Howard Lindsay, one of the cowriters of *A Slight Case of Murder*) enjoyed on stage but lost when transformed into a broader, more frenetic movie, and one that *never* sacrificed the chance for an obvious laugh. One has only to look at *Stop, You're Killing Me* (with Broderick Crawford and Claire Trevor in the Robinson/Donnelly roles), the 1952 remake of *A Slight Case of Murder*, to appreciate the grace—and the word is not inappropriate—that the original possessed.

MERRILY WE LIVE
(HAL ROACH–MGM, 1938)

Directed by Norman Z. McLeod; screenplay by Eddie Moran and Jack Jevne.

LEADING PLAYERS:
Brian Aherne, Constance Bennett, Billie Burke, Alan Mowbray, Bonita Granville, Tom Brown, Clarence Kolb, Ann Dvorak, Patsy Kelly.

Merrily We Live came so hot on the heels of *My Man Godfrey* and was so clearly inspired by it that most of the contemporary critics (and especially Frank Nugent in the *New York Times*) devoted virtually all of their reviews to noting the parallels and the overlappings, saying little about what a good comedy it was, and for that matter still is. True, if *My Man Godfrey* had not been made, the *idea* of making the remarkably similar *Merrily We Live* might not have occurred to Roach. Yet it is *not* a near-plagiarism. *Merrily We Live* is based on a 1924 novel and a 1926 play, *and* is a remake of a 1930 movie *What A Man* in which Reginald Denny essayed the Brian Aherne role. Not only was the plot the same, but most of the characters and character *names* were identical.

From a familiar pattern, Roach created a very different film. Even though one of the last

of his MGM films, and thus given a budgetary advantage that would be denied his upcoming *There Goes My Heart* (for United Artists release), it still couldn't hope to compete with the glitzy art deco gloss of *My Man Godfrey*, and Roach must have realized that. He must also have realized that there was no way to duplicate the inspired teamwork and expertise of William Powell. So from the start, it was a lower-keyed effort, with Roach taking up some of the slack by falling back on sight gags and even slapstick to keep the screwball quality even more physical than it was in *My Man Godfrey*.

Screen comedy is a curious animal that changes its spots along with audience moods and contemporary mores. There have been times when Chaplin's *Modern Times* and *City Lights* did not seem funny to newer audiences. Harold Lloyd's most popular silent, *The Freshman*, never seemed to work out of its twenties milieu and left fifties audiences cold when Lloyd reissued it. There was a brief period when *My Man Godfrey* seemed somehow forced and unfunny, and *Merrily We Live* much superior to it. The passage of time, and more perspective, has allowed both films to resettle into

MERRILY WE LIVE (1938) Sisters Bonita Granville (left) and Constance Bennett discover that the silver is missing—along with the latest in a long line of hobo-employees.

MERRILY WE LIVE Wealthy author Brian Aherne posing as a hobo is persuaded to become the new family chauffeur, in the face of Bennett's skepticism.

108

chauffeur by a screwball family with a penchant for "redeeming" hoboes, most of whom promptly take off with the silver. It's a rather endearing family: Constance Bennett assumes the Lombard role as the spoiled heiress; old-time vaudevillian Clarence Kolb plays the ill-tempered head of the family and despite his age seems to take some spectacular pratfalls himself; Billie Burke is his addle-brained but charming wife, both funnier and easier to take for the audience than the abrasive and perennially screeching Alice Brady of *My Man Godfrey*. Other family members include Tom Brown, Ann Dvorak, and Bonita Granville, playing the brat as amusingly as she did in *It's Love I'm After* the year before.

Godfrey's family gained a little depth by having Gail Patrick play the self-centered and dishonest sister who is eventually (and a little surprisingly) reformed. Without her, this family is broader and less subtle—but perhaps more

MERRILY WE LIVE   Bennett and Aherne: Despite the film's obvious influence from *My Man Godfrey*, it *was* officially based on a twenties novel and play that had been turned into a film *What a Man!* in 1930, and even made that same year in an alternate Mexican version.

their rightful (though not necessarily permanent) positions. *My Man Godfrey* certainly is the better film, but *Merrily We Live* shouldn't be underrated. It has much going for it, and if similar aspects of both films were compared, point by point, there are occasions when *Merrily We Live* would still emerge the winner.

Brian Aherne—a good substitute for William Powell—is cast as a famous author who is touring incognito in an old wreck of a car, disguised as a tramp, seeking material for his new book. (Actually this role and masquerade is far more of a forerunner to Joel McCrea's movie director in *Sullivan's Travels* than a steal from William Powell, whose Godfrey was a genuine victim of the Depression.) His car is wrecked, and when ultimately found, it is assumed that he is dead. In the meantime, he is taken in as a

MERRILY WE LIVE   As in *Godfrey*, the new employee creates turmoil, especially among the love-stricken female servants—a typical group being maids Marjorie Kane (left) and Patsy Kelly, butler Alan Mowbray, and frustrated head-of-household Clarence Kolb.

consistently appealing. The staff is well represented by butler Alan Mowbray, forever having his pomposity deflated, and forever resigning, and by Patsy Kelly as the maid, playing her typical Hal Roach comedy support. She's funny, her snappy comebacks are amusing, but her role is entirely predictable, losing out in direct comparison to Jean Dixon in *My Man Godfrey.* Dixon's wry, sarcastic comments were not only funny, but also kept up a sardonic and witty commentary on the foibles of the rich. Both films of course stressed the problems of the rich, and the solutions that could be bought not by money but only by friendship and loyalty. A brace of Great Danes added to the overall chaos of the quarters of *Merrily We Live*'s Kilbourne family, which was a comfortable country home as opposed to *My Man Godfrey*'s Bullock clan's magnificently palatial New York mansion.

Both films devote themselves primarily to the childish and self-indulgent lifestyles of these two families, though *My Man Godfrey* has a slightly more complex story line and does develop as it proceeds. *Merrily We Live* seems content to milk its gag situations for all they are worth, and then proceed to the next. Both films arrive at the same conclusion—the solution to a financial dilemma by the apparent hobo. Although realism is hardly a quality one looks for in this kind of comedy, it should be noted that the ending of *Merrily We Live* is at least marginally logical and possible, whereas the "solution" to *My Man Godfrey* is pure wishful thinking almost on a fairy-tale level. Incidentally, the similarity in the films even extends to their running times: both run just a few minutes over the ninety-minute mark.

BLUEBEARD'S EIGHTH WIFE

(PARAMOUNT, 1938)

Directed by Ernst Lubitsch; screenplay by Billy Wilder and Charles Brackett, from the play by Alfred Savoir.

LEADING PLAYERS:
Gary Cooper, Claudette Colbert, Edward Everett Horton, David Niven, Elizabeth Patterson, Herman Bing, Warren Hymer, Franklin Pangborn, Lawrence Grant, Charles Halton.

Originally a stage vehicle for Ina Claire in the early twenties, and two years later brought to the silent screen with Gloria Swanson under Sam Wood's direction, *Bluebeard's Eighth Wife,* marked the end of Lubitsch's "Riviera comedy" period. The changing face of Europe, and the onrush of World War II, were making this kind of material obsolete—at least until it reappeared, with a very different set of values, after the war. It was also Lubitsch's last comedy for Paramount, and while it was far short of the standards set by his 1932 masterpiece *Trouble in Paradise,* it was still so superior to *Design for Living* (1933) and *Angel* (1937) that it in no way indicated any kind of decline. It is usually referred to as one of the director's weakest comedies, but this may well be because the film was unavailable for reappraisal for many years, a problem with the literary rights keeping it on the shelf when most of the several books on Lubitsch were being written.

It is also the one Lubitsch comedy in which the elements of screwball are at least equal to those of elegant romantic farce.

Its basic plot is simple. Claudette Colbert, after an accidental meeting with multimillionaire Gary Cooper, is pushed into a romance with him by nouveau-poor father Edward Everett Horton. At first reluctant, she eventually falls in love with Gary and the marriage takes place. But she discovers that he is—to put it mildly—something of a romantic philanderer, and that she is wife number eight. She refuses to consummate the marriage and uses various ploys—including faked affairs—to drive him to jealousy and frustration so that he will divorce her and provide a handsome settlement. Poor Gary winds up in a straitjacket in an asylum, and Claudette gets her settlement. But now that she is independently wealthy she feels, through curious last-reel plot logic, that she can approach him on her own terms. A happy ending and reunion is brought about—with the guarantee that there is no possibility of wife number nine in the future.

Elegant from first scene to last (it boasts one of the most brilliant and provocative boy-

BLUEBEARD'S EIGHTH WIFE (1938) A family portrait: matriarch Elizabeth Patterson, eight-times married millionaire husband Gary Cooper, fortune-hunting father Edward Everett Horton, daughter and bride number eight Claudette Colbert.

BLUEBEARD'S EIGHTH WIFE With the aid of a right cross (and the off-screen Monsieur Pepinard, private detective, played by Herman Bing), Claudette Colbert tries to make husband Cooper jealous by pretending to have resisted the advances of David Niven.

meets-girl openings of any screwball comedy), brightly paced, written, and played, flawlessly constructed so that comedy specialists such as Herman Bing and Franklin Pangborn have their own highlights and moments of glory, and backed by a charmingly spirited musical score, it may not represent Lubitsch at his innovational best. But it does offer him the opportunity to glide comfortably and stylishly through a territory that he knew inside and out, offering, in a sense, a late-thirties apotheosis of a vanishing genre. If it remains a stage play at heart, it doesn't show: Lubitsch and writers Charles Brackett and Billy Wilder have obviously contrived dialogue and bits of business specifically to exploit the comic personas of Pangborn et al., and much of it is staged "on the move"—some of Pangborn's funniest lines take place as he is ushering his tenants up the stairs to view a new apartment. Scenes are set on the beach and even on a floating raft to which Cooper's secretary swims to check the exact wording on a dictated letter. A montaged honeymoon trip, shops, the boulevard, an asy-

lum, miscellaneous bedrooms, and stream-lined apartments, all provide backgrounds consistent in their luxury yet sufficiently varied in space and design to keep the theatrical origins well at bay. (The film is also substantially longer than its silent predecessor.) Its deftness and satiric use of music give it a comic gloss that would have been impossible onstage, and Claudette Colbert, who never looked lovelier nor was gowned more fetchingly, works wonders with her material. A would-be seduction scene is a masterpiece of its kind, quite worthy of ranking with Barbara Stanwyck's almost casually disinterested onslaught on Henry Fonda's virtue in Preston Sturges's *The Lady Eve* a few years later.

The film's introductory sequence is a gem of mood and plot-setting. Boy meets girl in a French haberdashery; Cooper wants to purchase only the bottom section of a pair of pajamas; Colbert wants only the tops. ("Love has its little secrets, m'sieur," explains a shopwalker coyly when Cooper takes him aside to ask why.) Banter about the respective price each purchaser should pay for his/her half, if they buy a pair jointly, leads to a discussion of the pattern (Colbert feels that he is "the stripey type") and a futile attempt on Cooper's part to find out for whom the pajama tops are intended. After ascertaining that she is not married, Cooper gamely struggles on, commenting that for someone as dainty and, as the French say, petite, as she is, to have a brother that large—whereupon, all wide-eyed innocence, Colbert interrupts, "Oh, I have no brother m'sieur." Cooper is allowed to think the worst about Colbert's male companion, but the audience is soon let in on the secret—the pajamas are for her father. All this follows Cooper's attempts to buy just "the *pantalons*," a ploy resisted by all the salespersons. Finally, Cooper's insistence on being able to buy just half a pair of pajamas is relayed to the managing director's home. Still in bed, he gets up to answer the phone. Played by prissy, tight-lipped Charles Halton, he is wearing only the pajama tops as he strides over to the phone, hears the request, denies it with a terse "But that is Communism!" and returns to bed.

Seldom has so much delightful comic footage been extracted from a single premise. Almost as good is the sequence wherein Colbert and Cooper, having arrived at a kind of a truce, but a strictly platonic one, decide to spend an evening at home rather than going to the ballet. Colbert is exquisitely gowned; Cooper, in a mood for romance, croons to her and plies her with liquor. Sensing that her defenses are crumbling, Colbert warns her amorous husband that the Russian Ballet is still waiting—that night they are dancing *A Toyshop in Old Moscow* and *The Glow-Worm's Birthday*—and when that ploy doesn't work, takes a healthy bite from a handful of spring onions, breathing hard into Cooper's face just in time to prevent the kiss that might well cause her to give in. Lubitsch is able to get away with these and other sexual piquancies because the battling couple are, after all, married and whatever happened would be both legal and morally acceptable to the Production Code.

Other delights of this charming film are the performances of Herman Bing as a private detective, Warren Hymer as a most unlikely professional corespondent, designed to make Cooper jealous and maybe rough him up a little, and David Niven, admirably in the spirit of things as Cooper's lazy male secretary, anxious to take advantage of the ruptured marriage and to move in on the wife. Niven's giggled suggestions of an affair (he is too embarrassed to get much beyond the giggle stage) is met by a giggled repudiation from Colbert. And then of course there's the reliable Edward Everett Horton, at one point reduced to masquerading as a man who thinks he's a dog, in order to gain admission to the asylum where Cooper is incarcerated.

Both as a breezy and physical screwball comedy, and as a sophisticated romantic farce, *Bluebeard's Eighth Wife* is a thorough (and totally undated) delight. One can attribute its generally apathetic reception from the critics only to the fact that comedic standards (both in quality and quantity) were so high in 1938 that it seemed far less remarkable than it does today.

The only criticism one can logically make of the film is that Gary Cooper seems miscast as a

Howard Hughes type who is a whiz at every kind of business, treats women in a cavalier fashion (generous in his settlements but unfeeling in his personal relationships), speaks appalling French, and is naive about every aspect of culture and history. It's difficult to accept Cooper in such a role, and if it were a serious, dramatic story, the miscasting would be fatal. But he plays it so amiably (if not as well as Henry Fonda in *The Lady Eve*) that it is asking little of an audience to accept that miscasting right away and then just settle back to enjoy the brisk eight reels that follow.

THE RAGE OF PARIS

(UNIVERSAL, 1938)

Directed by Henry Koster; screenplay by Bruce Manning and Felix Jackson.

LEADING PLAYERS:
Danielle Darrieux, Douglas Fairbanks, Jr., Louis Hayward, Helen Broderick, Mischa Auer, Charles Coleman, Samuel S. Hinds, Nella Walker, Harry Davenport.

One of the most engaging and above all one of the most charming of all the screwball come-

THE RAGE OF PARIS (1938)   Douglas Fairbanks Jr. and Danielle Darrieux.

THE RAGE OF PARIS   Helen Broderick, Louis Hayward (millionaire number one, soon to be discarded), Danielle Darrieux, and millionaire number two, Douglas Fairbanks Jr., to be wooed, lost, and won.

113

THE RAGE OF PARIS The inevitable screwball moment, when heroine and hero spent an innocent night together in a deserted cabin. Here, a pajama-clad Darrieux has a kink in her back straightened out by Fairbanks.

dies, *The Rage of Paris* is particularly difficult to describe since so much of its appeal is vested in the delicious performance of Danielle Darrieux (her first American film, and her only one until the postwar years), the suave collaboration of her romantic costar, Douglas Fair-

banks, Jr., and the expert ensemble playing of a small but handpicked supporting cast.

Darrieux is Nicole, a French girl stranded in New York who, in trying to get a job, innocently accepts one that entails near-nude modeling for dress designer Fairbanks. Their risqué dialogue, full of double entendres, culminates in Darrieux's taking flight and Fairbanks's being convinced that she was a gold digger.

Later, in one of those plot contrivances so beloved of screwball comedy, Darrieux teams up with an older woman, the caustic Helen Broderick, who persuades her, against her better judgment, to turn her youth and beauty into a mathematically precise campaign to win a rich husband. To do this, she has to seem rich herself. Enter headwaiter Mischa Auer, who has a small nest egg building up to open his own restaurant, and who is eventually persuaded to invest it all in luxury clothes and a regal living style so that Darrieux can go after millionaire Louis Hayward. Needless to say, just as Hayward is hooked, Fairbanks, a pal of his, reenters, gives the game away, rescues Hayward (who isn't at all sure he wants to be rescued), and in time falls for Darrieux himself. (Even though he's a working designer, and thus creative *and* gainfully employed during the Depression, he conveniently has even more money than Hayward!) As in so many screwball comedies of the era, boy kidnaps girl and takes her off to his hunting lodge in the mountains—although since the two are not married, unlike the couples in *The Awful Truth* and *My Favorite Wife,* the night spent there is a platonic one, chaperoned by caretaker Harry Davenport. And unlike those two films, where the closing lodge sequences were protracted wrapups to comedies that had already run their basic course, the last reel or so of *The Rage of Paris* is one of its comedic highlights, with Darrieux fetchingly (and amusingly) clad in oversize men's pajamas, and much visual (and painful) comedy involving a slipping window and the frustrations of trying to get to sleep.

With her impeccable comic timing and youthful beauty—and a perfect command of English, though with a delightful French accent—Darrieux had Hollywood at her feet with this film and would undoubtedly have consolidated her popularity with American audiences had not the war intervened. And Fairbanks, who has given some excellent comedy performances, was never better than with the comedy of exasperation that characterizes his role here.

The film begins with fashion-oriented credits, in which the title cards are extracted from coverings of tissue and tulle, and never loses its elegance once in its surprisingly short seventy-five-minute running time. With European expatriates Henry Koster (director) and Felix Jackson (writer) heading the creative credits, it's not surprising that the film gives off an aura of European sophistication. At times it looks as though it might have been planned as a Deanna Durbin vehicle, but that its risqué content was considered a little too near-the-knuckle for her wholesome image. Thank heaven it was left alone and turned into such a felicitous showcase for Darrieux. Despite the fortune-hunting theme, Koster's taste as a director and the total lack of sniggering in the comedy-of-misunderstanding situations that develop keep it all a model of decorum and stylish good taste without in any way minimizing any of the fun. (Surprising that such a silken web of comic froufrou should have been written by two men, while some of the rowdy, pre-Code longshoreman humors of such comedies as *Sailor's Luck*, a 1933 Raoul Walsh film, should be wholly the work of lady scenarists!)

Interestingly, *The Rage of Paris* was reissued in the early fifties by an independent company that changed its title to *Confessions of a Model* and concocted a whole new ad campaign, built around the "undressing" scene at the beginning, and suggesting that it was a lurid sex drama! It's a tribute to the film's appeal that audiences lured in by that advertising (which included frame blowups of the episode, tactfully not represented in the original stills) were still so captivated by it that they complained not at all at the total lack of the salacious material they expected.

Quite incidentally, *The Rage of Paris* lapsed into the public domain when its copyright was not renewed, as also happened to *My Man Godfrey, Nothing Sacred,* and *His Girl Friday,* making four of the all-time classic screwball comedies instantly and widely available to videotape collectors at nominal prices (and sometimes, alas, offering only nominal picture and sound quality, too!).

WIFE, HUSBAND AND FRIEND

(20TH CENTURY-FOX, 1939)

Directed by Gregory Ratoff; producer and screenplay, Nunnally Johnson, from an original story by James N. Cain.

LEADING PLAYERS:
Warner Baxter, Loretta Young, Binnie Barnes, Cesar Romero, George Barbier, Eugene Pallette, J. Edgar Bromberg, Ruth Terry.

On the surface one of the most genial of screwball comedies, yet beneath it (perhaps due to

WIFE HUSBAND AND FRIEND (1939)   Eugene Pallette sympathizes with business colleague Warner Baxter whose wife (Loretta Young) has decided on a singing career.

WIFE HUSBAND AND FRIEND   Baxter unexpectedly discovers that *he* has an operatic voice!

the original James Cain story) one of the most biting, *Wife, Husband and Friend* poses an interesting story line. Warner Baxter is a successful businessman and Loretta Young his beautiful, loving but essentially rather shallow wife. Their marriage is a happy one, marred only by her belief that she can be a great singer if given the chance. Actually she has virtually no talent, but out of a desire to let her prove it to herself, he allows her to put on a showcase concert— attended mainly by their friends. As she is on the verge of admitting that her dream was a foolish one, the husband accidentally discovers that *he* has a great voice—one capable of shattering glass in the bathroom. Although uninterested in a musical career, and inclined to pooh-pooh his chances, he is sufficiently irked by his wife's attitude to allow himself to be "trained" and presented. He is a huge popular and critical success, although his sponsor, Binnie Barnes, also has romantic designs on him. They are not reciprocated, but they cause a further rift in his household. Finally, unbecomingly bedecked in armor, he has his first flop in an operatic performance and wisely decides to use that as an excuse to renounce his musical career and return to the now welcoming arms of his wife.

It's a film that's alternately warm and human, and in some of its dialogue, tough and

WIFE HUSBAND AND FRIEND After both have had their flings, Loretta Young and Warner Baxter decide to abandon singing and settle down to domestic bliss.

116

relatively realistic. Its zany story idea, and a brief running time, keep it from ever being taken too seriously, yet it never becomes totally screwball either.

One can forgive audiences and critics for having overlooked and misplaced this delightful film. Warner Baxter was then within a year of ending his long extraordinarily prolific tenure at Fox and its successor 20th Century-Fox, and many of his films overlapped not only in content but in title. Earlier on he had made both *Such Men Are Dangerous* and then *Such Women Are Dangerous*. In memory it's almost as hard to separate his *Doctors' Wives* from *Wife, Doctor and Nurse* as it is to separate that latter film from *Wife, Husband and Friend*, and the Baxter vehicles at the end of the thirties, though still carefully made, were increasingly routine. Thus one had no reason for great expectations from a Baxter film with a title like *Wife, Husband and Friend*, but the combination of a good original story, a tasteful writer-producer (whose contributions and influence may well have been greater than those of the merely workmanlike director), the flawless typecasting of the Fox stock company (where would *any* screwball comedy be without the gruff tones of an irascible Eugene Pallette?), and the usual impeccable art direction (Richard Day and Mark-Lee Kirk), photography (Ernest Palmer), and even laboratory printing of the Fox organization, all team up to make it the superb piece of mechanism that it is. (Too often, that mechanism was called in to camouflage the unoriginal rehashes that characterized so much of the 20th Century-Fox product of the mid to late thirties, but here it had material worthy of its slickness.)

The writing is genial and civilized, never forcing likable characters into comic bitchiness or semivillainy to make for tidier (and more clichéd) construction, and even the choice of director seems right under the circumstances. With a bigger and more important director, the production would have been commensurately bigger, and longer. As it is, it never overplays its hand, content to remain short and snappy, and to settle for the continuous chuckle rather than aiming for the big laugh. It's a trivial and superficial delight, the kind of film that works as well as it does because it is smart enough not to try to outgrow its "programmer" category. It was remade, well, though not *as* well, and slightly longer in 1949 by Edmund Goulding as *Everybody Does It,* with Paul Douglas and Celeste Holm as the battling married duo.

BACHELOR MOTHER
(RKO RADIO, 1939)

Directed by Garson Kanin; screenplay by Norman Krasna, from an original story by Felix Jackson.

LEADING PLAYERS:
Ginger Rogers; David Niven, Charles Coburn, Frank Albertson, E. E. Clive, Ernest Truex, Paul Stanton.

BACHELOR MOTHER   Store owner David Niven (incognito) tries to prove to salesgirl Ginger Rogers that the customer is always right and that damaged goods will be replaced, although obstinate sales clerk Irving Bacon refuses to cooperate.

One of the movies' best years, 1939 was full of great comedies, screwball and otherwise, some of them—like *Midnight*—having made far greater critical and popular impact than *Bachelor Mother.* Yet few films could be more appropriate to signify both the change of pace, and

117

the step forward, that comedy had achieved by the end of the decade.

Just as film noir began the forties with a stress on expressionistic lighting and Germanic art direction, only to conclude the decade with a more realistic, subdued visual style, though with no radical change in plot or characters, so did screwball comedy gradually drop its physical lunacy to adopt a milieu more recognizable as the real world, but also without abandoning any of its key or most popular elements.

Bachelor Mother, a reworking of a 1935 Austrian film called *Little Mother*, deals with a shopgirl, Ginger Rogers, facing a department-store layoff after the Christmas rush. A baby is deposited outside a foundling home; Rogers, unfortuitously passing at that moment, is assumed to be the mother. Nothing she says can convince anyone otherwise. Her store is contacted, and the owner's son, David Niven, intervenes, getting her restored to a good job, and gradually becoming involved in her life and the baby's welfare. Jealous store employees assume the worst, that Niven is the father. Word gets back to *his* father, Charles Coburn, who is so overjoyed that his son is apparently settling down *and* providing him with a grandson all at the same time that he, too, refuses to accept the girl's denials. Other fake claimants to fatherhood appear just to prove Niven's innocence.

Needless to say, the outcome is a happy marriage between Rogers and Niven, and a secure future with them for the toddler.

Such is the casual maturity of the film that while the audience knows from the start that the girl is not the child's mother, nobody in the film itself ever does find out—nor does it seem to matter. A couple of years earlier the Production Code would have insisted on a scene in which everything was *fully* explained and the heroine's "innocence" proven beyond doubt.

While the plot is a good one, with many rich, human touches as boy and girl—both unfamiliar with the mechanics of raising an infant—wrestle with problems of feeding and dressing, it also allows for some marvelous set pieces. There's a New Year's celebration at a nightclub, where, unable to come up with a plausible explanation for his dating Ginger Rogers, David Niven introduces her as a friend from Sweden who cannot speak a word of English and translates all the small talk for—and from—her. One of the guests is a catty casual girlfriend of Niven's, whom Rogers squashes with a one-liner in perfect English just as she is leaving.

The department-store setting, and the petty jealousies and rivalries of the floorwalkers and clerks, produces several superbly comic scenes. In one of them, Niven, in order to prove to Rogers that damaged merchandise is "cheerfully" exchanged by his staff, masquerades as a

customer and tries to exchange a duck, only to be met by rudeness, antagonism, and of course ultimate refusal. He is even physically manhandled by the newly promoted Frank Alberton. "You've *disgraced* the toy department," snarls the priggish floorwalker as Albertson is demoted again. Another charming sequence has Niven and Rogers promenading their baby in the park, encountering another couple with a baby (the unlikely couple are Florence Lake and Chester Clute), and Niven, knowing little of the normal development of babies, countering their boasting with a counterclaim that *his* child can already recite most of "Gunga Din." This was easily comparative newcomer Niven's best comedy performance to date, and while one or two others (*Eternally Yours, Raffles*) followed, the war intervened, and he returned to see service with the British forces, interrupting a career that might well have established him as a major comedic romantic rival to Cary Grant.

Ginger Rogers at this time, via such near-screwball films as *Vivacious Lady* and *Fifth Avenue Girl*, was close to overtaking Lombard as Hollywood's premier comedienne. But she had a tendency to try too hard, to strain for effect, something that also overtook the later work of Garson Kanin. This was only his fourth movie as a director, and his first A; only a couple of years later when he and Rogers worked together again in *Tom, Dick and Harry*, the easy grace for both of them had gone, although Rogers regained it to a large degree under Billy Wilder's direction in *The Major and the Minor*, one of the best screwball comedies of the early forties.

Despite the Production Code, one gag did slip by—only to be discovered when preview audiences howled uproariously at the film's apparently innocent but treacherously loaded final line. As their wedding night approaches, Niven comments that he is glad that Rogers has finally given up claiming that the baby is not hers. Tired of arguing the point, Rogers merely nods but adds, "Are *you* going to be surprised?" Realizing what they had passed in script form, apparently surprised at the sophistication of audiences that "got" the line

immediately, and determined that American audiences just weren't entitled to such boisterous and bawdy laughter, the Code stepped in and demanded an alteration. In the milder, amended version with the same basic intent, Rogers merely looks sagely at Niven and the camera and murmurs quizzically, "Hmmmm-hmmmmm."

Bachelor Mother was remade semimusically in the midfifties as *Bundle of Joy* starring Eddie Fisher and Debbie Reynolds. Late in his career Garson Kanin returned, disastrously, to the near-screwball field with a generation-gap comedy, *Where It's At*, in 1969. Both outings were decided mistakes.

IT'S A WONDERFUL WORLD
(MGM, 1939)

Directed by W. S. Van Dyke; screenplay by Ben Hecht and Herman Mankiewicz.

LEADING PLAYERS:
James Stewart, Claudette Colbert, Guy Kibbee, Nat Pendleton, Ernest Truex, Sidney Blackmer, Edgar Kennedy.

One of the relatively few screwball comedies that was also a murder mystery and comedy thriller, *It's a Wonderful World* managed to be influenced by both *It Happened One Night* and Hitchcock's *The 39 Steps* without being in any way derivative or lazily imitative. MGM was fairly awash with somewhat standardized screwballs, thanks to the omnipresence of William Powell and Myrna Loy on their star roster, but here was one that was individual and different. Ironically, *It's a Wonderful World* was all but dismissed by contemporary critics as being fun but foolish, and movie audiences—all except hard-core screwball devotees, who always remembered it fondly—forgot it almost as soon as it appeared and invariably confused it later on with the more popular and similarly titled postwar Jimmy Stewart vehicle *It's a Wonderful Life.*

In this outing, Stewart plays the offbeat (for him) role of a private eye whose client, Ernest

Truex, is framed on a murder charge and sentenced to the electric chair. Due to be jailed for a short term as an accessory, Stewart escapes en route to prison, determined to track down the real killer—not out of any sense of loyalty to his client, but because he knows that he'll be paid well if he saves the guy's life. In the course of events, he commandeers the car of poet Claudette Colbert, and thereafter he is stuck with her as an often far from helpful cosleuth. It's a crazily unpredictable film—Stewart follows screwball precedent by socking her in the jaw and in a highlight sequence dons spectacles (which make him virtually blind) in order to masquerade as a Boy Scout master. In this episode the sleuthing duo meet a genuine Boy Scout who sees through their disguise; played by Leonard Kibrick, he bears the character name of Herman Plotka—a surname that presumably had some personal significance for screenwriter Hecht, or that he found somehow amusing, since it was the surname that he affixed to Carole Lombard before she was rechristened Lily Garland in *20th Century*.

The cross-country ramblings become a little more serious toward the end when the sleuthing zeroes in on a summer-stock theater group. But the mixture of callous indifference to Truex's plight, slapstick, and physical and verbal mayhem is maintained until the end. Reputedly made in less than twelve days by the always nonfussy, no-retake Woody Van Dyke, the production in fact benefits from his hurried schedule. Like all MGM productions, it has gloss—but it doesn't have the final polish that they would have liked. Some of the scenes still have a few rough edges, and the performances (Stewart's in particular) benefit, too, from not being honed through rehearsals or having time for mannerisms to develop. These rough edges give the film a vitality, a spontaneity, even a sense of urgency, that most MGM films (which means almost any *not* directed by Van Dyke) would have smoothed away.

Quite incidentally, the film's principal influence from *It Happened One Night* may well be in its choice of an equally meaningless and ambiguous title. The earlier Capra film was concerned with *not* using what it felt was a noncommercial and misleading title from the original story, "Night Bus," and its final title, if uninformative and unrelated to the plot, at least suggested a carefree and lightly romantic mood. *It's a Wonderful World* is even less related to its content—much less so for example than *San Diego, I Love You* (1944). In fact, with the Colbert-Stewart teaming to back it up, it suggests something that it most decidedly was not an upbeat romance. Perhaps a tougher, more appropriate title might have helped it at the box office.

IT'S A WONDERFUL WORLD (1939) Posing as a Boy Scout leader and nearly blinded by the glasses he wears, James Stewart enlists the unwilling aid of Claudette Colbert in solving a murder.

FIVE

THE THIRTIES—A LAST LOOK

THE MAD MISS MANTON (1938)   Henry Fonda's hopes for a reconciliation with
Barbara Stanwyck are very quickly dashed—or doused—by maid Hattie
McDaniel.

DUCK SOUP (1933) While devoid of the romantic complications so essential to screwball—except sometimes in burlesque form—the Marx Brothers (all four of them seen here in the film's mock musical number) certainly made their contribution to the zany genre.

DUCK SOUP With eternal vamp Lillian Miles in a typically broad bedroom scene with the boys.

When, near the end of 1938, *Variety* reviewed Paramount's *Say It in French*, it had this to say (as part of a much longer review):

> . . . latest in the apparently unending string of romantic screwball comedies . . . main trouble is that repetition has dulled the edge of all but the rarest and best screwball comedies. As a result, the harder *Say It in French* strives for harebrained badinage, the more labored it becomes. For the most part, it is very heavy indeed . . . related with such determined hilarity and energetic whimsy that it somehow succeeds only rarely in being even a little bit funny. If pictures like *It Happened One Night, My Man Godfrey,* and *The Awful Truth* hadn't already set such a lofty standard, *Say It in French* might be considered a regular side-splitter. But it doesn't even approach any of them.

The point in reviving this critical mauling over half a century later (actually the film was an entertaining enough trifle in its own way) is twofold: first as a reminder of how standardized the screwball comedy genre had become over just a few years, just as the Underground Resistance thriller would become standardized in an even more compressed period during World War II; second, as a warning note concerning the reliability of reviews—particularly those of publications like *Variety,* which sought to review everything. In the thirties and forties, thousands of theaters existed to gobble up all the product that was offered, and accordingly a lot of product was needed. Much of it was inevitably almost assembly-line produced. And reviewers for trade publications—more con-

BREAKFAST FOR TWO (1937) Typical of the standardization of the screwball genre: despite big names in Herbert Marshall and Barbara Stanwyck, this ran a brief sixty-five minutes. It had a certain amount of novelty in that *both* protagonists, were, unknown to the other, millionaires!

cerned with commercial value to exhibitors than artistic content, though of course aware that artistic content *could* have bearing on box-office value—naturally became jaded at repetitions and rip-offs. It's quite astonishing how many films then downgraded as bad are now regarded as classics; how many they damned with faint praise as films that might just get by because of their stars turned out to be box-office blockbusters and remained cult favorites through the years.

Because of the mass-production methods of the thirties, many interesting screwball comedies of the time have not been given individual attention in the preceding pages, not least because so many of them overlapped into adjacent areas. But in fairness, a few of them should be mentioned in passing. Some have already been arguably overpraised elsewhere. Others were enterprising misfires. Still more await rediscovery.

In the wake of *The Invisible Man* (1933), a number of "trick" comedies evolved, notably Hal Roach's duo *Topper* (1937) and its sequel *Topper Takes a Trip* (1939), both directed by Norman Z. McLeod. Because of the presence of Cary Grant, the former has remained the more popular. Grant and Constance Bennett are husband and wife ghosts who return to life— or more accurately, are prevented from entering the afterlife—to perform a good deed, and in doing so make life difficult and embarrassing for the meek Cosmo Topper, played by Roland Young. The comic ghost theme was a novelty in 1937, but the film does not wear well today. Much better is its sequel, less popular because of the absence of Cary Grant (except in a flashback sequence), but slicker in its camera trickery, and on surer comedic ground in its concentration on the comedy of embarrassment, always a Roach speciality. Constance Bennett as the female spirit, and Roland Young and Billie Burke as Mr. and Mrs. Topper repeated their original roles. The films could only hint at the sexual piquancies contained in Thorne Smith's original novel, but *Topper Takes a Trip* hardly needed them.

The screwball murder-mystery spin-offs from *The Thin Man* have already been noted,

TOPPER TAKES A TRIP (1939) Cosmo Topper (Roland Young) toasts his ghostly friend—and sometimes tormentor—Marion Kerby (Constance Bennett).

TOPPER TAKES A TRIP Mrs. Topper (Billie Burke) with family friend Alexander D'Arcy and ghost Constance Bennett.

but the comedy thriller independent of that inspiration did occasionally invade screwball territory. Sometimes the results were mixed. William K. Howard was a top director of stylish, well-photographed, rapidly cut mystery thrillers, and he brought those qualities to *The Princess Comes Across* (1936), but he seemed more interested in mood than laughs. Fortunately, Carole Lombard's stance was just the opposite: playing an American girl masquerading as Swedish royalty, she strikes sparks in a shipboard meeting with Fred MacMurray. Even though stars and director seemed to leave each other resolutely alone, each was so expert in his or her line that no cleavage showed, and the brief running time kept the fun and thrills evenly balanced. *The Mad Miss Manton*, a 1938 foray into screwball mystery, probably turned out far better than was expected or they'd have assigned a better director than Leigh Jason. The film tried hard to live up to its title, with

Barbara Stanwyck as a society debutante who gets her circle of friends—including Henry Fonda—involved in a murder mystery. It was a surprise hit at the time and certainly had some bright lines of dialogue, but it hasn't survived the years too well. However, a lesser-known Jason-directed comedy, 1937's *Wise Girl*, holds up rather better. At least it had some new wrinkles in its scatterbrained plot, which had heiress Miriam Hopkins masquerading as an out-of-work actress and infiltrating a Bohemian artists' commune in order to regain custody of a baby! Ray Milland was her romantic viz-a-viz in a comedy with more wit and warmth than this brief synopsis might suggest.

It's hard to disqualify films merely because their charm so totally overpowers their screwball content, but that, sadly, must be the fate of Frank Capra's *Mr. Deeds Goes to Town* (1936) and especially Richard Wallace's *The Young in Heart* (1938), a delightful film with wonderful ensem-

Can't Take It With You—with one of the zaniest of all screwball families—missed badly because (a) it tried too hard, and (b) it lacked the courage of its convictions, or the willingness to stand its ground with the Production Code boys. One of the most appealing aspects of the original play was the refusal of Grandfather (Lionel Barrymore in the film) to pay his income tax. The film gets its fun out of the situa-

PPER TAKES A TRIP With the help he invisible Marion, Topper oland Young) confuses bartender ul Hurst.

ble acting—Janet Gaynor, Douglas Fairbanks, Jr., Billie Burke, and Roland Young as a wacky family who live, somewhat illegally, off their wits, with Minnie Dupree, Richard Carlson, and Paulette Goddard as the outsiders who eventually reform them. Its large doses of sentiment are honest and enjoyable, but keep the hard edge of screwball very much at bay.

Another 1938 film, however, Capra's *You*

tion, particularly with Charles Lane playing an exasperated IRS investigator, and then pulls the rug out from us by having Grandfather admit later, "Oh, I was just funning with him— I don't owe the government a cent!" Capra regulars—Jean Arthur, James Stewart, Edward Arnold—and useful hangers-on (Ann Miller, Spring Byington, Mischa Auer, Donald Meek) kept its craziness noisily on the go, but it was a

125

YOU CAN'T TAKE IT WITH YOU (1938) Despite a classic screwball family, Frank Capra's adaptation of the stage hit was a watered-down disappointment, though it remained a good vehicle for (from left) Lionel Barrymore, James Stewart, Jean Arthur, and Edward Arnold.

disappointing film to which many of the *Variety* criticisms of *Say It in French* might well have been directed were it not for the saving grace of star value.

Nevertheless, it's a measure of the general paucity of good films in 1938 that this second-rate screwball comedy and third-rate Capra film still won the Academy Award as Best Picture of the Year.

Hands Across the Table (1935) was possibly one of the more underrated screwball comedies of the thirties, though again its claim to the genre is somewhat marginal. Its title is as elegant and subtle as its plot line, which deals with manicurist Carole Lombard out to snare millionaire Ralph Bellamy though she loves impoverished playboy Fred MacMurray. Even though that setup automatically doomed Bellamy's chances, for once he wasn't the dunderheaded other man, but a sensitive fellow who was also a semi-invalid and who immediately won audience sympathy. Mitchell Leisen directed with

charm and style; but his comedies really needed the bite of a Billy Wilder or Preston Sturges script to veer them in the direction of screwball. (When he remade his *Midnight,* a 1939 hit, several years later as *Masquerade in Mexico,* it was denied that bite and became one of his dullest and most meandering comedies.)

Warner Bros. made some commendable attempts to climb on the screwball bandwagon in the thirties, but only the already discussed *A Slight Case of Murder* could be considered a genuine classic. If nothing else, the Bette Davis–Leslie Howard theatrical romp *It's Love I'm After* (1937, director Archie Mayo)—a kind of echo of *20th Century* and a forerunner of elements of *The Man Who Came to Dinner* and *All About Eve*—demonstrated what a sprightly light comedienne Olivia de Havilland could be, a talent that Warners took too little advantage of when she was just the right age for such roles. Attempts to vary if not change Errol Flynn's image by putting him into such screw-

BOMBSHELL (1933) Jean Harlow literally playing herself and Lee Tracy playing the studio publicity man, in one of Hollywood's most pungent self-satires.

BOMBSHELL Franchot Tone—*his* masquerade as a society scion was one of the film's screwball elements, *and* one of its biggest climactic surprises—with Harlow.

IT'S ALL YOURS (1937)
Madeleine Carroll, Mischa Auer, and C. L. Dale in another enjoyable if standardized programmer, with a twist in that Madeleine's millionaire father disinherits her and makes penniless Francis Lederer his heir, in order to teach her responsibility.

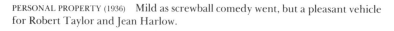

PERSONAL PROPERTY (1936)   Mild as screwball comedy went, but a pleasant vehicle for Robert Taylor and Jean Harlow.

THE COWBOY AND THE LADY (1938) A mild, predictable Gary Cooper–Merle Oberon teaming; most of the fun antics came from the supporting cast, among them (shown here) Walter Brennan and Patsy Kelly.

IT'S LOVE I'M AFTER (1937) Broadway matinee idol Leslie Howard deliberately makes himself disagreeable at breakfast (paraphrasing Shakespeare to criticize a kipper) in order to disillusion lovelorn Olivia de Havilland (standing next to him). Also shown, mother Spring Byington, outraged butler E. E. Clive, and blustery father George Barbier.

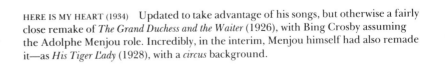

HERE IS MY HEART (1934) Updated to take advantage of his songs, but otherwise a fairly close remake of *The Grand Duchess and the Waiter* (1926), with Bing Crosby assuming the Adolphe Menjou role. Incredibly, in the interim, Menjou himself had also remade it—as *His Tiger Lady* (1928), with a *circus* background.

THE EX MRS. BRADFORD (1936) Jean Arthur and William Powell made a wonderfully charismatic team in one of the best *Thin Man* imitations.

THE EX MRS. BRADFORD The morning after too much liquor and a beating is treated with more liquor: William Powell and Jean Arthur.

THEODORA GOES WILD
(1937) Irene Dunne as the
small-town,
ultra-respectable church
organist.

THEODORA GOES WILD
Enjoying a fling in New York
with the artist who designed
the cover for her risqué
novel, Dunne and the
ever-present Melvyn Douglas.

TRUE CONFESSION (1937) John Barrymore returned to screwball comedy with a
decidedly over-the-top performance as an amiable nut who *might* be a murderer.

TRUE CONFESSION Best friend Una Merkel, wife Carole Lombard, and struggling lawyer husband Fred MacMurray.

TRUE CONFESSION An overdone running gag: Lombard's tongue in her cheek informs the audience that she's about to tell another whopper of a lie to MacMurray.

133

HOLIDAY (1938) Jean Dixon, Katharine Hepburn, and Edward Everett Horton.

BOY MEETS GIRL (1938) Pat O'Brien and James Cagney, as Hollywood scenarists based loosely on Hecht and MacArthur, outline a story idea to Western star Dick Foran (left), studio head Ralph Bellamy, and cafeteria waitress Marie Wilson, whose unborn child they plan to boost to stardom.

THE YOUNG IN HEART (1938) Douglas Fairbanks Jr. and Roland Young headed a wonderfully larcenous and zany family that was among the most engaging of all screwball families, but the film was too charming and pleasingly sentimental to qualify fully.

ETERNALLY YOURS (1938)   Another perfect marriage goes temporarily wrong; David
Niven as the illusionist husband, Loretta Young as his stage partner and wife.

ETERNALLY YOURS   Hugh Herbert is Niven's valet and adds
many of the laughs.

ball forays as Michael Curtiz's *The Perfect Specimen* (1937) and *Four's a Crowd* (1938) were fatal flaws in those otherwise enjoyable and amiable comedies.

There are a handful of films that *should* have worked, but just didn't—films that had the right combination of stars and director, and under normal circumstances, despite routine scripts, *would* have come to life on the screen. Typical of these is *Wedding Present*, a 1936 Paramount comedy of newspaper rivalry, directed by the usually reliable Richard Wallace, and costarring Cary Grant and Joan Bennett, backed by a strong cast of character favorites. Even in 1936 it was a dog. It's the kind of film that one expects to be more interesting today. After all, it reflects an era, its mass-production techniques are now almost an asset rather than a liability, it's a pleasure (or should be) to look

THE HOUSEKEEPER'S DAUGHTER (1938)   One of the oddest of all screwball comedies, this provided excellent opportunities for Adolphe Menjou and that excellent farceur John Hubbard, seen here with leading lady Joan Bennett, but its black comedy elements—including George E. Stone as a psychopathic killer—didn't always jell.

REMEMBER THE NIGHT   Fred and Barbara run afoul of small-town sheriff Thomas Ross; Stanwyck is about to effect their escape by starting a fire in his wastepaper basket.

REMEMBER THE NIGHT (1939)   One of the smoothest mixtures of screwball comedy and sentimental romance: Barbara Stanwyck and Fred MacMurray.

137

MR. SMITH GOES TO WASHINGTON (1939)   Capra's last film of the thirties had too much sentiment, too much patriotism, too much seriousness of purpose to be bona-fide screwball—but it certainly had its moments and some appropriate players, including (from left) Eugene Pallette, Claude Rains, Edward Arnold, and (seated) Guy Kibbee.

FIRST LOVE (1939)   A perfect climax to the thirties and a farewell to its innocence, orphan Deanna Durbin is introduced into the home of uncle Eugene Pallette—the only sane member of a family that is a reprise from *My Man Godfrey*.

back on the earlier yet already accomplished work of a player like Cary Grant. All those factors should work in its favor, but they don't. In the nineties it's *still* a dog, and one difficult to sit through.

Three Blind Mice, The Moon's Our Home, The Joy of Living, Love on the Run, very arguably *Holiday*—the list of near or potential screwballs from the thirties is endless. Nor would the problem—both of borderline cases and especially of overly prolific production in this field—be solved in the early forties. Both *My Favorite Wife* (Cary Grant and Irene Dunne) and the reverse side of the coin, *Too Many Husbands* (Jean Arthur and Melvyn Douglas, confusingly retitled *My Two Husbands* in Britain), were 1940 offerings, while Melvyn Douglas was still in harness in early 1941 in *Our Wife*. But these confusions must await examination, if not solutions, in the following chapter.

NINOTCHKA (1939)   More satire than screwball, Lubitsch's *Ninotchka* nevertheless had many traditional screwball elements. The zany family was replaced by a trio of Communists enjoying a spree in Paris. Shown here with Garbo are Felix Bressart (left), the incomparable Sig Rumann (with beard), and Alexander Granach, a fine dramatic actor in one of his few comic roles.

NINOTCHKA   "Garbo Laughs" was the catchline used to sell the film, implying that she had never done so before—she had—and this is the scene (with Melvyn Douglas) that justified the line.

139

As a link between the outgoing thirties and the incoming forties, a reminder that *dress*, especially in publicity stills, was a way of informing the public that stars not normally associated with screwball comedy were letting their hair down—or in the case of Red Skelton, that an established clown was going even more over the top.

Robert Taylor

William Powell

Spencer Tracy

Red Skelton
(with Esther Williams and Betty Garrett)

SIX

THE FORTIES

The two extremes of comedy with which the forties began: *The Philadelphia Story* (1940) with Cary Grant, Katharine Hepburn, James Stewart, and a resurgence in elaborate sight-gag and patter comedy by Bob Hope, Jack Benny and Bud Abbott and Lou Costello, still visually fresh in this scene from one of their best films, *Hold That Ghost* surrounded by Evelyn Ankers (left), Richard Carlson, and Joan Davis. Until the full ascendance of Preston Sturges, screwball comedy remained somewhere in between.

Just as the thirties could, filmically, be split into three basic sections—early sound, the peak of the pre–Production Code years, and (the biggest section) the Production Code period from late 1934 on—so do the forties divide themselves into three roughly parallel groups.

The first couple of years are clearly the pre-war years, with screwball comedy in a sense marking time, duplicating material from the thirties with perhaps greater sophistication and less censorship. With America's entry into the conflict at the end of 1941, war-oriented problems or themes provided fertile ground for new areas of comedy, their originality bolstered by the new confidence placed in writers like Billy Wilder and Preston Sturges who were now able to direct their own material.

Not unexpectedly, wartime box offices boomed and audiences increased. With the end of the war, Hollywood was anxious to maintain both its momentum *and* its new audiences, and to prepare for the upcoming battle against television. Comedy played a surprisingly small part in this campaign. Hollywood's main ploy seemed to be to stress its new maturity, and to utilize properties from the stage

Joel McCrea and the William Powell/Myrna Loy team continued to add polish and style to many screwball comedies of the forties.

Writer/director Preston Sturges, who revitalized screwball comedy in the forties, from . . .

THE LADY EVE (1941) with Henry Fonda and Barbara Stanwyck, his first major hit and still one of his best, to . . .

UNFAITHFULLY YOURS (1948), with Linda Darnell and Rex Harrison, his blackest and wittiest film.

that would entitle it to "respect." Many of these films were, however, watered down to popular taste (*All My Sons*) or were frankly top-heavy bores (*Mourning Becomes Electra*). In terms of comedy, Preston Sturges was past his peak and on the way out, although at least one classic, *Unfaithfully Yours* (1948), remained. Despite the wit in their writing, Billy Wilder and Joseph Mankiewicz could hardly be considered comedy specialists in those postwar years. Martin and Lewis were about to replace Abbott and Costello as the major comedy team, and screwball comedy was heading in the more sedate

direction of the Cary Grant, Doris Day, and Rock Hudson comedies of the fifties. The best of American screwball comedy in the forties can be found in the first half of the decade.

The early 1940 releases showed no specific pattern, other than that the old reliables—Cary Grant, Irene Dunne, Melvyn Douglas, Jean Arthur—were still able to deliver the goods. Howard Hawks's *His Girl Friday* got the decade off to a dazzling beginning, a highlight that was difficult to top. The echoes from the past appeared early: *Oh Johnny, How You Can Love!* was a spirited if routine B from Universal,

SLIGHTLY HONORABLE (1940)   Another black comedy of murders in the tradition of *The Housekeeper's Daughter*; the beginning of a trend. From left: Douglas Fowley, Ruth Terry, Pat O'Brien, Broderick Crawford, and Addison Richards. Edward Arnold also had a key role.

145

THE MAN WHO LOST HIMSELF (1941) Screwball in plot, characters like Kay Francis and Brian Aherne, everything except its pacing, which was short, leisurely, and left too many fine comic players with too little to do.

THE MAN WHO LOST HIMSELF S. Z. Sakall and Brian Aherne.

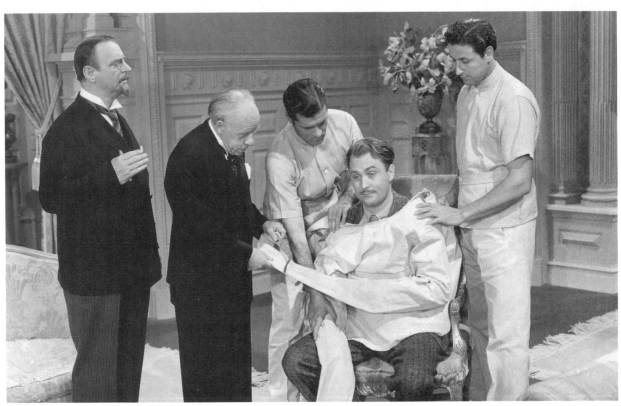

THE MAN WHO LOST HIMSELF Sig Rumann (left), the formidable doctor of so many screwballs, enlists the aid of Barlowe Borland in putting Brian Aherne in a straight jacket.

THE INVISIBLE WOMAN (1941)   A gag publicity shot of Charlie Ruggles being tormented by the Invisible Woman (Virginia Bruce), product of scatterbrained John Barrymore's experiments.

THE INVISIBLE WOMAN   The ubiquitous Charles Lane gets officious with Virginia Bruce. Next to her as an extra, with stardom only a year away, is Maria Montez (third left). Mary Gordon, at the far end of the line, looks sympathetic.

OUR WIFE (1941)   Ellen Drew, Melvyn Douglas, and Ruth Hussey.

directed by Charles Lamont. Its plot: a travel-ing salesman (Tom Brown) links up with a run-away heiress (Peggy Moran) hoping to elope with a fortune hunter frowned on by her fam-ily. The cross-country trip includes a stopover at an auto camp. If it sounds familiar, it cer-tainly should!

Enjoyable, if unmemorable, were *The Amaz-ing Mr. Williams* with the ubiquitous Melvyn

Douglas; *He Married His Wife* with Joel McCrea, not yet having hit his real comedy stride; *Slightly Honorable,* Tay Garnett's return to one of his directorial specialties, the screwball crime or mystery film, unnecessarily confusing per-haps but with a genuine surprise in its ulti-mate revelation of the unknown killer; and Wesley Ruggles's *Too Many Husbands,* a curious yet coincidental forerunner of *My Favorite Wife,*

WORLD PREMIERE (1941) Satirizing the anti-Nazi movies Hollywood couldn't yet make because America was still neutral; Ricardo Cortez strapped to the torture table, gloatingly watched by femme fatale Frances Farmer, listens to instructions from director Andrew Tombes.

WORLD PREMIERE Where would screwball comedies be without trains? En route to the premiere, studio executives John Barrymore, Cliff Nazarro, and Eugene Pallette.

HIRED WIFE (1943)   Indistinguishable from a dozen other big-business comedies, but a pleasant and zany time-killer, with Rosalind Russell and Brian Aherne going through their usual paces.

to be released in May. Based on an earlier Noel Coward play (and remade in 1955 as *Three for the Show,* a relatively unchanged Technicolor musical version with Betty Grable and Jack Lemmon), *Too Many Husbands* presents Fred MacMurray as a long-shipwrecked and presumed-dead husband who returns to civilization to find his "widow," Jean Arthur, now remarried to Melvyn Douglas. Legal procedure establishes and prioritizes MacMurray as the legal spouse, but complications don't end there since the wife now cannot make up her mind as to which husband she prefers. *My Favorite Wife* (about which more later) offered a parallel situation in that it was the shipwrecked wife (Irene Dunne) who returned just as former husband (Cary Grant) and new wife (Gail Patrick) were leaving on their honeymoon!

Many of the 1940 comedies, such as Robert Z. Leonard's *Third Finger, Left Hand* (Melvyn Douglas yet again, making a temporary substitute for William Powell opposite Myrna Loy), were essentially lighthearted romantic romps. Mitchell Leisen's *Remember the Night* is virtually unclassifiable, and therein perhaps lies its

TOO MANY HUSBANDS (1940)   Hitting the market at virtually the same time as *My Favorite Wife,* and not at all bad a reverse imitation: Melvyn Douglas, Fred MacMurray, and Jean Arthur.

150

HE STAYED FOR BREAKFAST
(1940) Melvyn Douglas, who
apparently never slept or took a
vacation, played a kind of male
Ninotchka in this curious comedy,
with Eugene Pallette, Alan Marshal,
and Loretta Young.

RINGS ON HER FINGERS (1942)
Rouben Mamoulian made a
rather surprising entry into
(restrained) Screwball with this
romantic comedy, one of rather
too many that Henry Fonda
made in the early forties, here
trying to make a point with
police chief Charles Wilson as
Spring Byington and Gene
Tierney support him.

RINGS ON HER FINGERS Spring
Byington, Laird Cregar, Gene
Tierney, and player.

151

MY SISTER EILEEN (1942)   Brian Aherne and Janet Blair await a take; Rosalind Russell also starred in this wild and entirely nutty comedy.

HI DIDDLE DIDDLE (1943)   Pola Negri, here with Adolphe Menjou, made a long overdue return to the Hollywood screen in this frenzied romantic wartime comedy that sought to extend the inspired insanity of *Hellzapoppin*.

charm. Thanks to Preston Sturges's script, there are certainly marvelous screwball highlights—a zany courtroom scene near the beginning, with Willard Robertson (normally a dour judge or a tight-lipped parole-board official) having the time of his life with the role of his life, as a flamboyant defense attorney concocting (and acting out) an incredible story to prove that his guilty-as-hell client, Barbara Stanwyck, did not steal some jewelry; or a later sequence in which Stanwyck and Fred MacMurray run afoul of a small-town sheriff and spin equally tall tales before they set fire to the office and escape in the confusion. Most of *Remember the Night* is however richly human, warm, and poignant, a perfect mating of the very different styles of Leisen and Sturges. (Sturges directing the same material would probably have fashioned a screwball masterpiece; as it is, it's a masterpiece of a quieter kind, and almost certainly Leisen's best film.)

Early 1940 also saw the distribution in the

THE BACHELOR'S DAUGHTERS Adolphe Menjou with Jane Wyatt, the most likable of the four "daughters."

United States of Alexander Korda's British Technicolor comedy *Over the Moon,* with Merle Oberon as the suddenly fantastically rich heiress, and Rex Harrison as the man who loves her but now can't (or won't) marry her because of her sudden wealth. Ant then there was the charming French *Battements de Coeur,* barely finished, in stops and starts, due to the war, but a delightful low-key screwball comedy later remade in Hollywood as *Heartbeat* with Ginger Rogers inadequately replacing Danielle Darrieux, Jean Pierre Aumont taking over from Claude Dauphin, and Basil Rathbone contributing a superb comedy cameo in the old Saturnin Fabre role as a modern Fagin who runs a school for pickpockets in Paris!

It would take time for the forties screwball cycle to get off the ground, and it would never quite match the quantity or overall quality of the thirties product, but thanks mainly to new talents like Preston Sturges, when it was at its best, it was terrific!

THE BACHELOR'S DAUGHTERS (1948) Like *Hi Diddle Diddle*, produced by Andrew Stone, this was a rather more successful welding of sentiment with zany comedy, much of it revolving around Billie Burke, who played a silent movie star, with excerpts from her silent work pleasingly interpolated. (Clockwise from left) Jane Wyatt, Claire Trevor, Ann Dvorak, and Gail Russell surround Adolphe Menjou as his unofficial daughters, among them purveying greed, ambition, sweetness and light, all of course mellowing for a happy ending.

153

TOO MANY BLONDES (1941) The same year that Lon Chaney did *The Wolf Man* he also played in this nutty "B" farce with Helen Parrish (left), Iris Adrian, Rudy Vallee, and (seated) Jerome Cowan. Thornton Freeland, a major comedy name from the thirties, directed.

By its very nature, the screwball comedy relies a great deal on the skill of specialized players, directors, and writers, all of them luxuries more or less ruled out by the economics of the B movie. Moreover, screwball comedy was eclectic, whereas the nature of the B was that it be universal, able to fit on the bottom of a double bill. Efficiency rather than artistry or individuality was the aim of the short B movie. Nevertheless, within its life span of a little more than twenty years, the B, almost accidentally, roped in its share of screwball material, most notably in the late thirties and very early forties when production costs were still reasonable and when the B was still important enough, collectively if not individually, to allow for the occasional experiment with a nonstereotypical script.

RKO Radio's *Curtain Call* (1940), a directorial debut for Frank Woodruff (from radio), was an unexpected pleasure. Like all RKO Bs, it was slick and streamlined, but for once the gloss did not serve only to cover up a paucity of story material. This film (probably) introduced what was eventually to become the old chestnut of two Broadway producers (in this case, Donald MacBride in a most welcome lead with Alan Mowbray) putting on a bad play that, for business reasons, they hope will be a flop. Apart from the unconvincing notion that extremely bad plays, performed straight, immediately become hilarious satires and big hits, it was a most diverting hour's entertainment, with a good supporting cast headed by Barbara Read as the victimized small-town playwright, John Archer (father of contemporary star Anne Archer) as her loyal boyfriend, and Helen Vinson at her bitchiest as a temperamental Broadway star. So popular was the film that RKO produced an equally glossy sequel in 1941, *Footlight Fever*, with MacBride and Mowbray. It, too, was amusing and unusual, but the originality and much of the charm had evaporated, and RKO wisely dropped the idea of a whole series.

If any studio could be said to specialize in the screwball B, then it was Universal, which not only had players like Mischa Auer and Hugh Herbert under contract, but also was

CURTAIN CALL (1940)   Barbara Read as the stage-struck writer, John Archer her small-town boyfriend.

doubtless encouraged to do further digging in the mines so profitably explored in Ole Olsen and Chic Johnson's *Hellzapoppin* (1941). Unfortunately, ultrastandardization was the rule at Universal, and even those Bs that seemed original at the time can't escape that classification today. *I Can't Give You Anything but Love Baby* (1940) was a Runyonesque comedy about a sentimental, pop-song-loving gangster (Broderick Crawford) who kidnaps a down-on-his-luck composer (Johnny Downs) to write a love song that the former hopes will restore his long-lost sweetheart to him. Even its climactic chase, with a car taking shortcuts on city sidewalks, is less exhilarating by far today, its back projection and other tricks much more apparent now. Universal also did a brace of authentic Damon Runyon adaptations, *Tight Shoes* (1941) and *Butch Minds the Baby* (1942), both made at the height of Runyon's popularity as a pithy short story writer. But the studio sold him short and exploited and exaggerated the colorful characters he had created, rather than playing them as normal—which is why Warners' earlier *A Slight Case of Murder* had worked so well.

SANDY IS A LADY (1940)   Jack Carson, Baby Sandy, Una Merkel.

BUY ME THAT TOWN (1941)   One of the best "B" comedies ever; a Runyonesque tale with Constance Moore and Lloyd Nolan.

Too many of Universal's potentially interesting semiscrewball comedies veered off in other directions. The zany Ritz Brothers found their films awash in musical numbers. The delightful Baby Sandy movies were too prone to turn their infant star into a diminutive Harold Lloyd, with skyscraper-ledge climaxes, al-

BROADWAY LIMITED (1940)   An example of the care, even in "B" films, of creating the illusion of reality. A mock-up in the Hal Roach Studios of New York's Pennsylvania Station.

though *Bachelor Daddy* (1941, directed by Harold Young) had a fine sequence wherein Edward Everett Horton took his young charge to a kiddie matinee and found himself wrapped up in, and trying to explain, the plot complications of a Johnny Mack Brown western. Another 1941 Universal release, *Cracked*

WEEKEND FOR THREE (1941)   RKO's "B"s always has class and talent; this screwball marital farce even had a screenplay by Dorothy Parker and Alan Campbell. Dennis O'Keefe and Jane Wyatt play a married couple whose happiness is almost inadvertently wrecked by friend Edward Everett Horton.

Nuts, directed by the veteran Eddie Cline, was at least a screwball comedy pure and simple, without side excursions into music. Stuart Erwin played a contest winner, a typical small-town hick in the big city, persuaded to back the development of a somewhat pointless robot that had the features of Mischa Auer, who was also starred. The film was almost as mechanical as the robot, but at least it never strayed from the path of genuine insanity, and it is one of the few bona fide B screwballs. It is rarely shown today because television, its only market, has little space for sixty-one-minute movies, and little patience with as much racial humor (mainly provided by Mantan Moreland) as this film provides!

Universal generally had better luck with its programmer screwballs—a decided notch above the Bs, yet hardly full-fledged As—films like William A. Seiter's *Hired Wife* (1940) and its interchangeable twin *Fired Wife* (1943), *Her Primitive Man* (1944), the various Hugh Herbert comedies like *Six Lessons From Madame La Zonga* (1941), the surprise hit *San Diego, I Love*

157

SIX LESSONS FROM MADAME LA ZONGA
(1941) Universal had a large
contingent of character comedians
that they kept busy in slick "B"
comedies, many of them of a
screwball nature. Here are Leon
Erroll (left), Helen Parrish, Charles
Lang, and William Frawley, and in
the other still, Guinn Williams and
Lupe Velez.

You (1945, and discussed individually later), and *The Runaround* (1946). Yet another derivation from the still potent *It Happened One Night*, this Charles Lamont comedy was a frenetically paced, fight-packed cross-country chase with two private eyes (Rod Cameron and Broderick Crawford) trying to outsmart each other in their efforts to return runaway heiress Ella Raines (who seemed far too sensible to fit into such a madcap role) to her parents.

Paramount always made some of the best and most stylish B movies, often in direct contrast to the economy-conscious quality of many of its As. In the thirties, many of the studio's Charlie Ruggles–Mary Boland comedies, or its Edward Everett Horton vehicles, had often approached screwball territory without ever really embracing it. The same might be said for *Buy Me That Town* (1941), directed by Eugene Forde. Long enough at seven reels to get the most out of its Damon Runyonish plot (about racketeers buying a small town, lock, stock, and barrel, to exploit it for taxes and as a haven for fellow gangsters needing a safe hideout, and finally being reformed by wartime patriotism), it could easily have been developed as an A for

BACHELOR DADDY (1941) The Baby Sandy comedies combined sentiment, screwball antics, and Harold Lloyd-like thrill material; in this between-scenes shot, Baby Sandy Henville is flanked by (from left) Donald Woods, Edward Everett Horton, Kathryn Adams, and Franklin Pangborn.

Alan Ladd and expanded by another thirty minutes. But in so doing it would have lost its easygoing charm and would have had less time for such wonderful comic types as Edward Brophy, Warren Hymer, and in a rare departure from more serious roles, Albert Dekker. Lloyd Nolan and Constance Moore were just fine in roles that, on an A budget, would have gone to Alan Ladd and Gail Russell or her equivalent. Among the joys of the B comedies was the opportunity they gave to attractive and talented players like Constance Moore, Peggy Moran, Jane Wyatt, and Louise Allbritton, all of whom deserved to be top-liners rather than second-stringers.

Another Paramount entry, somewhat higher up the budgetary ladder though still only a programmer, was *Murder He Says* (1945), directed by George Marshall. Clearly inspired by the mood and partially by the plot of *Arsenic and Old Lace,* it was about a murderous family of hillbillies (headed by Marjorie Main, Mabel Paige, and Porter Hall) whose lethal hobby causes their victims to glow in the dark. Fred MacMurray was the statistic-collecting insurance man dropped in the midst of their spiderweb, and Helen Walker was the one sane member of the backwoods family, whom he ultimately rescues. Like so many films that were virtually overlooked at the time of their release, it was later rediscovered, possibly overpraised, and now seems to have been forgotten again. Unsubtle perhaps, it's still one of the funnier comedies of murder that the forties gave us. Among the several other macabre and/or screwball comedies inspired by *Arsenic and Old Lace* was Columbia's horror spoof *The Boogie Man Will Get You* (1942, director Lew Landers). Foolish and heavy-handed, but at least fast and fairly different, it cast Boris Karloff (who had scored a big hit onstage in *Arsenic and Old Lace*) as a scientist trying to create a race of supermen, and Peter Lorre as the amiably corrupt local sheriff who joins forces with him, turning a blind eye to all of Karloff's unsuccessful experiments.

159

BUTCH MINDS THE BABY (1942)   Virginia Bruce and Broderick Crawford in a Damon Runyon adaptation.

It was economically sound for Bs to make movies *about* movies, since all they had to do was use the studio as a basic set. They were usually melodramas or action films, murder mysteries, or occasionally westerns about stuntmen and doubles. Paramount's *World Premiere* (1941), though admittedly a waste of all the talent involved, was still one of the best B screwball comedies about the movies. Had it realized quite what potential the movie had, the studio might well have elevated it to A status and given it some real bite. As it was, it was a way of introducing former cameraman Ted Tetzlaff into his new field as a director, and it was also a useful way of using up contractual commitments for "difficult" players like John Barrymore and Frances Farmer. Barrymore went way over the top as the embattled producer, and Farmer hardly tried.

Its plot dealt with Hollywood's attempt to make a vital, important anti-Nazi picture—and enemy agents' attempts to first wreck the picture and then sabotage the premiere. Much of the film took place aboard a train, reminding

THE BOOGIE MAN WILL GET YOU (1942)   Boris Karloff and Peter Lorre in a promising but not too well developed murder spoof, obviously influenced by the stage success *Arsenic and Old Lace* (in which Karloff appeared) but released *before* the film version.

one—not too favorably—of Barrymore's earlier *20th Century*. But its craziness was sustained without letup, it did have genuinely funny moments, and best of all it gave Fritz Feld possibly his best-ever role as the face-slapping Hitlerite spy, who contrives to have reels of a *heimat* movie inserted into the ersatz realism of the studio's concentration-camp film.

If few of Hollywood's Bs approach genuine screwball status, many of them are far more than mere poor relations. Midforties Bs from 20th Century-Fox's Sol Wurtzel unit were mainly a dull, threadbare lot, but one of them—*Arthur Takes Over* (1948)—a typical wartime comedy of marital misunderstandings and complications, had much of the charm and occasional comic frenzy that the same director, Malcolm St. Clair, brought to such silken silent comedies as *Are Parents People?* in 1925. Republic's *Rosie the Riveter* (1944) was George Stevens's 1943 *The More the Merrier* in miniature, with Jane Frazee making a sunny, smiling substitute for Jean Arthur. The same studio's *Steppin' in Society* (1945) with Edward Everett Horton was a pepped-up remake of, of all things, the French *Extenuating Circumstances* with Michel Simon! RKO Radio's frenetic and now almost indistinguishable from one another *Mexican Spitfire* series were basically mechanical bedroom farces tailored to the pantomimic talents and dialogue mimicry of Leon Errol—but all of them had moments of which no major screwball comedy would be ashamed.

The Bs have virtually disappeared from television now, and home video utilization of them is increasingly sparse, but it is to them that we now have to look for the few, unexpected, and often rewarding surprises in their unheralded and infrequent embracing of the screwball tradition.

EIGHT

INDIVIDUAL FILMS OF THE FORTIES

BALL OF FIRE (1941)

ROAD TO SINGAPORE (1940)   Dorothy Lamour, Bing Crosby, and Bob Hope meet in what no one dreamed would be a long-running series.

ROAD TO SINGAPORE

(PARAMOUNT, 1940)

Directed by Victor Schertzinger; screenplay by Don Hartman and Frank Butler, from an original story by Harry Hervey.

LEADING PLAYERS:
Bing Crosby, Bob Hope, Dorothy Lamour, Anthony Quinn, Charles Coburn, Judith Barrett, Jerry Colonna.

Judged by all normal standards, *Road to Singapore* is hardly a screwball comedy nor even a particularly notable film no matter to which genre one is inclined to assign it. Yet its popular and commercial success was so great that this slight and inconsequential movie was of influence in several substantial and variant ways. Like that other big hit *Casablanca*, its success was due largely to casting chemistry, and its production was almost a matter of luck. Ini-

ROAD TO ZANZIBAR (1941)   Funniest and craziest of the series.

tially it was designed as a vehicle for Fred Mac-Murray and Jack Oakie, who turned it down—since its original story was written by Harry Hervey (*Shanghai Express, Passport to Hell*), a specialist in exotic Eastern romantic melodramas, one must assume that somewhere along the line it was a more serious work. (For the record, however, it had no connection with the 1931 William Powell film of the same name.)

Curiously, Bing Crosby, Dorothy Lamour, and Bob Hope all received below-the-title *featured* rather than star billing. The film did much for all of their careers; Crosby had starred in some twenty features prior to this one, but had never become a superstar. After this, he was well on his way. Hope, whose decade-long career to that point had roughly paralleled Crosby's, was fresh from *The Cat and the Canary*. The unexpected success of *Road to Singapore* boosted Paramount's faith in Hope and paved the way for a long string of solo-starring comedy hits, with the periodic *Road* follow-ups as highlights. As for Lamour, Paramount was having trouble finding suitable vehicles for her outside of the jungle/sarong epics that she had made so popular, and to which she would make an occasional return. Comedies like *Road to Singapore* were an ideal solution, since her glamour and songs gave her equal footage with the two leading men, yet made no other demands on her—or the writers.

Plotwise, *Road to Singapore* is even less substantial than such earlier Crosby vehicles as *Waikiki Wedding* (1937). It has virtually *no* story; merely the Capra-like situation of Crosby rebelling against father Charles Coburn, who wants him to assume leadership of his shipping line, and opting for the life of wandering beachcomber, a footloose lifestyle supported by petty con-man activities in partnership with Bob Hope. The film is not only plotless, but also shapeless, without structure, without highlights, without even a real climax, merely a casual solution.

What makes the film work is the unexpected chemistry of the costarring trio, and an escapism so relaxed it almost amounts to torpor. Acceptance—even embracing—of the latter quality was probably partially a matter of timing. With the war in Europe having been under way officially for some six months, and movies (and plays, newspapers, novels) full of strong (but in those pre–Pearl Harbor days still somewhat detached) moralizing, propaganda, and heavy war themes, it was pleasant to find a movie whose hero resolutely turned his back on all responsibility and just wanted to enjoy himself. (The film was especially popular in Britain, where audiences enjoyed its relaxed escapism, but also recognized that its stance wasn't meant to be taken seriously or as a reflection of America's attitude to the war.) Oddly enough, although the harmonious chemistry between the stars was the element that made the film so likable, it was also the element that underwent the greatest change in subsequent *Road* pictures. Crosby exploits Hope to a minimum here, outsmarts him only once or twice. For the most part there is real camaraderie and devotion there. When it seems that Lamour (the most docile and unassuming of heroines, wanting *only* to please) is in love with Hope, Crosby withdraws and goes back to the life he loathes—although it's not such a bad life at that. His fiancée is played by the lovely (and at Paramount much underused) Judith Barrett. In contrast to most wealthy fiancées in films of this type she is neither bitchy, scheming, nor a fortune hunter, but a genuinely "nice" person who eventually realizes that Crosby could never be happy with her and doesn't try to stop him when he heads back for a reunion with Hope and Lamour. Clearly not anticipating the film's success or the sequels it would spawn, *Road to Singapore* concludes with an implied Crosby-Lamour wedding, and a continuation of his happy-go-lucky life with Bob Hope in tow.

With a series in mind, the reconstituted differences were immediately apparent in the next entry, *Road to Zanzibar* (1941), arguably the best of the series, although since it is the one with the most visual and slapstick comedy, it is also the one most dependent on audience reaction. Here, Dorothy Lamour is partnered by Una Merkel and they are con women who are almost a match for Crosby and Hope, whose schemes are by now more grandiose and far more questionable legally. Too, no doubt influenced by the popularity of the new comedy team of Abbott and Costello, the Crosby-Hope comedy relationship seemed to be patterned on theirs, with Crosby (like Abbott) continuously and sometimes viciously exploiting his partner. The warmth from the original film was gone, and the tone of mutual distrust, suspicion, and double-crossing became a leitmotiv of the remaining *Road* films, though softened by the appealing personas of the two stars, which always remained above the brittle, impersonal, vaudevillian level of Abbott and Costello.

The mildly screwball elements of the first film were centered around comic violence (fisticuffs as a running and funny gag, much modified in the second film, and soon to disappear almost entirely) and inside-gag references that demanded audience sophistication. There were few of the latter in the first film though, surprisingly, rather more in the trailer, which comes "out" of the film to have Hope talk about Crosby. This angle would be exploited more and more in later films in the series—direct movie references, insane visual gags, asides to the audience, and in the case of *Road to Utopia*, a running commentary by Robert Benchley. And of course the success of this kind of comedy, which included unbilled guest appearances, recognizable stock scenes from other films, and Crosby doing gag guest spots in the individual starring vehicles of Hope, invariably helped to spread the use of this kind of gagging (originally creative and with genuine surprise value, ultimately rather pointless and ineffectual) in other forties comedies.

Probably the second in the series, *Road to Zanzibar* (with the same director and writers as the first), is the only one that can make any kind of claim to screwball legitimacy. The pairing off of two comedians and two comediennes provides the requisite battle-of-the-sexes footage, and the set-piece gags—among them Bob Hope as a human cannonball in a carni-

ROAD TO MOROCCO (1942)   Slickest and glossiest; thereafter the series remained popular but less inspired.

val, and later fighting a giant ape in a native village—have a near-surreal quality. The supporting cast, too, boasted some "appropriate" names, headed by Eric Blore and Iris Adrian. With or without an audience, and on television or via home video it loses much of its impact, it is probably the funniest of the group.

The third entry, *Road to Morocco* (1942), was the biggest box-office hit of them all and the slickest, most streamlined-looking production. By now, Paramount, assured that the series was coasting on its own momentum, and in need of little help other than title and stars, economized somewhat on production and comedy set pieces. The production slickness helped cover those economies, and on television the skimping hardly shows at all. The desert backgrounds allowed for the logical insertion of a number of harem beauties, and sex appeal plus good songs were the mainstay of the production. The Hope-Crosby clowning contained more inside jokes than before.

After a hiatus the next in the series, *Road to Utopia* (1945) appeared and was worth the wait. A satire on Klondike melodramas, it was the zaniest of the group thus far. Even Paramount's trademark mountain was brought into the action as a gag, the trick effects from the *Speaking of Animals* series of shorts came into play with talking bears and the like in the backup comedy, and Robert Benchley, often seen via an irised-in insert at the top of the frame, commented on the plot and action throughout. It came to its close with a punchline gag of questionable taste (involving presumed sexual dalliance on Crosby's part) that was rather amazing for that still Production Code–dominated period, but certainly raised a hearty laugh as it segued into the end title.

As with so many successful series (Universal's *Frankenstein* films fell into the same trap), its reshuffling of a single basic story idea couldn't survive too long, and the fourth entry was the last good one. *Road to Rio* (1947, and at one hundred minutes the longest of the series), *Road to Bali* (1952, the only one in color, and already having to retread some of the territory of the first in the series), and *The Road to Hong Kong* (1962) all suffered from diminishing returns.

Overall, while none of them qualified 100 percent as an orthodox screwball comedy, they contributed enough to the genre in inspiration and influence to rate this acknowledgment in passing.

MY FAVORITE WIFE

(RKO RADIO, 1940)

Directed by Garson Kanin; a Leo McCarey Production; screenplay by Bella and Samuel Spewack, based on a story by the Spewacks and Leo McCarey.

LEADING PLAYERS:
Cary Grant, Irene Dunne, Randolph Scott, Gail Patrick, Donald MacBride, Ann Shoemaker, Scotty Beckett, Granville Bates.

My Favorite Wife is one of those irritating films that was a huge popular success at the time of its release, but that for reasons not immediately apparent falls far short of expectations (and memories) today. In May of 1940, when it opened at the Radio City Music Hall to rave reviews, it had a great deal going for it. For one thing, its sophisticated escapism was a major plus (especially in Britain) in those tense early days of the war. And as a Cary Grant vehicle it was riding on the momentum of the earlier 1940 release of *His Girl Friday*, and with a reunion of such names as McCarey and Kanin, and Grant and Dunne (Kanin excepted, all from the still well-remembered *The Awful Truth*), it seemed to suggest a full-scale resumption of the screwball cycle, a renaissance merely hinted at in *Too Many Husbands*.

The only notes of mild criticism in the reviews were directed at relative newcomer Garson Kanin, who had hurriedly taken over from Leo McCarey when the latter had been injured. The direction was labeled "uneven"—an odd complaint since that was a perennial flaw of McCarey's direction, except that he was such a popular comedy director that "uneven" was usually reinterpreted as "unpredictable," deemed a positive quality, by most critics. Critics had presumably forgotten Kanin's expertise on *Bachelor Mother*, and the directorial com-

166

MY FAVORITE WIFE (1940)   Cary Grant in one of many harried moments.

plaints were probably concocted to express a measure of sympathy for McCarey in having lost one of his pet projects.

The aborted remake with Marilyn Monroe and Dean Martin (*Something's Got to Give*) and the subsequent *Move Over, Darling* (1963), an efficient and amusing redo with Doris Day and James Garner, only served to upgrade the reputation of the original film, then not generally available for reappraisal.

Why then, *does* it disappoint today? Even admitting that it remains a slick and entertaining film, probably because of the expertise of its ensemble playing, it fails for much the same reasons that *Bringing Up Baby* fails. Considering its popularity, it is perhaps somewhat harsh to refer to *Bringing Up Baby* as a failure. But it was a flop initially, and its current inexplicable success can probably be attributed largely to brainwashing from cult critics, and partly to the enormous popularity of Grant in comedy, a condition that did not yet exist in 1938.

Basically *My Favorite Wife* has no surprises and takes no chances. For one thing, Gail Patrick is established in her very first scene (as wife number two) as selfish and thoughtless. At least in the parallel situation in *Too Many Husbands,* both husbands were equally likable. Audiences either had to fall back on their personal preferences for the stars' personas, or weigh one against the other in the narrative, to decide which one to root for and enjoy the suspense of not knowing for sure until the final reel. In *My Favorite Wife* there is no question that Gail Patrick is unworthy and will be jettisoned as soon as feasible, hence no audience involvement or suspense. Second, the film is awkwardly scripted and paced. It puts off confrontation between the two wives as long as possible. Randolph Scott, as the potential other man (he'd spent seven years on the desert isle with the shipwrecked Irene Dunne) doesn't arrive until the halfway point, and the jealousy and suspicion that he creates in Grant's mind is sufficiently funny that it could well have been utilized earlier. A particularly amusing though underplayed highlight is when Grant strives mightily to prevent Scott from being left alone with Dunne for a brief period and asks why Scott is chuckling. "I was just thinking," replies Scott, "after seven years, what's another half hour?" Some good comedy is also derived from Dunne's trying to allay Grant's fears about those seven years on a desert isle, and attempting to palm off diminutive, henpecked-husband stereotype Chester Clute as her desert-island companion! When, later, Grant tries to look him up at a country club, he meets the *real* companion—Randolph Scott, attired in brief bathing trunks, surrounded by adoring women, and performing impressive gymnastic and diving feats to the musical ac-

companiment of "The Skater's Waltz." Echoes of this sequence are used later to torment Grant further when, alone in his office, he is haunted by tiny inserts of the Scott prowess, speeded up and accompanied by equally speeded-up renditions of "The Skater's Waltz." This Grant-Scott dominated portion of the film is by far the best, and it is too brief.

For a protracted climax, the film basically repeats the last reel or so of *The Awful Truth*: husband and original wife spending the night at an out-of-the-way lodge, wife Dunne insisting on all the proprieties, husband Grant being forced to sleep on a couch and finding all sorts of excuses to invade her bedroom, hoping he'll be invited to stay . . . as of course he finally is. The earlier portions of the film are

MY FAVORITE WIFE One of the film's funniest and calmest comedy scenes: new wife Gail Patrick, husband Cary Grant, returned-from-the-dead wife Irene Dunne, and hopeful husband-to-be Randolph Scott are interrogated by a blasé and impatient judge Granville Bates.

at least so superficially sparkling that the ending seems especially lame and devoid of inspiration. And unfortunately the genuinely amusing third quarter, so dominated by Grant and Scott, takes on a potentially different subtext today with the revelations of Grant's very close offscreen friendship with Scott. Such reinterpretations of basically innocent material have, sadly, become far more common as the scandal magazines and books have toppled so many formerly untouchable stars from their thrones.

Gail Patrick gets some fun out of the situation of the newly married second wife, who cannot understand why on their wedding night her husband finds so many excuses to be temporarily and then permanently absent. But as written, it's a one-dimensional role, giving Patrick few of the opportunities that she enjoyed (and played to the hilt) as the other woman in *My Man Godfrey*.

Despite the experienced work of the four troupers in the leads, some of the most amusing moments come from two of the supporting players. The use of Granville Bates in the opening scenes is a stroke of writing and casting genius. Playing an irritable, bored, slightly deaf but withal not unjust judge, he has a courtroom scene that not only provides the audience with all the information it needs and helps to establish the unsympathetic nature of Gail Patrick in a deft scene or two, but also is extremely funny . . . quieter in its humor than the showcase courtroom scene written by Preston Sturges for *Remember the Night*, yet as much of a classic in its own way. Bates also figures later in the film in a similar scene working toward a solution of the triangular puzzle.

More familiar in his comedy but no less effective is Donald MacBride as the exasperated and ultimately admiring reception-desk clerk who welcomes Grant back to the Yosemite inn, to the same room that he'd booked for his first honeymoon years earlier . . . and then moments later finds Grant booking a second wife into a second room. Dunne's arrival at the honeymoon inn in the nick of time also allows for a wonderful moment when Grant catches a glimpse of her standing in the lobby just as the elevator door closes to whisk him up to the honeymoon suite. The combinations of movements—Grant, his face a picture of bemusement and disbelief, straining his neck to make the most of the diminishing space as the elevator closes and moves upward—remind one of the best sight gags in some of McCarey's silent Charley Chase comedies.

His Girl Friday, which received relatively lukewarm reviews at the time by critics, who felt that the classic stature of *The Front Page* had been diminished, seems to get better and in many ways even more topical in its satire with the passing years. Much better received but really little more than fluffy froufrou, *My Favorite Wife* loses a little each time one sees it . . . but thanks to the warmth and camaraderie of Grant and Dunne—one of the most felicitous (if least heralded) of all screen teams—and that wonderful support work from Donald MacBride and Granville Bates, it will always have much to delight the eye and ear.

TURNABOUT
(HAL ROACH–UNITED ARTISTS, 1940)

Produced and directed by Hal Roach; screenplay by Mickell Novak, Berne Giler, John McClain, and Rian James, from the novel by Thorne Smith.

LEADING PLAYERS:
Carole Landis, John Hubbard, Adolphe Menjou, Mary Astor, Verree Teasdale, William Gargan, Donald Meek, Berton Churchill, Franklin Pangborn.

ROAD SHOW
(HAL ROACH–UNITED ARTISTS, 1941)

Produced and directed by Hal Roach; associate director, Gordon Douglas; screenplay by Arnold Belgard, Harry Langdon, and Mickell Novak, from the novel by Eric Hatch.

LEADING PLAYERS:
Carole Landis, John Hubbard, Adolphe Menjou, Charles Butterworth, Patsy Kelly, George E. Stone, Florence Bates, Polly Ann Young, Edward Norris, Willie Best.

TURNABOUT (1940)   A posed publicity still that nevertheless captures the essence of the sex-change plot of the movie. John Hubbard, left, and Carole Landis.

TURNABOUT Carole
Landis and John
Hubbard.

These two films with the same three leads, both produced in 1940 although the second was released in early 1941, represent a commendable if somewhat misfire effort by Hal Roach to return to the screwball comedy field he had mined rather more successfully in the thirties with *Topper, There Goes My Heart, Merrily We Live,* and *Topper Takes a Trip.*

Though not enthusiastically received by the press, both films were popular with audiences, and it is easy to see why. *Turnabout,* based on a risqué Thorne Smith novel (he had written the *Topper* stories, too), was slightly more suggestive than the Production Code usually allowed at that time. Moreover, it was a slick, good-looking production, its bright art deco sets of luxury homes and big business offices the work of art director Nicolai Remisoff. One wonders why Roach hadn't given the assignment to Charles D. Hall, a comedic and art deco specialist who had worked on Chaplin's *Modern Times* and would work on *Road Show,* although it gave him few opportunities. The explanation may be that Remisoff was a newcomer of note whose first American assignment had been on Roach's 1939 *Of Mice and Men,* a brilliant job of

art direction. Roach may have been either rewarding him or testing his versatility on a totally different kind of film.

Both *Turnabout* and *Road Show* benefited from audience needs for escapism and laughter in the tense prewar period in the United States, and of course from those same but even greater needs in the British market, where war was already a reality. *Road Show* in particular was a big hit in Britain, where it was double-billed on the huge Gaumont-British circuit with a topical Hitchcockian comedy-thriller *Cottage to Let.* Neither was a major film, neither had a single front-rank star, but both were peppered with some of the best second-echelon players (Alastair Sim, John Mills, and Leslie Banks were in the British film), and together they made up one of the most enjoyable double bills of the early war years, an enormous morale-boosting program since the British movie, a spy story, contained a modicum of propaganda, too.

Turnabout, the first of Hal Roach's forties screwball duo, dealt with an attractive but bored young couple (Landis and Hubbard, an admirable if too often wasted farceur) who,

171

ROAD SHOW (1941)   Adolphe Menjou provides another of his eccentric near-Barrymore comedy performances as a (not entirely crazy) Colonel hiding away with a small circus operated by Carole Landis, right.

due to having uttered a casual wish in the presence of an idol possessed of mystic powers, find their personalities reversed. The husband thus finds himself in the body of his wife and is forced to stay home, taking care of wifely chores, sitting in on bridge games, etc., while she goes to business in her husband's body, raising not a few eyebrows at her sudden feminine traits—such as a full-blooded scream when a crony accidentally taps his/her derrière. Censorship of the period didn't allow for a full exploration of the comic potentials of the situation, and the humor for the most part was broad and tasteful, yet certainly in the screwball manner.

Actually the biggest laughs came from Adolphe Menjou as a wife-hating business executive, who at one point has a secretary call his home, ask his wife what they're having for dinner, and then tell her that it'll be no good! Menjou was a delight, and in supporting roles Verree Teasdale (the real-life Mrs. M.) and Mary Astor beautifully if stereotypically upheld the causes of working and nonworking women. Not a long film (at eighty minutes) it still takes half of that running time to get to its sex-change gag. Since its plot was novel and well-publicized, the initial reels seem padded, and after that, it all moves too quickly to its fade-out, which leaves the husband in a state of pregnancy!

ROAD SHOW   In support, Charles Butterworth repeats his famous shy-millionaire characterization—much interested in girls but not too sure of what to do about it. Margaret Roach (Hal's daughter) is the attractive vamp.

Road Show was a less opulent production and seemed determined to succeed as a screwball comedy in areas where *Turnabout* might have failed. It starts off promisingly with a typical screwball comedy launch, but with the novelty of the genders reversed.

At a big society wedding, it is millionaire Hubbard, a big-business whiz and by no means as scatterbrained as most of his heiress predecessors, who flees marriage. In a frenzy of immediate activity, the film never bothers to explain why the wealthy and engagingly named Drogo Gaines is wearing an aggressively nonmatching coat and trousers. Immediately he feigns insanity (the first of several obligatory masquerades in the film) and is carried, swooning, into an anteroom. There, his avaricious in-laws-to-be — Florence Bates, bride Polly Ann Young, and her brother, Edward Norris — thinking him unconscious, bemoan their fate at the delayed wedding and all of the Gaines millions that might slip through their hands. Drogo of course is only faking; he comes out of his swoon to reveal that he has heard everything. Curiously it doesn't seem to surprise or bother him, merely confirming his long-held belief that he was not meant for marriage. Fiancée Polly Ann Young tries to convince him that she does truly love him, then threatens to have him confined in an insane asylum if he doesn't go through with the marriage. In the physical fracas that follows — she manhandles *him,* screaming for help because *she* is being attacked — Drogo is knocked unconscious and awakens, trouserless, in an asylum, the exterior of which bears the comforting but ambiguous inscription "For the Rest of Your Life."

This is probably the most amusing section of the film, and possibly the sequence that most closely adheres to the original story by Eric Hatch, who had also written *My Man Godfrey.* Drogo encounters the usual collection of rather amiable and harmless lunatics — Johnny Arthur, Maurice Cass — and is treated condescendingly by asylum director Paul Stanton, tight-lipped and smug as always. On the grounds, Drogo also runs into crackpot inventor Colonel Carraway (Adolphe Menjou), and the two hatch a plot to escape.

The aura of enjoyable insanity is well sustained during the escape, accomplished on a fragile raft, and to the accompaniment of much noise and unnecessary complications created by the colonel to make the getaway exciting and worthwhile. But he has miscalculated: the river that runs through the asylum grounds heads straight for a large waterfall, and they escape disaster only by heaving their anchor to the shore — and catching the rear of a passing circus truck, part of a small-scale carnival operated by Penguin Moore (Carole Landis).

The establishing material is thus out of the way quickly and efficiently with the three main characters and the story line proper (if one can call it that) brought together. Unfortunately, from here on the influence of Eric Hatch's story diminishes and the number of Hal Roach characters and gags increases.

Drogo and the colonel join the carnival, and sensing that in Penguin he may have found a girl he could truly love and who knows nothing of his millions, Drogo keeps his identity a secret, though helping out with small amounts of money when the show runs into process servers. This second masquerade as a "nobody" is transformed into that of a world-famous lion tamer, seemingly safe since the show has no lions — until Penguin buys some for him, hoping to restore his self-esteem and also put her show back on its feet. Nobody expects too much logic from a screwball comedy, but unfortunately *Road Show* takes the old scattershot vaudevillian approach of providing too much material on the theory that some of it is bound to fall on fertile ground. The constant run-ins with and flights from the law are repetitious. Patsy Kelly as a fake Indian princess peddling patent medicine attracts the admiring attention of a genuine Indian (George E. Stone), who attaches himself to the show and pursues her as a literal running gag. (Nothing comes of it other than a segue into an end title of questionable taste.)

Other well-known comedy faces are spotted merely for punctuation. Jack Norton performs his usual dapper-drunk act. Black comedian Willie Best prompts the usual "scared darkie" antics with an escaped lion, and at least one racially stereotyped gag typical of the period. When the carnival camps on ground familiar to Menjou, he tells the collective colored contingent, "The watermelons are *that* way!" and as they all rush off eagerly, he stops Best and in a tone suggesting that this is a special favor, adds, "And the chickens are *that* way!" The stolen-chicken gag is then reworked for rather more than it is worth.

Standing out among the byplay, possibly as a relic of the original Hatch story, is Charles Butterworth as Menjou's nephew, another eccentric millionaire who travels everywhere in a fire truck and burns down a barn every Saturday night so that his weekend guests can rush to put it out. Butterworth does extract the maximum from his small role and is especially amusing in his scenes of infatuation with a taffy-pulling machine, in which of course he becomes messily entrapped.

There's a vigorous if rather pointless "Hey, rube!" all-in fight at the carnival, and the colonel sees to it that the battered remnants of the show are stored in the barn that is due to be burned down that weekend. When the burning takes place, the fire engines speed off in a mad chase, but are actually diverted to a brand-new, deluxe carnival that Drogo has bought for Penguin—and that they plan to run jointly as husband and wife. This climactic dash is turned into a slapstick chase (and slapstick was never Roach's forte) for no apparent reason other than to have some kind of a climax. All of the gags (principally involving acrobatics atop a raised fire-truck ladder, and cars just missing each other on the highway) had been done better by Sennett in a midtwenties two-reeler *Galloping Bungalows* and would be done much better later in 1941 as virtually the definitive such chase, as the climax to the W. C. Fields feature *Never Give a Sucker an Even Break.*

Perhaps a major problem with both *Turnabout* and *Road Show* was that Hal Roach was essentially a producer, and a good one, and never a very inspired director. In fact, he was not even interested in directing, but returned to it periodically, merely to keep abreast of changes in production techniques. It's a pity that he chose to direct these two particular comedies himself. His motivation for doing so was probably based on the apparent expansion of his production schedule for United Artists, and the lack of sufficient good directors under contract to him. Actually that expansion was short-lived, and Roach soon reverted to smaller and cheaper pictures, little more than featurettes, which warranted neither *his* time or the uneconomical hiring of directors from outside his unit. A third 1941 comedy, *Topper Returns,* was more comedy-thriller than screwball, and under the more expert hands of director Roy Del Ruth was the best if the most traditional of the three.

Curiously, since it was not stressed, the most pleasing aspect of *Road Show* was the songs by Hoagy Carmichael. If anything, they slowed the pace and didn't really belong in a screwball comedy, but they weren't intrusive either and added charm and originality to what was basically pretty familiar stuff. One of them, performed by the Charioteers, a Negro group who also appeared in *Hellzapoppin,* was sung as they pounded pegs and raised tents and was introduced by an extremely fast-cut montage; the whole episode seems to have inspired a virtually identical sequence and similar song in Disney's later *Dumbo.*

It's a pity that one can't be more enthusiastic about *Turnabout* and *Road Show* since they did try hard—perhaps too hard—to make a major contribution to the screwball renaissance of the period. But if they weren't as good as they could have been, they were also better than most reviews indicated and were solid audience-pleasers.

THE GREAT PROFILE
(20TH CENTURY-FOX, 1940)

Directed by Walter Lang; screenplay by Milton Sperling and Hilary Lynn.

LEADING PLAYERS:
John Barrymore, Anne Baxter, Mary Beth Hughes, John Payne, Lionel Atwill, Gregory Ratoff, Charles Lane, Marc Lawrence.

John Barrymore admirers are usually saddened by this, his first capitulation to self-

174

THE GREAT PROFILE (1940) Actor John Barrymore throttles actress wife Mary Beth Hughes.

The plot revolves around that old reliable, the "artistic" play written by an idealistic small-town girl, played by Anne Baxter, which is so awful that it can only succeed when played for laughs. Barrymore latches onto it as a vehicle for himself and his estranged wife, Mary Beth Hughes. Their particular battle of the sexes is quite as violent (though seldom as funny or skillfully written) as the Barrymore-Lombard pairing in *20th Century* a mere six years earlier. Although it does run out of steam before the end, it has so much gusto, ribaldry, slick one-liners, and uninhibited Barrymore byplay and pantomime that one can't help but regard it as a not unworthy if lesser cog in Barrymore's chronological wheel. Backed by Fox's usual solid production values and a particularly strong supporting cast, even the criticism of its running out of steam before the end seems a little unfair. After all, it runs for only some seventy-odd minutes, and if the loss of

mockery, and they tend, too, to resent its tactless exploitation of Barrymore's contemporary (alcoholic, marital, and other) problems. But it is so much fun and such an enjoyable if unsubtle Barrymore farce that it is hard to bear the film any ill will, especially so long after the fact. (The later *Playmates* is something else again and deserved all the scorn that was piled upon it and eventual oblivion.)

If nothing else, *The Great Profile* is an invaluable if quite unofficial record of what went on, daily, during Barrymore's run in *My Dear Children* at New York's Belasco Theatre the previous year, when every performance was different. Audiences came not to see the play, but to see what Barrymore did to it in terms of ad-libbed dialogue, jovial drunken slapstick, and sundry mayhem.

Initially *The Great Profile* was intended as a quiet, subtler vehicle for Adolphe Menjou, but he was tactfully paid off and the script revamped to match Barrymore's much-publicized stage antics.

THE GREAT PROFILE The great actor Evans Garrick (John Barrymore) reenacts a "lost weekend" for manservant Willie Fung and agent Gregory Ratoff.

175

momentum toward the end is a necessary pause to tie up loose story threads, then by the last scene—the curtain rising on Barrymore performing in tights with acrobats and jugglers—the energy has been restored. Whether by accident or design, Gregory Ratoff—an excellent foil for Barrymore—plays the same character that he did in *Broadway Thru a Keyhole* seven years earlier.

When released in New York, *The Great Profile* suffered the undeserved indignity of playing the lower half of a double bill at the Palace. True, it's rough-and-ready, often rather cruel to Barrymore's actress-wife Elaine Barrie through her screen counterpart, Mary Beth Hughes, and unsubtler by far than it needs to be. It cries out for Preston Sturges, and with his unique and much surer blending of slapstick and satire it could have been a screwball classic. But on its own boisterous level it's an enjoyably insane frolic that survives much better than might have been expected, especially as one gets further away from the pain and sadness of Barrymore's personal and professional decline.

ELSA MAXWELL'S PUBLIC DEB NO. 1

(20th CENTURY-FOX, 1940)

Directed by Gergory Ratoff; screenplay by Karl Tunberg and Darrell Ware, from an original story by Tunberg and Don Ettlinger.

LEADING PLAYERS:
Brenda Joyce, George Murphy, Ralph Bellamy, Elsa Maxwell, Charlie Ruggles, Mischa Auer, Maxie Rosenbloom, Berton Churchill, Franklin Pangborn, Ivan Lebedeff.

Although a bona fide screwball comedy, *Elsa Maxwell's Public Deb No. 1* is neither particularly funny nor a very important movie; yet it deserves this space if only so that it can be a spokesfilm for all the movies, particularly of 1940–42, that can be justified as screwball yet really did nothing new or distinctive to the genre. Most of the proliferating semiscrewballs

of the early forties were either coasting on the reputation of a star (Irene Dunne), possibly a costarring team (Henry Fonda and Barbara Stanwyck, whose *You Belong to Me* of late 1941 hoped to suggest that it was a continuation of their inspired teaming in *The Mad Miss Manton* and *The Lady Eve*), or the known association with the genre of a given director (Mitchell Leisen for example).

There was nothing unethical about this; it was merely good movie showmanship, and in an era when serious film study of genres or directors was virtually unknown, there was no intent to lure in "serious" filmgoers by misleading advertising. The confusion arises only today, when one can recognize screwball elements in early forties comedies as disparate as Lubitsch's *That Uncertain Feeling*, Hitchcock's *Mr. and Mrs. Smith*, LaCava's *Unfinished Business* and *Lady in a Jam* (both sad disappointments from the director of *My Man Godfrey*), Keighley's *The Bride Came C.O.D.*, Cukor's *Two-Faced Woman* and *The Philadelphia Story*, and the endless and interchangeable comedy vehicles for Joan Crawford, Melvyn Douglas, William Powell, and Myrna Loy turned out on a virtual assembly-line basis by MGM and Columbia, some with light romance dominating, some veering to farce. Several of the films now loosely roped into the screwball corral, such as Rene Clair's *I Married a Witch* and Alexander Hall's *Here Comes Mr. Jordan*, are basically whimsies and fantasies, more fruitfully studied as part of that curious war and postwar subgenre about life, death, combinations thereof, and life after death, a group of films that would also encompass Powell and Pressburger's often comedic (but definitely not screwball) *A Matter of Life and Death* (aka *Stairway to Heaven*), the curiously concurrent French *Les Jeux Sont Faits*, and Victor Fleming's *A Guy Named Joe*.

It is perhaps only the cinema-studies mentality that approaches film history today in terms of auteurship and groupings that could be responsible for hailing 1940–42 as representing a kind of peak period in the renaissance of screwball comedy. Yet there is a way of sorting things out. It's not official, it's not exclusive, and it's certainly not infallible. But basically (and without recourse to reviews and other memory-jogging aids), if one can remember the plots, in essence if not in detail, then you probably have a true screwball comedy. It's not difficult to recall both plots and highlights of films like *The Lady Eve, The Major and the Minor,* or *Ball of Fire* (just as one can never forget the basic elements of such earlier classics as *Nothing Sacred* or *My Man Godfrey*), but try to remember the plot lines of *They All Kissed the Bride, Third Finger, Left Hand,* or *Love Crazy.* It doesn't diminish them as films to be hazy about their plots; it merely puts them in their proper place as first and foremost star vehicles in which the narrative was reduced to a far lower priority than it would have enjoyed in the screwball genre.

This rather lengthy preamble is by way of introducing *Elsa Maxwell's Public Deb No. 1* as a film that, while a genuine if not very notable screwball, can represent all the tangential would-be screwball comedies that surrounded

PUBLIC DEB #1 (1940)   In a street rally, Communist agitator Grisha (Mischa Auer) gets belted by an American legionnaire.

177

it on all sides, without being dealt with individually in these pages.

A perfect example of how minor movies can record, reflect, and capture the essence of their time, this film—an enjoyable enough wacky comedy—achieves some historical importance as a time capsule of Hollywood's self-imposed anti-Communist crusade.

Its plot is simple and traditional, if not very believable. Brenda Joyce is the madcap heiress whose family (headed by Charlie Ruggles) has made a fortune from soup. Unfortunately her espousing of Communist causes, in which she welcomes being arrested and sent to jail, is generating bad publicity that is hurting soup sales. The family wants to marry her off to likable, all-American Ralph Bellamy, and when she has a run-in with waiter George Murphy and causes him to be fired, he is given the job of (secretly) weaning her away from the Reds. During the taming-of-the-shrew narrative she inevitably falls in love with him, though not until after he has kidnapped her to prevent her marriage to Bellamy. Ultimately the Com-

PUBLIC DEB #1   Elsa Maxwell, as Benjamin Franklin, dances with Uncle Sam (Charlie Ruggles) at a fancy dress party.

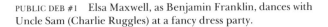

PUBLIC DEB #1   Elsa Maxwell, as Benjamin Franklin, dances with Uncle Sam (Charlie Ruggles) at a fancy dress party.

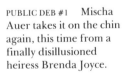

PUBLIC DEB #1   Mischa Auer takes it on the chin again, this time from a finally disillusioned heiress Brenda Joyce.

munist hypocrisy in Finland causes all her ideals to be crushed, and she rushes into the arms of Murphy, and a new embracing of the advantage of capitalism!

The whole ebb and flow of Hollywood's attitude toward Russia and Communism (which it never understood, other than being sure that it disapproved of it!) is a fascinating one. Although there were one or two earlier forays into the field, it really started with the use of the Russian Revolution as the background to an extraordinarily prolific group of melo-

179

dramas and romances during the years 1927–33, in which heads of state and other key Russian figures were used with impunity as puppets of fiction writers. These films segued into the hysterically anti-Communist blasts of the midthirties, such as the previously discussed *Red Salute*, curious for their implied approval of FBI strategies that are now regarded as very dirty pool, and for their aggressively nonintellectual stance. There was a tentative thawing-out with 1939's *Ninotchka* (significantly, written, directed, and largely played by Europeans) and the subsequent *Comrade X*, but almost immediately thereafter a switch to anti-Red-by-ridicule propagandist methods.

He Stayed For Breakfast (1940, directed by Alexander Hall), though based on a French play, seemed merely an opportunistic follow-up to *Ninotchka*, though as often happens in screwball variants, with the sexes reversed. This time it is Melvyn Douglas who is the dedicated Communist, and Loretta Young the glamorous capitalist in whose apartment he hides while on the run for shooting a banker. Just as Douglas seduced Garbo to the ways of the West in the earlier (and much superior) film, so here Young has the same effect on Douglas. This and *Elsa Maxwell's Pubic Deb No. 1* were the most blatant of the let's-ridicule-the-Reds subgenre. With America's involvement in the war at the end of 1941 came another about-face: fervently pro-Russian films, *Days of Glory, Song of Russia, Mission to Moscow,* and *The North Star,* that were as naive in their espousal of the Communist cause as the earlier films had been vicious in their repudiation of it. Then of course in the postwar period came yet another reversal to a long-standing but now happily terminated series of unrestrainedly "anti" films: *I Married a Communist, The Red Menace, Big Jim McLain.*

Public Deb No. 1 is from that curious and uneasy period at the beginning of the war when America was still neutral. Hollywood recognized that it wasn't supposed to take a political stand and was still committed to purveying propaganda-free entertainment, though now almost entirely for the home and British market. Yet with world affairs as they were, it was felt that films had to say something of significance. Most attempts to weld entertainment to "statements" were not too successful; there were too few talents around to match Preston Sturges's, so there tended to be more films like *Public Deb No. 1* than *Sullivan's Travels.* And since Hollywood wasn't supposed to be actively anti-Nazi, the Communists were fair game, and fashionable besides. (Plus, offending the Russians didn't pose much of a threat to Hollywood's income since it collected but little from the USSR, which often chose not to recognize the legality of copyrights.) The ploy at this particular time was to expose Communism as a sham and a racket, and to show that if people of integrity were lured into it, then it would be only a matter of time before they realized they had been duped.

There was never any allowing for the possibility that Communist ranks *might* include philosophers and/or statesmen of genuine integrity, not even "misguided" ones. Brenda Joyce here is an even more scatterbrained reincarnation of Barbara Stanwyck's relatively serious Red disciple in *Red Salute.* The film is of course quite inconsistent: at the beginning, when we are supposed to accept the heroine's idealism with sympathy, the oafish American Legionnaires are redneck caricatures, yet presumably their actions and attitudes are justified by later events in the movie.

It was not, needless to say, a marked box-office hit, although doubtless audiences were flattered into thinking that they were getting a little political "depth" along with their comedy. In England, where Communism was briefly fashionable, never particularly popular but never a subject for ridicule either, the film got a fairly wide initial exhibition (since comedies were especially popular in a country already at war) but disappeared quickly. The British had never really understood what debutantes were, understood party-giver extraordinaire Elsa Maxwell's apparently pivotal role in American society even less, and at that particular time had no real desire or need to find out. (That Elsa Maxwell's name was a part of the main title bemused the British even more.)

Of course, one cannot—and should not—analyze a film like this too carefully on purely

180

political grounds. But therein, too, lies its danger, since its political irresponsibility could sway and inflame judgments of those who knew even less about the issues at hand than the makers of the film.

However, despite the occasional and sometimes embarrassing pauses for speeches on Americanism, it's an amusing comedy in the Capra tradition if not up to Capra standards. (Gregory Ratoff was hardly a sophisticated comedy director, yet his batting average was surprisingly high.) The cast is full of familiar character people, some of the dialogue has real snap and punch, and there are a number of wacky highlights—including Elsa Maxwell's appearance at a masquerade party as Benjamin Franklin!

Restraint is never much in evidence, except perhaps for the climactic gag where (presumably) the Production Code put its foot down and left a basically offensive and cheap gag largely to the imagination, although the groundwork is certainly set up. A book on Communist doctrine—frequently referred to in the film—is finally thrown out the window and winds up in the gutter, next to a tree. A passing dog inspects it curiously, obviously

with a certain act in mind, but fortunately the gag is muted at that point.

With a subtler director and some more imposing star names (and Brenda Joyce never quite fulfilled the promise she showed in *The Rains Came*), this could well have been a much better comedy, one that might have avoided its now almost total obscurity. But then—possibly—it might also have been a far less accurate barometer of its time, and that, in the long run, may be its major contribution.

HELLZAPOPPIN

(UNIVERSAL, 1941)

Directed by H. C. Potter; screenplay by Nat Perrin and Warren Wilson.

LEADING PLAYERS:
Olsen and Johnson, Robert Paige, Jane Frazee, Martha Raye, Hugh Herbert, Mischa Auer, Shemp Howard, Clarence Kolb.

Hellzapoppin, inspired by rather than based on the aggressively insane Broadway smash with and by Ole Olsen and Chic Johnson, must be

HELLZAPOPPIN (1941)   Ole Olsen and Chic Johnson: creators, stars, and their own best audience.

unique in the annals of screwball comedy as being virtually unclassifiable except as certifiably crazy. Its absurd story is presented as an unfolding description of a script that Olsen and Johnson hope to sell to Hollywood. Unlike most genuine screwball comedies, it has nothing of significance to protest against—unless it be the hidebound traditions and clichés of Hollywood moviemaking. These it proceeds to demolish and ridicule, yet at the same time it uses them almost as extensively as a "normal" Hollywood film. The battle of the sexes is notably absent, though mainly because the lead romantic couple (Robert Paige and Jane Frazee)—and the involved hangers-on—are used to lambast those boy-meets-loses-gets-girl clichés, and the hero is so insufferably sacrificial that he backs away from all confrontations, let alone battles.

The film is virtually shapeless, and to its credit, while it uses most of the putting-on-a-show and social-status differences so common to Hollywood musical comedy, it manages to

HELLZAPOPPIN   Production of the movie within a movie is held up; director Richard Lane (right) listens as, under Olsen's watchful eye, Johnson helps sort a box of strawberries by phone.

HELLZAPOPPIN   An obvious and predictable gag but it works: "May I take your picture?" asks the cameraman, and when Olsen and Johnson assent, he removes a painting from the wall. Richard Lane looks on.

HELLZAPOPPIN   An early appearance of one of the film's running gags: Frank Darien is trying to deliver a tree. It, and its tub, increase in size during the film; in the last reel delivery is still being attempted via a truck. Richard Lane (left) continues to look on.

CRAZY HOUSE (1943)   Olsen and Johnson's sequel had an inspired opening reel, but thereafter became essentially a musical. This time Shemp Howard (left) is the onlooker.

interrupt them constantly. No romantic exchange is allowed to proceed without surreal gag interpolations, and one really charming musical number is played out as Paige and Frazee are putting up decorations and paint illustrations of their song directly on the screen. A glass slide is repeatedly thrust in front of them informing Stinky Miller that he has been in the audience too long and has to go home. Annoyed at the continued intrusion into their song, the lovebirds finally address the audience directly—and Stinky obligingly if reluctantly rises from his seat and walks in front of the screen to the exit. It is the continued disregard of the screen as a presence and barrier that makes *Hellzapoppin* unique.

There is continual exchange between characters on-screen and the audience, though on at least one occasion this is marred by an attempt to explain it. In one of the funniest sequences in the film, the projectionist (Shemp Howard) gets involved in a fight with his piqued girlfriend (Jody Gilbert, a mountain of flesh at least twice his size). In the ensuing melee, the reels are mixed up, an Indian attack from a western appears out of nowhere, the film is projected out of frame (causing Olsen and Johnson to bump their heads on the top of the screen as adjustments are made) and even upside down (though with normal sound, a mechanical impossibility). Director H. C. Potter—a good comedy director, but hardly an inspired one—rather surprisingly wanted to shoot this sequence only from the audience's viewpoint and without cutbacks to the projection booth. From the point of view of innovative comedy he was undoubtedly right, and a brilliant sequence was minimized, assuming it could have been carried off.

But Universal was right, too; audiences then knew little of the intricacies of film projection, probably not even what a projection booth looked like. The gag had to be understood to be really funny, and without the cutbacks the bulk of the audience probably would not have known what was going on. The Howard footage was funny in itself: he complained about the impossibility of the actors talking back to him, and the gag continued to be milked even after it was over, with an Indian from the stock footage turning up to take umbrage at Olsen and Johnson's scornful reference to Hollywood Indians and taking a potshot at them.

Olsen and Johnson were not particularly funny; they had gotten nowhere as movie comedians via several aborted tries in the thirties at Warners and Republic. They seemed even less funny (or appealing) in the early forties when the new team of Abbott and Costello, also working for Universal, were taking box-offices by storm. Subsequently there was an attempt to tame Olsen and Johnson's antics, to make their use of musical numbers more conventional, and to fit them into a pseudo-Abbott-and-Costello slot. This was a major mistake since they weren't supposed to be funny or likable; they were merely the catalyst by which funny things happened. The only problem with *Hellzapoppin* was that most of the funny things were mechanical ones: tampering with the physical qualities of film, or with the traditions of filmmaking. Once those surprises had been revealed, there wasn't an awful lot left but many familiar faces and a great deal of energy. Thus *Hellzapoppin* doesn't reward too many repeat viewings. Admittedly, it wasn't intended to. But with a major comedian at the helm—Buster Keaton for example—it would have had some heart as well, and then *Hellzapoppin* could be reseen as often and as profitably as Keaton's silent *Sherlock Jr.,* likewise a comedy built around the mechanics of filmmaking.

However, when *Hellzapoppin* was good it was very good, and some of its gags were so up-to-the-minute that they were only appreciated years later. In one of the funniest scenes, Olsen and Johnson traipse through a series of studio sets as they converse, emerging properly garbed as they walk across each soundstage—itself a derivation of Keaton gags. As they walk across a Far North set, clothed in voluminous Eskimo sealskins, they notice a sled with the painted word *Rosebud.* "I thought they burned that thing," one of them remarks casually, a throwaway gag lost on most of the audience which still hadn't seen *Citizen Kane*. (Welles's film had been released several months earlier in 1941, but it took time to build an audience, and that audience was not necessarily the same one that flocked to *Hellzapoppin*.

Hellzapoppin apparently starts out in hell, but after a bizarre episode involving music, sight gags, and chorus girls being roasted on spits, it all turns out to be a sequence for Olsen and Johnson's new film. Richard Lane, as their director, throws up his hands in disgust and claims that it's impossible; Olsen and Johnson then explain their story to him via stills, which eventually segue into a live-action enactment of the film to be. Apart from a thin connecting story line, it is all a farrago that permits comedians like Hugh Herbert and Mischa Auer to kid their own specialties, allows the Frankenstein monster to turn up casually, and packs in a never-ending array of running gags old and new—such as Frank Darien trying to deliver a small potted plant early in the film, which (along with its box-container) grows each time it reappears during the film and winds up a huge tree in the last reel, the delivery still being attempted, via truck.

For plot reasons, the final big show has to be sabotaged, which allows for an even more accelerated pace in the gagging, the introduction of a talking bear, invisibility, and sundry other gags, many involving interchange between audience and film. Some of the gags fall flat, but as in old-time vaudeville, most of them work at least nominally through their sheer energy and the confidence that their perpetrators have in their material. When the tale is told and the film seems set for production, cameraman George Chandler commits suicide, and assistant director Elisha Cook, Jr., is shot full of holes by his superior. "I always wear a bulletproof vest on the set," he explains, drinking a glass of water, which then pours out of the dozen or so bullet holes in his body as the film segues into its end title.

Despite the nonstop activity, elaborate comic set pieces, and frequent pauses for song and dance (one jazz number by the Harlem Congaroos is especially lively, splendidly edited, and the only musical sequence in the film allowed to play through without comic intervention), *Hellzapoppin* runs only for a tight eight reels and has no slack moments apart from the old, overly familiar backchat gags that don't always work. Although nothing in it was actually new, the concentration of gags of shock and insanity that in other films had only been used for punctuation made it all seem fresh. Although there was never another film quite like it—Olsen and Johnson's next one, *Crazy House,* was much more orthodox, being a traditional musical comedy after a marvelously satiric opening in which the two zanies march on Universal and the studio and its stars marshal their defenses—*Hellzapoppin* was of major influence in establishing the orthodoxy of insanity in Hollywood comedy. *Hi Diddle Diddle,* W. C. Fields's *Never Give a Sucker an Even Break* (made almost concurrently), and many of the Bob Hope films owe a great deal to it. It is rarely seen today, mainly because its ownership is split several ways (including the widows of Olsen and Johnson) and clearances are time-consuming. When it is shown, it sometimes disappoints—but it always demonstrates what all the shouting was about.

LA NUIT FANTASTIQUE

(FRANCE, 1941)

Directed by Marcel L'Herbier; screenplay by Louis Chavance, Maurice Henry, Marcel L'Herbier, and Henri Jeanson.

LEADING PLAYERS:
Micheline Presle, Fernand Gravet, Saturnin Fabre, Bernard Blier, Maurice Schutz.

France was not noted for screwball comedy; its preference was for pantomimic romantic farce, something it had done best in the silent period via such films as Rene Clair's *The Italian Straw Hat.* While not a classic example of the genre, *La Nuit Fantastique* is probably the best of France's few forays into screwball, though more tinged with fantasy and whimsy than its Hollywood equivalent.

Made under the Nazi occupation, *La Nuit Fantastique* was determinedly escapist. While a certain amount of freedom was extended to French producers, clearly contemporary anti-Nazi stories would not be countenanced, nor did French audiences, already hard-pressed by the austerity and grimness of occupation life, want a return to the poetic-realism tragedies so popular in the immediate prewar years. One solution was for escapism via fantasy, costume romance, or modernized legend as in Cocteau's *L'Eternel Retour.* Light comedies, especially those with Danielle Darrieux, were extremely popular, too.

But *La Nuit Fantastique* was unique in that it created its fantasy escape world out of the reality of the contemporary scene. Fernand Gravet played a porter in a bustling Parisian market; always tired, he was forever falling asleep in the piles of empty baskets. In his dreams, he is haunted by the white-clad, fairylike figure of a woman, played by Micheline Presle. Ultimately he encounters her in his waking hours, follows her, and is thrust into a bizarre romantic adventure—she works for a colorfully mad magician—which involves midnight rooftop chases, is never far from the spirit of the old Méliès fantasies, and is deliberately vague about separating reality from dream. Much of it had a near-surreal quality, but the magnificent bravura hamming of Saturnin Fabre as the menacing but still funny magician kept the overall tone light. Presle plays with the same delightful sense of fun that her compatriot Danielle Darrieux had brought to *The Rage of Paris,* but Darrieux had suggested innocence and gaiety, while the actually younger Presle was able to suggest a woman of mystery and allure. And, in the best screwball tradition, she had to pose as a madwoman at one point in the plot!

At the time it was highly acclaimed in France, winning no less than two Grand Prizes as well as a Best Actress award for Presle. These awards were probably an acknowledgment of how well the film served the needs of entertainment-starved occupied France, although director Marcel L'Herbier was held in high esteem—and had been since the silent days. When the film was unveiled at British and

LA NUIT FANTASTIQUE (1941) An inspired screwball comedy from Nazi-occupied France gets under way when market porter Fernand Gravet is intrigued by a white-clad figure flitting through the stalls at night.

The bizarre, dreamlike action, over a single night, takes the two protagonists through the streets of Paris, to a magician's cellar and to an insane asylum.

American art houses after the war, critics were not exactly ecstatic, but audiences took the film to their hearts. Most audiences were seeing (and being impressed by) Presle, a new star, for the first time, and they were also applauding the spirit of a country that could produce such a gay and charming film under conditions of such adversity. The film has been unseen for many years, and possibly a reappraisal might be less generous today, for it was in many ways a too economical production, its trick and fantasy scenes lacking slickness and expertise.

Micheline Presle could have become France's Carole Lombard if that country had had an appropriate comedy tradition. However, she was such a superb dramatic actress, so capable at taking on the walk, stance, and diction of much older women, that she tended to be restricted largely to much more serious works such as *Le Diable au Corps, Felicie Nanteuil,* and *Les Jeux Sont Faits,* in which her dramatic talents were certainly not wasted. But, like Lombard, she was something of a madcap offscreen, too, and it's a pity that this aspect of her personality wasn't exploited more on film. (In due time, as French television inevitably aped American situation-comedy series, she starred in a series not too unlike *I Love Lucy.*)

TOM, DICK AND HARRY

(RKO RADIO 1941)

Directed by Garson Kanin; screenplay by Paul Jarrico.

LEADING PLAYERS:
Ginger Rogers, George Murphy, Burgess Meredith, Alan Marshal, Phil Silvers.

The quantitative zenith of the screwball comedy cycle, and, in terms of its continuous production as a major genre, its climax, was reached in 1941–42. With America at war, comedy took a very different turn, and though there were interim highlights, traditional (and top-bracket) screwball really breathed its last with Preston Sturges's *Unfaithfully Yours.*

Tom, Dick and Harry, released in the second half of 1941, undoubtedly profited by public response to its particular brand of comedy. At the time it was highly popular, and big at the box office. Today it seems inventive but somewhat labored, and much of its charm has evaporated. It marked the last of a string of interesting and mainly comedic works by writer/director Garson Kanin before he joined the army, and also the last film Ginger Rogers would make for RKO, under her original contract. She'd be back, but as a bigger-name star in such films as *Once Upon a Honeymoon* and *Tender Comrade.* It was both a curious echo of *Kitty Foyle* (1940)—for which she won an Academy Award—and a forerunner of two later Rogers films, *Lady in the Dark* and *It Had to Be You.* In all four films she was cast as a girl unable to make up her mind which marriage suitor to select, and in the latter three, all comedies, much of the decision-making was guided by elaborate dream sequences.

Actually, *Tom, Dick and Harry* would have had much more screwball bite if it had been daring enough to parody the rather stodgy (and certainly overrated) *Kitty Foyle.* But since the earlier film had been parlayed to box-office success by an unusually elaborate publicity campaign, and Rogers probably exercised enough clout to deny the possibility of kidding a film that had just won her stature as a major dramatic actress, the opportunity was bypassed. The only hint of potential parody lay in the way the dream sequences were introduced, via Rogers staring into her mirror and musing as to her future.

Her three suitors were Alan Marshal, a debonair and charming millionaire who, on their first date, whisks her off in his private plane; George Murphy, the longtime boyfriend who is a hardworking, ambitious car salesman; and shiftless, jobless Burgess Meredith, whose only apparent asset is that he causes invisible bells to ring when he and Rogers kiss. The dream sequences are near surreal in their design, and not particularly funny due to Roger's developing tendency to mug badly in comedy. (This was the first film to display that weakness; her prior film with Kanin, *Bachelor Mother,* dis-

TOM, DICK AND HARRY (1941) (From left) George Murphy, Alan Marshal, and Burgess Meredith in the title roles, as suitors to Ginger Rogers.

TOM, DICK AND HARRY Millionaire Tom (Alan Marshal) whisks Ginger off in his private plane.

played an under-control talent for comedy that resulted in a performance that was funny, dramatic, and moving without any apparent shifting of gears.)

In the funniest single sequence, the penniless Meredith, seeking to size up his opposition for Rogers's hand, strolls past the car showrooms where Murphy is the ace salesman. Murphy lures him inside, then proceeds to

TOM, DICK AND HARRY Dreams of an idyllic future with super car salesman Dick (George Murphy).

189

TOM, DICK AND HARRY   And dreams of a carefree but none too secure future with unemployed Harry (Burgess Meredith).

high-pressure him into buying a car that he cannot afford and of course has no intention of purchasing. Just as Murphy reaches a subclimax in his sales pitch, he remembers to add on the "slight additional" charges, then proceeds to the next plateau, with more charges, until the car's price has virtually doubled. Meredith's underplaying, and Murphy's necessary high-pressure overplaying, mesh beautifully in this sequence. Meredith was always a magnificent low-key comedy performer, rather like an even more laid-back James Stewart and without the Stewart mannerisms. It's a pity that his comedy performances were so few, though one can be grateful to Lubitsch's *That Uncertain Feeling* (with Meredith as the neurotic pianist who comes between psychiatrist Melvyn Douglas and his wife, Merle Oberon) and H. C. Potter's *Second Chorus* (Meredith's a jazz trumpeter who tries to double-cross partner Fred Astaire, professionally with bandleader Artie Shaw, and romantically with Paulette Goddard).

Audiences familiar with Hollywood plot construction knew that Rogers would wind up with the least worthy but most engaging of the trio, namely Meredith. A last-minute attempt at a twist had her accepting George Murphy— but a farewell kiss from Meredith produced those bells again, so off went Ginger and Burgess in a cloud of dust to the surprise of absolutely no one.

MR. AND MRS. SMITH

(RKO RADIO, 1941)

Directed by Alfred Hitchcock, original story and screenplay by Norman Krasna.

LEADING PLAYERS:
Carole Lombard, Robert Montgomery, Gene Raymond, Jack Carson, Philip Merivale, Lucile Watson.

Although not overused in film, the old saw of the happily married couple who suddenly discover that through a legal loophole they are not wed at all was a fairly reliable device on the stage. Once the situation was established, the plot could go in any number of directions— one partner wants to legalize the situation immediately while the other isn't so sure, or both partners have the opportunity to weigh their new freedom against the responsibilities and restrictions that have just been lifted from them. In the movies at least, to placate the censors, the bureaucratic mistake is often found to have itself been a mistake. Climaxes usually found the couple—or couples—happily reunited. One of the best forays into this kind of comedy was in the British *When We Are Married*, a 1943 comedy based on the popular J. B. Priestley play that is frequently revived on the London stage, not least because it is a wonderful showcase for ensemble playing. However, this British film is by no means a screwball comedy; set in the north of England at the turn of the century, it satirizes small-town life and politics, and the "respectability" automatically gained by regular attendance at church. A similar Hollywood film, but essentially modern and zany, was *We're Not Married* (1952) in which a stellar cast including Ginger Rogers, Fred Allen, Victor Moore, David Wayne, Eve Arden, Eddie Bracken, Marilyn Monroe, and Paul Douglas acted out a story idea fragmented into individual episodes.

As virtually the first major A production to handle this theme, quite distinct from the complicated marital-problem films (exemplified by *My Favorite Wife*), *Mr. and Mrs. Smith*—especially given its two leads, and the novelty of Alfred Hitchcock involving himself in a comedy—should have been a bigger hit than it was. Underrated or not, it was a very good comedy rather than an outstanding one, and the rug was rather pulled out from underneath its mildly creaking legs by the almost concurrent appearance of Preston Sturges's *The Lady Eve*. The Sturges film—his third as a director, but his first A film with appropriate box-office stars—opened a few weeks later. The critics had undoubtedly already seen it when they wrote their *Mr. and Mrs. Smith* reviews; they

MR AND MRS SMITH (1941)   Robert Montgomery and Carole Lombard are the bickering but much-in-love couple who suddenly find that their marriage is invalid.

MR AND MRS SMITH   While Montgomery tries to woo and win her back, Lombard enjoys her new-found freedom and becomes the sexual aggressor determined to have love on her terms.

knew Hitchcock's was merely good, and Sturges's not only brilliant and fresh, but also confirming him as a master of screwball comedy who in many ways (especially as writer of his own material) had surpassed Lubitsch. The critics wanted to be fair to the Hitchcock film and for the most part they were, but there remains the suspicion that they were pulling their punches in order that their paeans of praise to Sturges would be that much more spectacular. Undoubtedly, if *The Lady Eve* had arrived six months later, and the press screenings of the two films had not overlapped, *Mr. and Mrs. Smith* would have been received, if not more rapturously, then certainly less casually.

Disliked by Hitchcock fanciers because it seemed devoid of his tricks (though actually more of them are apparent today than seemed to be the case in 1941), it was nevertheless a popular comedy and a respectable addition to the screwball cycle. That smooth and polished

191

romantic comedian Robert Montgomery was restored to the kind of role he did best; here he's the earnest husband trying to rekindle his wife's love by repeating their courtship days—revisiting favorite restaurants for example. Lombard, on the other hand, has a field day as the newly liberated wife who is not so sure that she *wants* to get back into marriage again. Utterly scatterbrained, she doesn't really seem worthy of Montgomery's love and devotion, and one almost wishes that the script had had him seek solace from and remarriage to Jane Wyatt, Anne Shirley, Anna Lee, or other attractive young ladies then available on the RKO lot.

However, Lombard's energy and charm enabled her to carry off the rather silly role with aplomb, and it was an appropriate farewell for her to screwball comedy. (The classic *To Be or Not to Be* followed, her last film before her tragic wartime death, but that was essentially a masterpiece of black comedy).

As so often happens with this kind of comedy (especially those written by Norman Krasna, though a number of the best examples occurred in *Tom, Dick and Harry*, which he had *not* written) some of the funniest moments had little to do with the basic story line. An interlude at an amusement park was especially effective, but best of all was a brief visit to a temperance lecture, at which the speaker, with all the fire and brimstone of a preacher, rails against Montgomery's fondness for liquor and climaxes his spiel by throwing liquor into Montgomery's face. The latter is clearly in some discomfort. "If that's what it does to your face, imagine what it does to your stomach!" the lecturer intones. Montgomery leaves in high dudgeon, only to return a moment later with what he announces to be a big bag of crinkly, crunchy potato chips. The speaker seems unimpressed and doesn't see the point, whereupon Montgomery takes a huge handful of the chips and rubs them violently into the speaker's face. "If that's what they do to your face, imagine what they do to your stomach!" is his exit line.

THE LADY EVE
(PARAMOUNT, 1941)

Written and directed by Preston Sturges, from a story by Monckton Hoffe.

LEADING PLAYERS:
Barbara Stanwyck, Henry Fonda, Charles Coburn, William Demarest, Eric Blore, Eugene Pallette, Robert Greig.

Early in 1993, at the Library of Congress in Washington, the newly established National Film Preservation Committee was charged with selecting twenty-five American films (*representative* films as well as classics) to be placed on that year's listing of preserved and protected films—"protected" also taking in hoped-for resistance to colorizing or reediting, and legally enforced labeling of those practices when they do in fact take place.

Sullivan's Travels by Sturges had automatically been voted onto an earlier list. Clearly, most of Sturges's films are national treasures that should be revered, protected, and enjoyed. But with the Library limiting itself to twenty-five titles annually, and so much of Hollywood's past not so recognized, it would have been reckless to add more than one Sturges title at a time. There was heated discussion about the respective merits of various Sturges films. Committee member and actor Roddy McDowall seemed to settle it all, however, when he argued that while other Sturges films might well be funnier, *The Lady Eve* was perfect in every way—in writing, in acting, and especially in its construction. He carried the day, and *The Palm Beach Story* and possibly *The Miracle of Morgan's Creek* will get their share of the limelight in a later year.

Unless one was around and a regular cinemagoer at the time, it's difficult to imagine the impact that Sturges, and this film in particular, had in 1941. Even though we weren't exactly starved for comedy then, Bosley Crowther in the *New York Times* was moved to remark:

> Preston Sturges is definitely and distinctly the most refreshing new force to hit the

American motion picture in the past five years . . . with *The Lady Eve* Mr. Sturges is indisputably established as one of the top one or two writers and directors of comedy working in Hollywood today. A more charming or distinguished gem of nonsense has not occurred since *It Happened One Night.* Superlatives like that are dangerous, but superlatives like *The Lady Eve* are much too rare for the careful weighing of words. And much too precious a boon in these grim and mirthless times. For this bubbling and frothy comedy-romance possesses all the pristine bounce and humor, all the freshness and ingenuity, that seem to have been lacking from movies since way back—we don't know when. Suddenly the art of comedy-making is rediscovered.

If Orson Welles and John Huston were not to make their directorial debuts later in that same year, Preston Sturges would have wrapped up 1941 easily as the director of the year. As it was, the success of *The Lady Eve* carried Sturges along on its momentum for a brief but heady series of triumphs at Paramount. (Ironically, the Academy Award for direction that year went to none of these dynamic newcomers but to the deserving traditionalist, John Ford, who probably didn't care that much whether he got another Oscar or not!)

At heart, *The Lady Eve* is formula stuff. Charles Coburn, daughter Barbara Stanwyck, and their valet/troubleshooter, Melville Cooper, are cardsharps plying their trade on luxury liners. On this occasion they encounter millionaire Henry Fonda and plot to take him. True love intervenes, but before Stanwyck can confess her past, Fonda finds out about it. Hurt beyond measure—this was his first real romance—Fonda breaks everything off and won't listen to Stanwyck's explanations. Equally hurt, but also angered, she decides on a unique revenge. Posing as Lady Eve Sidwich, a wealthy British aristocrat, she arrives at Fonda's high-society home, confuses him, finally convinces him that she is a totally different woman from the shipboard cheat, gets him to fall in love with her all over again, and marries

him. Then on their wedding night she spins such a tall (but to him convincing) tale of her previous marriages and amours that he is disillusioned once again and leaves her a second time. In a brief interim—similar to the one in *It Happened One Night*—it is established that both parties do in fact love one another, and that monetary gain was never Eve's aim. As we segue into another shipboard meeting, Eve has reverted to her former self, contrives to meet Fonda "accidentally," and their original romance is on again, he being too lovesick to really care who she is, but dumb enough to believe that he has been lucky enough to be reunited with his initial love.

This kind of material has been played straight—for light comedy or serious dramatics—any number of times. *Shady Lady* (1945) was the same kind of film, with Charles Coburn playing a similar role. But Ginny Simms (though she sang pleasantly) was no Stanwyck, and likable Robert Paige was too obviously a B stand-in for Fonda. Most critical of all, director George Waggner was no Sturges. The delight of *The Lady Eve* is that it toys with clichés that the audience knows by heart, comes up with a happy ending that the audience could likewise foretell from scene one, yet fills the intervening nine reels with so many surprises, such charm and wit, and such wonderful utilization of beloved character players like Eugene Pallette that one feels with Bosley Crowther that the art of comedy is being reborn. Charm and wit are essential ingredients, for while the film is funny and has consistent chuckles, it doesn't aim for the *big* laugh and, moreover, doesn't need it. Afterward, one feels that one has enjoyed a magnificent gourmet meal—but not one that was too fancy or had one course too many.

While Preston Sturges obviously rates most of the praise for the success of *The Lady Eve,* it is still difficult to (fairly) distribute the praise. The performances are uniformly excellent, yet they depend so largely on Sturges's wonderful dialogue and his directorial guidance. Henry Fonda had made comedies before—at least a quartet of them—but his performance (and timing) under Sturges were as much a revela-

THE LADY EVE (1941)
Con-man and daughter
(Charles Coburn and
Barbara Stanwyck),
sucker-about-to-be-trimmed
(Henry Fonda) and his
sceptical manservant
(William Demarest,
standing).

THE LADY EVE   An
innocent suggestion by
Eve (Stanwyck), "Don't
you think we should go to
bed?"—ostensibly
referring only to the
lateness of the
hour—turns poor Jonesey
(Fonda) into a nervous
wreck.

THE LADY EVE   William Demarest and ship's officer Torben
Meyer bring Fonda news of Stanwyck's criminal past, and
scuttle his marriage plans.

THE LADY EVE
Assuming a new guise, that of the very English Lady Eve Sidwich, Stanwyck sets herself up in New England society and prepares a new snare for Fonda. Joining her (from left) are Charles Coburn, Melville Cooper, and Eric Blore.

THE LADY EVE
Humiliation is part of the battle plan; one of a series of mishaps that befall the hapless Fonda. His father, Eugene Pallette (with cigar), is much amused; butler Robert Greig is scornful.

THE LADY EVE   The wedding finally comes off, but . . .

. . . the honeymoon is aborted when Eve—in a Pullman car speeding through the night—feels compelled to confess all her previous indiscretions to Jonesey. However, Sturges wraps up separation and reconciliation at his usual lightning speed.

tion as Joel McCrea's acting for Sturges. And while to Sturges writing was perhaps more important than direction, many hilarious moments in *The Lady Eve* are totally without dialogue and reveal his knowledge of and respect for the silent cinema. The pratfalls in *The Lady Eve*—with Fonda, falling into mud or food, the butt of most of them—are pratfalls of the sight gag rather than the sheer slapstick variety. As with Laurel and Hardy, each such moment is connected to another elsewhere in the film, so that the laughs are compounded into a combination of echoes and anticipations, along with a direct response to the gag itself.

Sturges, more than any other screenwriter, mastered the skill of manipulating words to comic effect. He had no trouble tossing off one-liners as virtual throwaways, and Charles Coburn's character has a plethora of them: "Let us be crooks but let us not be common"; "The tragedy of the rich is that they don't need anything"; "The trouble with reformers is that they always rain on somebody else's parade." But Sturges could make ordinary words and commonplace dialogue seem funny. In one of the highlights of the film, a crooked card game where Coburn is trying to "take" the innocent Fonda and has him in a spot to lose thousands, Stanwyck constantly interferes to spoil his scheming. Just before Coburn is about to wipe out his opponent with a stunning hand (most of the cards for which came from inside pockets or were hidden in a handkerchief), Stanwyck "accidentally" drops an ace out of the pack from which she is dealing and disarmingly remarks, "Now I could have sworn one of you had four aces," forcing Coburn to throw in the towel before his cheating is revealed. Afterward, Fonda tells Stanwyck that, while he hopes she doesn't mind him saying so, he thought her father wasn't playing very well that night. "Oh, he was a little uneven tonight," she replies brightly, adding, with a sarcasm lost on him, "only sometimes he's a little more uneven than others." "That's what makes him uneven, of course," says Fonda blandly—in a delivery that suggests that Rudy Vallee studied Fonda's performance carefully before doing *his* bland millionaire for Sturges in *The Palm Beach Story* (1942).

Without seeming to do so deliberately, the film divides into two parts, each equally long but somewhat different in style. The first half takes place aboard a luxury liner that Fonda as Charlie Pike, heir to the Pike's Ale millions ("The Ale That Won for Yale," one of the many slogans that decorate Sturges's films), joins after a long sojourn along the Amazon. He's been pursuing his lifelong ambition to study snakes and has brought one along with him. (The waiter in the ship's restaurant is somewhat nonplussed when asked to provide four houseflies and a cockroach for breakfast.) Everything about the film's shipboard sequence has a luxury even most luxury liners wouldn't contemplate: staterooms the size of presidential suites, bay windows opening directly on ocean views, all underscored by Paramount's usual lush reworking of its old Rodgers and Hart and other melodies, with "Isn't It Romantic?" from *Love Me Tonight* particularly in evidence.

The battle of the sexes becomes in this instance a slaughter of the innocents, with Stanwyck relentlessly stalking her prey, commenting occasionally on the futile and obvious methods employed by the shipload of women all intent on landing the millionaire, and using completely unpredictable shock tactics to trip, hook, and reel in her totally helpless victim. Two mock seduction scenes manage to be both pricelessly funny (thanks to the subdued, low-pressure playing of both stars) and genuinely steamy. One even finishes with Stanwyck looking directly at Fonda and saying forthrightly, "I think it's time we went to bed." The shock effect on Fonda is no less than that on the audience, and one can only conjecture by what circuitous persuasion it got past the Production Code. Subsequent events show that she was referring to their retiring separately because it was late, but there's no such inference in the look on her face, nor is there the usual line of dialogue to tidy up and clarify.

The second half of the film shifts gears with the lessening presence of Coburn and Stanwyck's appearance at the Pike mansion masquerading as the Lady Eve. Here one finds some halfhearted recognition of the war in Europe; the suspicious William Demarest points out to his boss that masquerades are easy and proves it by doing a Hitler impersonation. That U.S.—Britain luxury liners have stopped running is noted several times, and also that the Lady Eve was sufficiently high up in British aristocracy to manage to come over on a battleship!

Although the film certainly doesn't need it, it gets a vigorous infusion of new blood at this point from a whole new gaggle of characters: Eric Blore as an English con man who helps Eve in her masquerade; Eugene Pallette, archetypal screwball-family head as Fonda's father; and a wonderful retinue of Sturges servants including Robert Greig (butler), Luis Alberni (cook), and other faces, familiar, bizarre, lovable. Pallette's role is interestingly off-center for him, after following in the pattern of his *My Man Godfrey* role for so many years. He still stomps through the house muttering that it's a madhouse; and he has a wonderful sequence (intercut with other scenes, so that it grows in intensity) where his growing impatience at not being served breakfast climaxes in his clanging metal pot-lids together like cymbals, rhythmically and exasperatedly as he strives vainly for attention. But otherwise his Pike senior is more blessed than most of his predecessors: his wife (Janet Beecher) is sensible and little seen; his business is in good shape; and he has no Depression-era worries from which he needs to be rescued.

Whereas part one of *The Lady Eve* was as ruthlessly methodical as Stanwyck's pursuit of Fonda, part two is as fanciful and nutty as her masquerade—done, by the way, with an incredibly effective accent and a deft combination of the democratic with the condescending that is the mark of the true British aristocrat.

After a zany and satiric courtship sequence—one of Sturges's many writing skills was in using clichéd Hollywood dialogue in such a way that the audience knew it was meant to be taken as satire, and yet having it move the plot forward at the same time—the film arrives at its probable comic highspot, the wedding night aboard a speeding train.

About to exact her revenge and break up *his* happiness as he once destroyed hers, Eve drops casual, unintended hints about a previous love—and then, saying that it wasn't important or worth mentioning, snuggles down into Pike's arms. But once again the bait has worked and he is hooked. He insists on knowing all—and when Eve obliges him, he squirms but forgives and delivers a little speech about the distinction between man and beast being man's ability to be noble and to forget. Thus encouraged, Eve drops the next shoe . . . and the next. Sturges constantly cuts away to the train speeding through the stormy night, or, that oldest sexual cliché of all, through a tunnel. Each time he returns to the battling couple, it is to find that Eve's reminiscences have just gotten as far as the groom—"well, not really the groom, he was just a stable boy"—and thence to twins, to John, and to complicated relationships that don't bear thinking about.

When the train comes to a halt, Pike escapes hastily from the nuptial chamber, still clad in pajamas, clasping his belongings—and falls flat in the mud beside the tracks.

The often close relationship between screw-ball comedy and noir films with themes of madness is borne out by Luis Buñuel's classic *El* (1953), in which one sequence, though totally reversed, is obviously patterned on this honeymoon episode from *The Lady Eve*. As a happy couple prepare for their wedding night on a train roaring through the countryside, the apparently normal husband (first revealed as neurotic, then eventually as totally insane), played by Arturo de Cordova, first gently asks his wife if she had been in love before. Not taking him too seriously, and being entirely innocent, she replies no. Then he reminds her of a man she had once been engaged to—a man *he* took her away from. Again, but increasingly concerned, the wife denies any wrongdoing. Incensed, the husband insists that she tell all, that he will forgive her so long as she confesses. Solely to pander to his concern, she admits that, yes, once she did love Raoul—but nothing ever came of it. Triumphantly the husband pounces; if there had been one, there must have been others. He wants names, details. Again, this is intercut with night exteriors and tunnel symbolism. De Cordova's mania is an exact reversal of Stanwyck's casual confession, but there seems little doubt that Buñuel borrowed at least this sequence from Sturges. (Ironically, *El* contained sequences that suggested Hitchcock did some borrowing for the later *Vertigo!*)

It has taken far too many words to explain highlights of *The Lady Eve* that Sturges achieved with fewer words, nuance of expression—and perhaps a pratfall. It remains as fresh and innovative today as when audiences first saw it in February of 1941—and if it's possible, it seems even funnier.

ARSENIC AND OLD LACE
(WARNER BROS., 1941)

Release delayed until 1944; produced and directed by Frank Capra; screenplay by Julius J. and Philip G. Epstein, from the play by Joseph Kesselring.

LEADING PLAYERS:

Cary Grant, Priscilla Lane, Raymond Massey, Peter Lorre, Josephine Hull, Jean Adair, Jack Carson, Edward Everett Horton, Grant Mitchell, James Gleason, John Alexander.

Although also a black comedy (of murders), *Arsenic And Old Lace* was in a sense one of the most legitimate of screwball comedies in that for once the members of its crazy family were all genuinely insane. Its plot, too well known to need detailed repetition here, concerned two well-loved and elderly sisters, known for their charitable works, among which—not so well known—is their systematic killing (via elder-berry wine laced with arsenic) of lonely old gentlemen to whom, in their eyes, death would be a blessed relief. Their more flamboyantly crazy brother, Teddy—who believes he is Teddy Roosevelt—buries all the "fever victims" in the "Panama Canal" down in the cellar. To this macabre household comes another member of the family, Jonathan Brewster, a sadistic serial killer looking for a hideout from the police, and his crony, Dr. Einstein. Caught in the middle, especially when he finds out what is going on, is nephew Mortimer, a drama critic who comments at one point, "Insanity runs in our family; it practically gallops!" and has second thoughts about getting married since the family taint may soon affect him as well.

The film was made in 1941, in less than a month, partly because the two sisters of the Broadway show—Josephine Hull and Jean Adair—were only free at that time, and partially because director Capra was under pressure of time too, due to report for army service. Contractually the film could not be released while the play was still playing in New York. Its unexpected popularity extended the Broadway run, and the film's release was delayed until 1944. This was unfortunate, since while not markedly affecting its commercial success—if anything the film was enhanced by Cary Grant's growing popularity—it did hurt it in other ways. When Capra made it, America was only on the verge of entering World War Two. It was a comedy about death, but the approach was distanced, and it was played largely as

ARSENIC AND OLD LACE (1941/1944)   Cary Grant as Mortimer Brewster, with homicidal aunts Jean Adair (left) and Josephine Hull.

ARSENIC AND OLD LACE   The arrival of Jonathan Brewster (Raymond Massey) interrupts the aunts' current funeral. Mortimer tumbles to the fact that there's a body in the window seat.

farce. In the interim, with America in the war while the film sat on the shelf, black comedies became, if not commonplace, then at least more frequent. Lubitsch's *To Be or Not to Be* and

199

ARSENIC AND OLD LACE Teddy (John Alexander) explains how fever victims must be buried in the cellar; Dr. Einstein (Peter Lorre) is amused; Jonathan realizes how he can now dispose of *his* latest corpse.

ARSENIC AND OLD LACE Jonathan is constantly irked by references to his resemblance to Boris Karloff; Mortimer doesn't help matters when he asks, "Where'd you get that face, Hollywood?"

McCarey's *Once Upon a Honeymoon* (also with Grant) were subtle and sophisticated, signposts on an increasingly traveled road to comedies about murder that would reach their full flowering in such postwar films as Chaplin's *Monseur Verdoux*, Robert Hamer's *Kind Hearts and Coronets*, and Alexander Mackendrick's *The Lady Killers*.

The fault was not so much in the play itself or in the public's changed attitude and a more casual acceptance of stories dealing with death, but in Capra's treatment. To provide some box-office insurance, the role of Mortimer Brewster was built up so that the play/film became a vehicle for star Cary Grant. Thus an extra reel was added to the beginning, establishing the Grant character as a former woman-hater about to marry, and creating a zany caricature of Brooklyn, against which the insane activities of the Brewster household seemed (unwittingly) almost normal, at least until the arrival of mad nephew Jonathan. Also, since in the play the character of Mortimer is relatively passive, Grant was encouraged—apparently even *ordered*—by Capra to mug the role far beyond the needs of comic pantomime. As a result, he brought a frenzy to the comedy that was uncalled-for and appeared to be much nuttier than the genuine lunatics! Grant himself was well aware of this, and later felt that it was easily his worst comedy performance, but being a professional and recognizing the tight shooting schedule, he went along with Capra's demands. The casting of this role originally on the New York and London stage was quite inspired; Allyn Joslyn played it in America and Naunton Wayne underplayed it superbly in the English edition. Even in the matter of the two old ladies, the film version suffered a little. Josephine Hull and Jean Adair had played it on stage, and perfected their mannerisms (such as Adair's way of scuttling rather than walking), and since they were returning to the stage version, clearly had no wish to unlearn those tricks. Too, since they were essentially stage rather than film players, they had mastered the technique of underplaying their best lines but with a theatrical emphasis so that nobody would miss the point. In the London version, Lillian Braithwaite and Mary Jerrold were veterans of both screen and stage, and played their roles in a naturalistic low-key that blended well with Naunton Wayne's restrained comic exasperation.

None of which is to say that the film fails. Its basic plot and dialogue are still very funny, and the ensemble work from a group of key Warner character players and comedians is superb. Raymond Massey and Peter Lorre, playing it (relatively) straight as Jonathan and Dr. Einstein, are particularly effective and amusing, especially in their scenes with the over-the-top Grant. There is delightful "professional" jealousy when Massey discovers that his aunts have disposed of one more body than he has, and with a baleful glare at Grant announces that all he needs is "one more." And when Grant is trussed up for treatment by Massey with his assortment of knives and scalpels, but time is short because the police are closing in, Lorre has a wonderful self-parodying scene where he pleads with Massey to "get it over quick" and not use the messy, long-winded "Melbourne method."

With an extremely elaborate Brooklyn backdrop set and a frenetic pace, the film manages to cover its theatrical origins surprisingly well, despite the reliance on dialogue and restriction of movement. In fact it's so consistently funny, thanks mainly to Joseph Kesselring's original writing and the fine ensemble playing, that one just wishes it also had the subtlety and style of the stage version. Compromises are actually fairly limited. The stage original meticulously avoided showing any bodies, and they were carted hither and yon from the window seat in darkness; the idea of also avoiding bodies in the film was a good one, but the retention of stage technique in indicating their transference, is rather clumsily done. The play's closing scene was of the sisters—now about to be taken away, quite happily, to an insane asylum, administering their poisoned wine to the lonely old asylum official, was un-

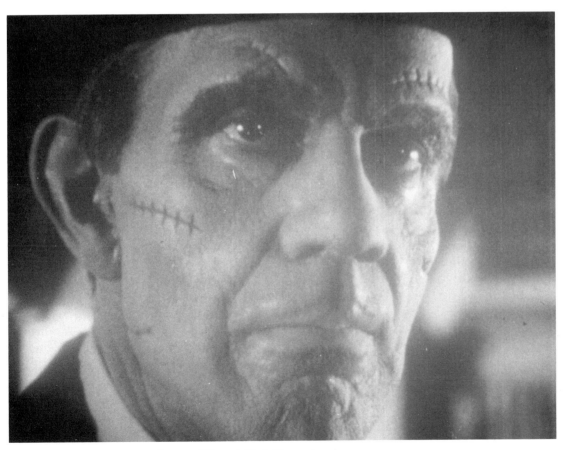

ARSENIC AND OLD LACE   A rare closeup of Massey's Karloffian makeup.

201

derstandably altered since the official was played by Edward Everett Horton who could hardly be killed off just for a climactic joke.

The play's concluding punch line also had to be removed due to then prevailing censorship. At the very last minute, just before being carted off to the asylum, the two old ladies confide to Jonathan that he isn't a Brewster at all, but a child of dubious parentage that they raised. They expect him to be dismayed; instead he is delighted that he is thus freed from the taint of insanity, and rushes after his fiancée, yelling, "Elaine—I'm not a Brewster, I'm a bastard!" In 1941, the line was still enough of an eyebrow raiser to be a sock curtain line. On film, it was toned down to "I'm not a Brewster—I'm a son of a sea cook!"

Perhaps the saddest omission from the film, however, was the play's biggest surprise, a gimmick that the critics sensibly kept to themselves so as not to spoil the fun. After all the curtain calls are over and the audience is expecting one more appearance by the whole cast, the curtain parts on an empty stage. A trap door from the cellar is pushed open, and up troop the dozen or so "fever victims," perfectly chosen "lonely old men" who make a joint curtain call to a mixture of delightful applause and laughter. It wouldn't have been at all difficult to have added this wonderful surprise to the film's post-End Title cast list . . . though admittedly, impatient projectionists might well have sabotaged the gag by switching off too early.

THE DEVIL AND MISS JONES

(RKO RADIO, 1941)

Directed by Sam Wood; original screenplay by Norman Krasna.

LEADING PLAYERS:
Jean Arthur, Charles Coburn, Robert Cummings, Spring Byington, Edmund Gwenn, S. Z. Sakall, William Demarest.

A big hit in its day, though rarely revived now (and usually in edited form), *The Devil and Miss Jones* was considered by the *New York Times* to be the best comedy of its type since *The Lady Eve.* That's not an unfair assessment, but neither is it a markedly grandiose one, since the Preston Sturges classic had preceded it into release by only a few months.

Mildly Capra-esque in manner, *The Devil and Miss Jones* gives the standard screwball themes some novel twists. The battle of the sexes this time is not so much between girl and boy as between girl and boss—although, another twist, the girl doesn't know that the older man she has befriended *is* her boss. In what is virtually the key role—rare in screwball comedy—the older man is both catalyst and lead. Charles Coburn, repeating (with variations) his millionaire store-owner role from *Bachelor Mother* (also scripted by Norman Krasna), is dismayed (and angered) to find that his store workers hate him so much that they have burned him in effigy and constantly attack him at labor meetings. So that he may gather evidence for revenge and a wholesale purge of recalcitrant employees, he takes a job as a shoe salesman in his own store . . . rather like Gustav Froelich going to work in the machine rooms in Fritz Lang's *Metropolis,* although Froelich's motives were humanitarian, whereas Coburn's, initially at least, are vindictive.

Inept as a salesman, Coburn is guided and helped by salesgirl Jean Arthur, with whom he strikes up a firm friendship. Since her boyfriend is Robert Cummings, leader of the labor agitators, the stage is set for humanizing, apparent betrayal, and ultimately reform and happiness all around. Coburn gets to savor the pleasures of Coney Island and also winds up with a (mature) girlfriend himself in Spring Byington.

The Devil and Miss Jones works on so many levels that it's sad that it doesn't work *totally* as a screwball classic. The fault lies squarely with Sam Wood, a dull, plodding director who was extremely fortunate in that his career was dotted with box-office hits, most of which owed their success to someone other than himself. The Marx Brothers' *A Night at the Opera* (1935) could hardly fail as entertainment with its particular ingredients, regardless of *who* directed.

King's Row (1942) likewise had a top cast, a good script, stunning production design by William Cameron Menzies, and outstanding camerawork by James Wong Howe to camouflage its directorial lack of inspiration.

The Devil and Miss Jones similarly has a good script, a fine cast, and impressive production design by Menzies. However, Menzies's sets, especially for the secret labor-union meetings held in the store basement (again a parallel with *Metropolis*) are essentially realistic, though very slightly stylized. Harry Stradling's photography lights them for drama rather than comedy. At moments like this, the mood changes for too long a period and the pace flags (as it never did with Sturges, as witness the firebrand sermon by the preacher in the flophouse of *Sullivan's Travels*). There are times when, despite a great cast (though Jean Arthur was rather going through the motions as before) and technical expertise, the director needs to step in with some flair of his own. Wood never did; the films that had nothing extra going for them and relied a great deal on his talent alone were usually exceptionally weak. Ironically, the best Wood films were those that were the most routine in concept—like *Lord Jeff* (1938)—and that made no de-

DEVIL & MISS JONES (1941)   Family retainer S. Z. Sakall and lonely millionaire Charles Coburn.

DEVIL & MISS JONES
In order to find out why he is hated by his employees, Coburn takes a job in his own store.

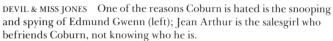

DEVIL & MISS JONES   One of the reasons Coburn is hated is the snooping and spying of Edmund Gwenn (left); Jean Arthur is the salesgirl who befriends Coburn, not knowing who he is.

DEVIL & MISS JONES   The equally inevitable moment of slapstick violence, Coburn (right) tries to rescue Jean Arthur from Walter Kingsford's clutches, while in the background, Edmund Gwenn is on the painful end of a wrestling hold from Robert Cummings.

DEVIL & MISS JONES   The inevitable humanizing process includes an outing on the subway; Coburn, with Spring Byington as the elderly employee who takes a romantic shine to him, and Jean Arthur.

mands on a director other than that he be an efficient traffic cop and keep the action moving. *The Devil and Miss Jones* is so good that with an inspired director it could have been a major work in its genre. Even as it is, it has quite enough to keep audiences happy. The masquerade aspect is more novel (and satisfying) than usual, and the supporting cast is full of familiar faces playing sneaky store employees, directors, detectives, and a fussy customer— the latter role in the always capable hands of Florence Bates.

BALL OF FIRE
(GOLDWYN–RKO RADIO, 1941)

Directed by Howard Hawks; screenplay by Billy Wilder and Charles Brackett, from a story by Wilder and Thomas Monroe.

LEADING PLAYERS:
Gary Cooper, Barbara Stanwyck, Oscar Homolka, S. Z. Sakall, Henry Travers, Tully Marshall, Leonid Kinsky, Richard Haydn, Aubrey Mather, Dana Andrews, Dan Duryea, Allen Jenkins, Elisha Cook, Jr., Kathleen Howard, Gene Krupa's Orchestra.

Barbara Stanwyck's career reached an amazing zenith in the forties, during which she starred

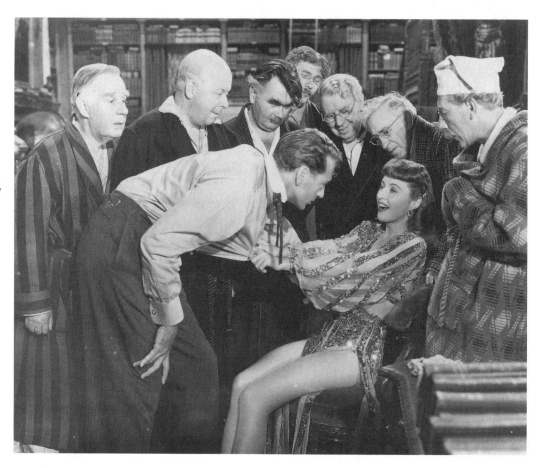

BALL OF FIRE   Sugarpuss O'Shea (Barbara Stanwyck), a stripteaser, captivates the professors whose home she invades: Gary Cooper and (from left) Henry Travers, Aubrey Mather, Oscar Homolka, Leonid Kinskey, S. Z. Sakall, Tully Marshall, and Richard Haydn.

in well over twenty grade-A films, a remarkable mixture of screwball comedy, suspense melodramas, westerns, and film noirs. The last comedy of these was *The Bride Wore Boots* (1946), essentially a scatterbrained romantic comedy rather than a bona fide screwball entry. *Ball of Fire* appeared within the same year as her *The Lady Eve* and is often cited as being the last screwball comedy, the genre allegedly being brought to a close by the advent of World War II. The idea is probably appealing to Howard Hawks's devotees, since he can then be credited with (arguably) opening the cycle with *20th Century* and completing it with this film. However, the claim does not hold water: far too much still lay ahead, including the funniest (if not the best) of all forties screwballs, Sturges's *The Palm Beach Story*, and beyond that, at least two more contenders from Hawks himself: *I Was a Male War Bride* (1949) and *Monkey Business* (1952).

Ball of Fire (later remade by Hawks as a Danny Kaye vehicle, *A Song Is Born*) is certainly one of the glossiest and glitziest of the screwballs of the forties. Stanwyck (at her most glamorous) is Sugarpuss O'Shea, on the run from an unwanted marriage to gangster Dana Andrews. She takes refuge in the near-monasterial retreat of Bertram Potts (Gary Cooper) and his seven absentminded-professor colleagues, only one of whom has ever been married. They are compiling a dictionary and are currently up to S—which takes in *slang, sex,* and *swing,* three areas that Sugarpuss insists she can be a big help with in completing. She moves in, to the consternation of housekeeper Kathleen Howard, the only woman to cross their threshold in years.

Billy Wilder made no secret of the fact that while the script was based on an old European story of his, it also drew deliberate parallels with *Snow White and the Seven Dwarfs,* with Homolka, Sakall, Travers, Haydn, Marshall, Kinsky, and Mather playing relatively close parallels to the well-varied dwarfs; Cooper as a very shy Prince Charming; Stanwyck as a decid-

FEATURE PRODUCTION

BALL OF FIRE   Many critics astutely "revealed" or guessed that the seven professors were "suggested" by Disney's Seven Dwarfs. Here's proof positive that writers Brackett and Wilder and director Hawks had that in mind all along: the seven stuffy professors, (from left) S. Z. Sakall, Leonid Kinskey, Richard Haydn, Henry Travers, Aubrey Mather, Tully Marshall, and Oscar Homolka posed by their cartoon prototypes.

edly more worldly-wise Snow White; and Dana Andrews, combining both charm and vicious sadism, as a neat male counterpart to the Wicked Witch.

The trouble is that *Ball of Fire* eschews most of the basics of screwball comedy. There is hardly a battle-of-the-sexes element, since Stanwyck, to protect her position, must win over her Prince and "the little men." Even her masquerade is limited to not revealing the true reason for her intrusion into their household. Certainly, there is no rule that says that screwball comedy *has* to follow any rules. But there is little that is lunatic about *Ball of Fire* until its climax of confrontation between professors and gangsters. Mostly it is amiable, witty, sometimes quite touching (as when the professors serenade their formerly married colleague with a rendition of "Genevieve"), and essentially a charming character-study comedy in which performers like Aubrey Mather and Tully Marshall are given rare opportunities to indulge in comedy. And like all Goldwyn productions of the forties, it is somewhat overproduced: overlong at nearly two hours, superbly photographed by Gregg Toland (with a gloss that removes the rough edges that sometimes give screwball comedy its bite), and with a spectacular nightclub set for a sequence in which Barbara Stanwyck is established as a sexy singer/dancer who performs to Gene Krupa's "Drum Boogie." The sequence does appear early in the film—later it would have been more intrusive—and is certainly entertaining, not least for Krupa's frenetic drum performance. But it's typical of a size that the film does not need.

As a comedy the film is always entertaining, often enchanting. As a screwball comedy, it is overrated, misses too many bets, and makes one wish that Billy Wilder had held on to his property and made it himself just a couple of years later when he was promoted to director, at Paramount, and proved his directorial/comedic mettle with *The Major and the Minor*.

THE LADY HAS PLANS

(PARAMOUNT, 1941; rel: 1942)

Directed by Sidney Lanfield; screenplay by Harry Tugend, from a story by Leo Birinski.

LEADING PLAYERS:
Ray Milland, Paulette Goddard, Roland Young, Albert Dekker, Cecil Kellaway, Margaret Hayes, Edward Norris, Addison Richards, Gerald Mohr.

Although released early after America's entry into World War II, *The Lady Has Plans* was produced in "peacetime 1941," when Hollywood was still playing it safe and not officially taking sides. But fortunately it was a spy tale set in Lisbon—by Hollywood standards second only

207

THE LADY HAS PLANS (1941) Ray Milland
sketches phony plans onto the back of
comely Paulette Goddard.

to Trieste in being a hotbed of espionage and intrigue—and it was also a spoof. Thus it was able to indulge in well-established stereotypes that made its choice of allies obvious without propagandist underlining. The British, as represented by Roland Young, were urbane, unruffled, and in a pinch, reliable. The Germans only had to be represented by Albert Dekker as "the baron," stiff-necked and monocled, for reference to Germany or the Nazis to be virtually unnecessary. And since that market was lost to them anyway, the producers had no qualms about making one of the chief espionage villains, whose guilt was kept secret until late in the proceedings, a *French* officer.

The plot rehashes that old gimmick from silent farce, the plans copied onto a lady's back. (Hence the title, both subtle and accurate.) The lady in question is Margaret Hayes, but through a mix-up in the States (one of her cohorts is arrested, and her passage to Lisbon slightly delayed), everybody—in the tradition of screwball comedy, without any really sub-

stantial evidence—assumes that Paulette Goddard, newly arrived in Lisbon to take up a newspaper post, is the spy. Dekker's faction figures that a deal has already been made; the British are out to upset the apple cart; the Americans, headed by Ray Milland, want to stop their military secrets from being sold.

Goddard is at first amazed at the attention she is getting: luxury suites, fancy clothes, an unlimited expense account, unheard of perks for a relatively untried reporter. Eventually, however, she is made aware that she is constantly being trailed by Europeans with highly charged libidos. The German confronts her and bluntly tells her to take off her clothes; Roland Young's Britisher more coyly and almost shyly suggests that she "drop her robe." The series of piquant encounters—playfully raunchy, but within the bounds of good taste demanded by the Production Code—is constantly interrupted by the timely arrival of one of the other parties. Eventually Milland comes to realize that Goddard is *not* a spy, and the two join forces with the British contingent to outwit the Axis.

A fake set of ancient mechanical plans is transferred to Miss Goddard's back, and she dutifully reports to the Nazi agents. Dekker is full of admiration (and bemusement) over the complicated plans that he cannot understand, but for the time being his aggressive tactics are halted. Not for long, however, for soon Margaret Hayes shows up with the genuine plans; waylaid by Milland, she is rescued by one of Dekker's men, and the chase is on again.

Until this point the emphasis has been lightly screwball. The attempts to get the clothes off Goddard's back, the suspicion at one point that the plans may actually be tattooed lower down, romancings, druggings, all of the trappings of the typical spy thriller are approached from a comedic viewpoint. The development is sprightly (the film runs less than eighty minutes), and Paramount's then popular costarring team of Millard and Goddard (*Reap the Wild Wind, The Crystal Ball, Kitty*) plays it on just the right level of mock seriousness.

Surprisingly, there are no major highlights

THE LADY HAS PLANS Nazi thugs restrain Ray Milland while Paulette Goddard watches helplessly and number-one spy Albert Dekker (right) glowers.

couple, and the film thus something of a trailer for their teaming in DeMille's period extravaganza *Reap the Wild Wind,* which was released in the same month (March of 1942). If so, the speed of production doesn't show—except possibly in the lack of any big-scale comedy sequences—and the zippy pace that results certainly helps. A lesser screwball to be sure, but an honorable one.

ROXIE HART

(20TH CENTURY-FOX, 1942)

Directed by William Wellman; written and produced by Nunnally Johnson, from the play *Chicago* by Maurine Watkins.

LEADING PLAYERS:
Ginger Rogers, George Montgomery, Adolphe Menjou, Lynne Overman, Nigel Bruce, Phil Silvers, Sara Allgood, William Frawley, Spring Byington, Iris Adrian, George Chandler.

It comes as rather a shock to realize that *Roxie Hart* was far, far closer to the roaring twenties

or comic set pieces, but the sexual undertones (it was still rare for such undertones to be sustained throughout the bulk of a film) keep it spicy if not as naughty as the ads suggested. Once the cat is out of the bag, however, and good confronts evil for the climax, the screwball element is largely dropped, and the final set piece is pure Hitchcock; Milland and Goddard trapped in the spies' headquarters while a major social function is in progress, not knowing who is friend and who is foe, and having to trick their way out. Actually its closest Hitchcockian parallel is in *Saboteur,* wherein Robert Cummings and Priscilla Lane find themselves in a similar predicament and, unpredictably, since it is not yet the climax, do not manage to make good their escape. However, Hitchcock's film was not released until several months later, so one can't accuse *The Lady Has Plans* of plagiarism.

Although never hilariously funny nor unusually suspenseful, *The Lady Has Plans* works well on both levels and is still entertaining. There are signs that Paramount made it fairly quickly so that Goddard (formerly established as a screen partner of Bob Hope's) and Milland could be introduced as a *modern* romantic

ROXIE HART (1942) In jail, Ginger Rogers (left) has her thunder temporarily stolen by new inmate Helene Reynolds, who shows her who's boss.

ROXIE HART Lawyer Billy Flynn (Adolphe Menjou) wins the sympathy of jury foreman William Frawley (right) with Roxie's "demure" behavior on the stand . . .

it depicted than we are today to the forties that produced it.

At the time, definitely outshone by the subtler satires that Preston Sturges was making at Paramount, *Roxie Hart* seemed amusing enough, surprisingly brief for an A film (a mere seventy-four minutes), and another step up in Ginger Rogers's at that time very variable comedy performances. Yet in retrospect it seems one of the better comedies of the forties, with a zest, crackle, and black quality not at all common then.

It is not as good a screwball comedy, nor as successful a satire, as Wellman's earlier *Nothing Sacred*, which played and underplayed its satire with irony. *Roxie Hart* tries hard for laughs and certainly gets them—but its approach is broader and more obvious. It attains its screwball quality through the exaggeration of clichés that are actually funnier when attention is not called to them. And like *Broadway*, a 1929 film (as was *Roxie Hart's* original, *Chicago*) remade in the early forties, it wraps it all up in nostalgia by making the whole story a flashback.

It takes longer to get off the ground, and it slows down occasionally to remind you that it's a flashback, and at the same time unavoidably tips off the probable outcome. But while the remake of *Broadway* pulled most of its punches and made sure that everybody abided by the Code, *Roxie Hart* does retain the authentic spirit of the original. Typecasting works against it somewhat. The film is a satire of yellow journalism and corrupt politics and of the public's insatiable demand for quick sensation—elements basically as topical today as they were in the twenties and to a lesser degree in the forties when the bigger issues of the war brought a certain dignity to the tabloids. Roxie Hart in the original play and film may or may not have been a murderess and certainly was an adulteress. As played in the earlier film by Phyllis Haver, she was attractive but tough, her potential lethal nature quite believable.

Audiences of the forties knew that Hollywood wasn't going to cast Ginger Rogers as a killer and that she certainly wouldn't accept such a part. This rather changes the concept of the role: as rewritten and played, Roxie is now dumb but likable, crude but attractive, and is persuaded to confess and play the role of murderess in a trial, the notoriety from which is

. . . which however does not preclude displaying a trim leg to the appreciative jurors.

supposed to boost her show business career. An element of mild suspense is introduced when the joke appears to go too far, and Roxie seems to be facing a guilty verdict and the noose. (The best gag in the film is also the only underplayed one. Back home, Father reads the news in the paper and tells Mother excitedly, "They're going to hang Roxie!" Mother just continues her rocking on the porch and calmly replies, "What did I tell you?")

Roxie's husband (George Chandler) is a minor opportunist with relatively little footage. In the silent film he (Victor Varconi) was a focal character, a sympathetic victim of Roxie's unfaithfulness who finally finds happiness with another woman only after he has thrown his wife out.

Subtlety is not a major asset of this *Roxie Hart,* and running gags are repeated too much: Roxie carefully hiking up her skirt to charm the jury with her knees, the judge rushing to strike a pose and making sure that he's in every picture the newsmen take. Of the players, only Sara Allgood (as the prison matron who casually knocks out both Roxie and Two Gun Gertie, a rival for Roxie's notoriety, when they get into a hair-pulling fracas) underplays in the tradition of good satire. But at least the other roles *can* be played for flamboyance, and what they lose in subtlety they gain in energy. Adolphe Menjou, as the totally unethical defense lawyer Billy Flynn (a role that John Barrymore could have played magnificently in the thirties), has some beautiful dialogue to which he does full justice. Lynne Overman as a crime reporter always looking for an angle to make the story even more sensational; William Frawley, as the lead jurist, using his flexible face to create some magnificent expressions of distaste and disapproval as he disagrees with the prosecutor's condemnation of Roxie; Iris Adrian as the strident Two Gun Gertie; and dear old, bumbling Nigel Bruce—all lend magnificent support to Rogers.

If her comedy work is a little loud and obvious here, it can be argued that it is entirely consistent with the role Rogers plays, and she certainly rates credit for agreeing to a frizzy hairstyle and unattractive gum-chewing mannerisms that were a far cry from her usual ladylike comedy performances. (Perhaps to make up for the negative qualities of the role, she is

211

given an impromptu tap dance on the iron stairs of the jailhouse, a charming piece of punctuation in an otherwise ceaselessly noisy and frenetic comedy.) George Montgomery must surely rank as the most passive of all screwball heroes; as an admiring cub reporter, he has little involvement with Roxie, and his main function is to provide continuity and a link with the flashback framework.

THE MAJOR
AND THE MINOR

(PARAMOUNT, 1942)

Directed by Billy Wilder; screenplay by Wilder and Charles Brackett, from a story by Fannie Kilbourne and a play by Edward Childs Carpenter.

LEADING PLAYERS:
Ginger Rogers, Ray Milland, Rita Johnson, Robert Benchley, Diana Lynn.

Preston Sturges's success as a screenwriter turned director made it easier for his studio—Paramount—to offer the same opportunity to Billy Wilder. While Sturges had to prove himself by two smaller films first, before being rewarded with *The Lady Eve*, Wilder was able to make the leap straight from screenwriter of *Ball of Fire* to director of a prestige A, *The Major and the Minor*.

The Major and the Minor is perhaps more technically than accurately a screwball comedy, by virtue of its overriding masquerade plot. Ginger Rogers, a manicurist who runs afoul of the lecherous Robert Benchley in his apartment (though had she stood her ground, she should probably have found him quite harmless), is fed up with the big city, pines for home, but lacks the fare to get there. So she masquerades, complete with lollipop and pigtails, as a twelve-year-old in order to get a half-price ticket on the train—and because of wartime space shortages ultimately finds herself sharing quarters with Ray Milland, an officer at a military school.

The sexual implications of their sharing

THE MAJOR AND THE MINOR (1942)   Ray Milland and Ginger Rogers in the title roles.

quarters, and the major's growing fondness for a girl he believes to be only twelve, are surprisingly risqué for a film of 1942 and in later years would certainly have been expanded beyond the bounds of good taste. However, the limitations of the period prevent the film from, in a sense, letting loose and becoming a full-fledged screwball comedy. It succeeds as much on wit and charm as it does on zaniness. Benchley reappears and is bewildered at why the girl seems so familiar. Diana Lynn is particularly appealing as the teenager who befriends Ginger and helps her in her masquerade.

Ginger's child masquerade is hardly convincing, although to her credit she pantomimes well and avoids the mugging of *Tom, Dick and Harry*. Also, the script contrives a Jekyll and Hyde angle so that she appears occasionally as an extremely well-groomed and gowned adult, effortlessly wooing Milland away from his unsympathetic fiancée, Rita Johnson. The extreme contrast between the adult Ginger and her child masquerade makes the latter seem a more impressive acting feat, even if it doesn't add to its conviction.

Despite offering one of the craziest of all

screwball comedies that year, Paramount's 1942 comedic releases nevertheless offered definite signs that the screwball cycle was leveling off. *The Lady Has Plans* and *Take a Letter, Darling* both pulled their punches, and *The Remarkable Andrew* and *I Married a Witch* (though the latter was eventually sold to United Artists because of a product surplus) stressed whimsy and fantasy. Another Ray Milland starrer, *Are Husbands Necessary?* was straight romantic farce.

One of the most pleasing aspects of *The Major and the Minor* is that it still presents Wilder as a writer-director with the writing half dominant, recalling the sophistication of such earlier credits as *Bluebeard's Eighth Wife* and *Midnight*. It has none of the leering heavy-handedness that would dilute the charm of many of Wilder's later directorial works, even though that heavy-handedness in many cases, especially with *Some Like It Hot*, added to the commercial success of the films.

THE MAJOR AND THE MINOR   Without enough money for a full fare home, Ginger masquerades as a twelve-year-old to ride at half fare, and arouses the paternal (?) instincts of Tom Dugan.

THE MAJOR AND THE MINOR   Robert Benchley is a shade too amorous for part-time stenographer Ginger, who beats a hasty retreat from his apartment.

THE PALM BEACH STORY

(PARAMOUNT, 1942)

Written and directed by Preston Sturges.

LEADING PLAYERS:
Joel McCrea, Claudette Colbert, Rudy Vallee, Mary Astor, William Demarest, Franklin Pangborn, Robert Dudley, Robert Greig, Sig Arno, Jimmy Conlin, Jack Norton, Robert Warwick.

Many latter-day critics and historians, seeking to tidy up the field of screwball comedy, point to *Ball of Fire* as being the "official" end to the cycle. Why they should be so anxious to *find* an exact end to such a wonderful group of films is puzzling; even harder to understand, since the war was supposedly the catalyst, is why they

213

PALM BEACH STORY (1942)   The Wienie King (Robert Dudley) stakes Tom (Joel McCrea) with enough money to follow the latter's errant wife to Florida.

ning with a crazy-quilt slapstick sequence behind the credits—a sequence that doesn't make sense until it is explained in the very last scene, and even then makes *little* sense—the film builds like a snowball, accelerating its pace and its fun as it progresses. It introduces new characters purely for the sake of having them solve an immediate plot problem, then moves on to the next insane sequence, arrives at Palm Beach at the approximate midway point, and changes pace yet again as a whole new set of characters are brought on. Of all the screwball comedies, it is the one where the plot should be (at best) hinted at, never described.

Joel McCrea's idiotic invention is taken seriously by everyone, and even eventually financed. The film's major set piece—the Ale and Quail gun club running amok aboard the night train to Florida (with conductor Alan Bridge finally abandoning their car in the middle of nowhere)—is really just an expansion of

should select a film made *before* America's entry into the war.

Quite certainly the war brought to an end a way of life that had been a mainstay of the screwball comedy. (But after all, the western depicted a way of life long extinguished, and it was going stronger than ever in the early forties.)

If there had to be an official end to screwball comedy, then *The Palm Beach Story* is the most likely candidate. By switching his field of operations to Palm Beach, Florida, Sturges was able to satirize—*demolish* might be a better word—a lifestyle of the rich that did still exist. And no screwball comedy was more determined to be fun from the word go, without regard to logic, and without even a hint of an inner meaning or a social criticism. While the comparisons are pointless, it is probable that, purely as films, *Sullivan's Travels* and *The Lady Eve* are Sturges's best. But there can be no question that *The Palm Beach Story* is his funniest. Begin-

214

PALM BEACH STORY
Stranded without clothes or money en route to Florida, Gerry (Claudette Colbert) fabricates an outfit from train curtains, and is championed by John D. Hackensacker III (Rudy Vallee). Waiter Mantan Moreland looks on in amazement.

PALM BEACH STORY   In Florida, Tom catches up with Gerry, but Priness (Mary Astor) is determined to land him as a husband, over the objections of unspecified-nationality foreigner Toto (Sig Arno).

a single situation set up to get Claudette Colbert from New York. One of Sturges's most inspired and lovable characters, the semideaf Wienie King (Robert Dudley), likewise exists only to appear at the right moment to finance McCrea's pursuit of his wife. And one of the funniest single lines in the film—the train porter's put down of millionaire Rudy Vallee—would require a paragraph of explanatory buildup to make it explicable, and it would spoil all the fun. Analyzing *The Palm Beach Story* is rather like dissecting an artichoke; pull all the individual leaves away and you know what you've got—but you no longer have an artichoke—or any fun.

Perhaps the biggest comedic surprise of *The Palm Beach Story* (and one that can be discussed, in moderation, without spoiling the fun) is Vallee, hitherto a pleasant crooner and a totally bland player. Under Sturges's direction, his blandness is exploited, and Vallee, bright enough to know what is happening, goes along with it and turns his millionaire into such a brilliant piece of comic invention that it became his stock-in-trade ever after. Sturges himself had Vallee repeat the role (though with subtle variations) in *Unfaithfully Yours*, while less imaginative directors merely had him copy the performance verbatim. As an incredibly rich, sloganeering, and patriotic American, Vallee uses his unemotional voice to deliver a running commentary on the foibles of the super rich and the character weaknesses of virtually everybody he doesn't like. Buying a breakfast for Colbert on board the train, he pontificates on the relative merits of the fifty-cent and the seventy-five-cent meal, yet later spends thousands of dollars buying her new clothes, carefully listing every purchase in a little notebook, commenting that he often wonders why he does it since he never bothers to add the figures up. Anything that he disagrees with is "un-American"; of McCrea (believing Colbert's absurdly manufactured tale of his abuse and neglect) he says in a burst of outrage, "Why, chivalry is not only dead, it's decomposing!"

Vallee is only one member of a screwball family that seems to have none of the problems of the Bullocks in *My Man Godfrey*. There's Mary Astor, his sister, and a thinly disguised nymphomaniac, who keeps Toto (Sig Arno) around like a pet dog, forcing him into easy submission to her whims by threatening to get rid of him entirely. Toto speaks no English, but grunts and whimpers expressively. McCrea, whose performance is Sturges's *Sullivan's Travels* the year before was something of a revelation and easily his finest acting to date (in a serio/comic role), is here rewarded with a purely comedy role, and proves once again that the old adage that it takes a great actor to play comedy well is entirely true. His timing, his double takes, his nuances of expression, facial as well as vocal, are nothing short of superb.

Underappreciated for too long, *The Palm Beach Story* is one of those few comedies that isn't hurt by television viewing (apart from the fact that its glossy sets and art direction will be lessened in their impact). In fact, seeing it without an audience will enable you to hear and savor all the great lines that you'd partially miss in an enthusiastic theater audience. The question of who was our greatest comedy performer—W. C. Fields, Keaton, Chaplin, Lloyd,

Laurel and Hardy, even some from later generations—will probably never be settled, nor can it or should it be. But there can surely be no dispute as to who was our funniest, cleverest, wittiest screenwriter. If not Preston Sturges, then who?

TO BE OR NOT TO BE
(ALEXANDER KORDA—
UNITED ARTISTS, 1942)

Directed by Ernst Lubitsch; Screenplay by Edwin Justus Mayer, from an original story by Melchior Lengyel and Lubitsch.

LEADING PLAYERS:
Jack Benny, Carole Lombard, Robert Stack, Stanley Ridges, Sig Rumann, Lionel Atwill, Charles Halton, Felix Bressart, Tom Dugan, Henry Victor.

Time has more than vindicated *To Be or Not to Be*. While always regarded as a major Lubitsch comedy, it was initially attacked for being "tasteless" and for exploiting the plight of occupied Poland during World War II. The shocking death of Carole Lombard immediately prior to its release also placed an unfair burden on the film's reception. In vain Lubitsch protested that he was saluting the heroic spirit of the occupied Poles, and that one of the best propagandist methods to combat Nazism was to satirize its own rigidity, fears, and insecurities. Regardless of a mixed press, it was a success, and after the war came to be regarded as one of Lubitsch's finest films on several levels. It was both a screwball comedy and a black comedy—areas not unrelated, but here seeming to work on separate and mutually effective levels. It was also an engrossing Resistance suspense drama, sometimes so holding that one hardly noticed that comedy might be lacking entirely and deliberately for quite long stretches, but it also welded comedy and suspense effectively when required. Far from least, it proved to be an almost perfect screen vehicle for Jack Benny, adapting his radio persona to a role and a narrative where his special style could be utilized to the maximum, but

TO BE OR NOT TO BE Schultz (Henry Victor) interrupts a tete-à-tete between Professor Siletzsky (actually Joseph Tura, the Great, GREAT Polish actor in disguise, played by Jack Benny) and Mrs. Tura (Carole Lombard).

TO BE OR NOT TO BE (1942)   Jack Benny (right) and aide Peter George Lynn offer a toy tank to a Hitler Youth to betray his parents.

TO BE OR NOT TO BE   The corpse of the real Siletzky (Stanley Ridges) lies in the chair, and imposter Benny has remarked on their slight resemblance. "Oh, so you *noticed* that?" smirks Ehrhardt (Sig Rumann, second left) who is flanked by Hans Schumm at extreme left, and Henry Victor, next to Benny.

TO BE OR NOT TO BE   Robert Stack (wearing cap) is given instructions by Charles Halton and Peter George Lynn (left) and Benny for his part in the final escape.

TO BE OR NOT TO BE   One of the film's delights was its use of character actors who played their roles straight or with a subdued sense of fun: left, Charles Halton as the manager of the troupe; right, Lionel Atwill as its leading "ham."

not in an obtrusive star-vehicle role. Benny himself was delighted with the film, considered it easily his best work, and later allied himself with Lubitsch and Lombard against prerelease attempts to change or soften it. As for Lombard, while not her best role (and to her credit, she was content to let much of the funniest material go to Benny), it was a wonderful swan-song, showing her at her glamorous, wittiest, and zaniest best. (Former Lubitsch star Miriam Hopkins had been considered for the role and immediately began jockeying for more footage and the dominant half of the costarring duo, whereupon she was dropped from the running. Teamwork was both the essence of the film's modus operandi and an important theme within the film; a temperamental star could have wrecked both.)

To Be or Not to Be is a complex story about a troupe of actors in occupied Poland who join forces with a Polish flier with the RAF to stop a spy (Stanley Ridges) before he can expose the underground leaders, and then escape to England. It is broken down into a series of suspenseful encounters with the Nazis, most of them comic as well as thrilling, and despite a long running time (99 minutes) it builds up an almost breathless excitement to its closing escape and chase, but still taking time out to punctuate that excitement with individual gags. Unusual for Lubitsch, he was not working from a play or novel, but from an original story of which he was one of the authors. His love of acting as a profession (he had been an actor before turning to directing, albeit not a very *good* one!) and his obvious sympathy for the fate of occupied Europe is apparent throughout, both attitudes usually expressed through

TO BE OR NOT TO BE   The great set of an important public square in Warsaw for the film's
opening sequence. Cameraman Rudolph Maté and, a few steps below him, Ernst Lubitsch,
can be seen to the right of the camera operator.

the mouth of Felix Bressart, one of his favorite character actors and here playing a bit player with the Polish acting troupe. Looking at the film through postwar eyes, and especially the eyes of the eighties and nineties when we have so much more perspective on those war years, its poignancy and sincerity are so genuine, and the most jagged barbs of its wit directed so firmly against the Axis invaders, that the earlier complaints now seem more than a little picayune.

Despite the wartime background and the intrusion of action melodrama, the essentials of screwball comedy remain firmly implanted. Benny and Lombard play egotistical actors, much in love and married, yet subject to fits of personal and professional jealousy—rather like Leslie Howard and Bette Davis in *It's Love I'm After* in the thirties (except that *their* marriage, planned for the start of the film, was delayed until its conclusion). The marriage in *To Be or Note to Be* is solid, but threatened by the fanatical devotion to Lombard of the young pilot (Robert Stack). Masquerades and deceptions abound and rebound. An early scene shows Jack Benny apparently as a Nazi officer trying to persuade a young boy to betray his parents. Only after some minutes does the camera pull back to reveal that it is a scene in a play. Hitler appears on the streets of Warsaw. It too is (after a big build-up) revealed as a masquerade—which later is repeated in the film's climax, Tom Dugan posing as Hitler as part of the escape ruse. Actors of the troupe masquerade as Nazis, almost giving the game away by their need to "make the most" of their parts. In order to gain time, Lombard poses as a woman willing to be a spy. And the most complicated masquerade of all is Benny's as the traitor spy, Stanley Ridges. Incredibly, Ridges (who was an excellent character actor and almost a double for writer Ben Hecht, who used Ridges as a spokesman for some of his best lines in the films he'd produced in the thirties) *did* look remarkably like Benny in height and stature and when both were fitted up with a trick beard. Ridges is murdered on stage (in an eerie scene worthy of Lang or Hitchcock) and Benny replaces him.

The masquerade is convincing, but also funny since Benny has no information to impart to the Gestapo and has to feed the ego of head Nazi biggie Sig Rumann (one of his greatest comedy roles) by telling him that he is known everywhere as Concentration Camp Ehrhardt. Rumann's pleased response, and his self-satisfied, oft-repeated, "So, they call me Concentration Camp Ehrhardt!" became a catch-phrase with lovers of the film—and still is. The masquerade goes through many twists and turns including one when the Nazis discover the body of the traitor, and place it in a room where Benny, in disguise, is waiting. Thinking quickly, Benny shaves the corpse's face, replaces the shaved beard, and later is able to talk his way out of the embarrassing situation with Rumann by pulling off the "fake" beard and reestablishing his own "genuine" identity, to Rumann's embarrassment. Whereupon Lionel Atwill, one of the acting troupe, acting on a wild plan of his own, rushes in dressed as a Nazi officer to arrest impostor Benny and spirit him away to safety. But Rumann won't be fooled again, and protests. In one of the film's great non-sequitur lines, Atwill pulls off Benny's fake beard and says witheringly to Ehrhardt/Rumann, "You mean you saw a *beard* and you didn't *pull* it?" Rumann's constant switches from sly menace to abject confusion and sheer terror (when he makes an innocent remark that might be considered belittling to Hitler) and his plaintive cries for "Schultz!" create a comic masterpiece out of the role . . . no small achievement in wartime when any Nazi, even a foolish one, was automatically hated. Rumann is so endearing that it's both a big laugh and a relief when in the film's climax, in complete disgrace (at having apparently tried to seduce Hitler's girlfriend, not knowing that both she and Tom Dugan as the tip-toeing Hitler are more masquerades), he shoots himself behind closed doors—but after the echoes of the shot die down, we hear again the pitiful cry, "Schultz!"

If this book had to limit itself to only ten screwball classics, then *To Be or Not to Be* would certainly be one of them. Whatever merits Mel Brooks's 1983 remake possessed were gleaned from following the original almost scene by scene. But it couldn't copy wit or style (or Rudolph Maté's stunning camerawork) and was forgotten as soon as its End Title hit the screen.

SAN DIEGO, I LOVE YOU
(UNIVERSAL, 1944)

Directed by Reginald LeBorg; written and produced by Michael Fessier and Ernest Pagano, from an original story by Ruth McKenney and Richard Bransten.

LEADING PLAYERS:
Louise Allbritton, Jon Hall, Edward Everett Horton, Eric Blore, Buster Keaton, Irene Ryan, Florence Lake, Chester Clute, Tom Keene, Vernon Dent.

When *San Diego, I Love You* appeared, unheralded, in late 1944, it was acclaimed as something of a sleeper. It was especially popular in England, where it even rated a major London premiere in Leicester Square, and where its freshness and lack of pretention made it a pleasant change from the endless grind of service comedies (Betty Hutton in A movies, Elyse Knox in B counterparts) or the aggressive knockabout of Abbott and Costello and

SAN DIEGO I LOVE YOU (1944) Louise Allbritton and Jon Hall, a likable romantic comedy team.

SAN DIEGO I LOVE YOU Another screwball family, but without a mother or lazy brothers. Ambitious Louise Allbritton and inventor/father Edward Everett Horton raise a brood of lovable tykes.

SAN DIEGO I LOVE YOU Aboard the inevitable train, railroad tycoon Jon Hall is gypped out of his private compartment—but is eventually glad to share the family's food.

221

Red Skelton. Perhaps because it *was* such a refreshing change of pace, it tended to be overrated by the critics, although it caused no great stir at the box office (nor had it any need to, since it was an economical production) and was soon forgotten again. And largely forgotten it has remained, only owing its occasional return to life to a charming sequence with Buster Keaton, which sometimes causes it to be included in the more imaginative and comprehensive Keaton retrospectives.

One of the genuine without-reservations screwball comedies of the war years, *San Diego, I Love You* tells of the adventures of the motherless McCooley brood, ruled by big sister Virginia (Louise Allbritton) and supported by the barely adequate earnings of teacher/father Edward Everett Horton. When one of his inventions—a new kind of life raft—is apparently accepted by a San Diego company filling war contracts, daughter Virginia takes the bull by the horns, tenders his resignation to the school board, and dips into the family savings to take them all to San Diego. (The family is rounded out by four small boys.) Apart from Virginia's lack of caution and her father's bumbling excess of it, it's a fairly normal family, given the boys' periodic pranks against the neighbors and the occasional explosions and clouds of black smoke caused by Horton's experiments. They pick up the obligatory screwball retinue when they arrive at San Diego and buy a house, virtually governed by a crybaby valet, Nelson (Eric Blore), who refuses to be fired and sabotages all attempts to sublet or sell the house, and is soon joined by Irene Ryan, she of the perpetually quivering lower lip, who mistakenly comes to the wrong house having rented a room by phone, and once installed refuses to be moved, despite the peculiar behavior of the family, who have no idea who she is!

Prior to arrival in San Diego, the necessary battle-of-the-sexes motif is set in motion by having the family move into and take over the temporarily vacant train compartment of John Caldwell (Jon Hall), who not only virtually owns the railroad, but also is of course the businessman they are en route to see.

Most of the wartime comedy ploys of unavailable train space and virtually nonexistent hotel accommodations are brought into play, but usually with unexpected touches of warmth or twists of humor that keep them fresh. The invention, it turns out, is no good—its manufacture authorized by the well-meaning but totally inefficient Chester Clute. Refusing to accept the exasperated Caldwell's word for it, Virginia tries it out in the Pacific Ocean and is saved from drowning only after a hectic last-reel chase. Fortuitously, some of the powder used in the flares she sets off to signal her position turns out to have potential as a deadly new explosive, so the family fortune is made, and a new matrimony-minded Caldwell succumbs, as the screwball heroes always do. But this story line and the attendant wranglings at home with Nelson and the mysterious lady tenant (one notes that the script is based on an original story by Ruth McKenney, author and protagonist of *My Sister Eileen*) are merely an excuse to offer a series of amusing, bizarre, and even wistful set pieces that have little to do with the plot proper and do not even relate to the wartime milieu, yet somehow never seem contrived or out of place. They include a visit to the San Diego Zoo; a hilariously written and staged barbershop brawl in which sundry stuntmen (Dave Sharpe, Richard Talmadge, and Dale Van Sickel among them) refuse to believe Virginia's protestations of Caldwell's innocence in the matter of her black eye and decide to mete out rough justice to him; and best of all the happily not overdone (through possibly overpraised) bus sequence.

In this touching and funny episode, Virginia muses about the tedium of the bus following the same route day in and day out, and how nice it would be to drive along the beach instead. At first hostile, then adamant in his refusal, but finally weakening, bus driver Keaton gives in. The weak and henpecked passengers apologize for their lack of backbone and leave. A housewife plans to leave to cook her husband's supper, then argues aloud with herself about how he'll be dissatisfied no matter what she does and resolutely sits down again. A husband complains about his wife's wet, slobbering kisses and looks forward to escaping them at least once. Two homely, lonely souls (Hobart Cavanaugh and Victoria Horne) sense adventure and possibly romance and eventually wind up in each other's arms. The longest single segment is when the passengers plead or justify their cases, and because the dialogue is so genuinely funny, it doesn't seem overlong. The sequence under way, it is over all too soon—like the adventure itself—but is all the more effective and touching for *not* dwelling on aftermaths. One wonders whether Keaton contributed anything to this gem of a sequence other than his presence.

To a degree, *San Diego, I Love You* suffers from the same malady that afflicts George Stevens's wartime comedy about housing shortages in Washington: those elements are no longer topical and date, leaving entertainment to other elements of the script and to the warmth of the playing. Much of the reflexive pace and gusto that kept these films on the go during the war translates into mere energy and noise today. Fortunately *San Diego, I Love You* transcends its wartime framework, especially in the second half when the mechanics of plot establishment are pushed aside and the individual (and in many cases timeless) sequences get a chance to work on their own merit. The fact that the screwball family seems to have the family of Capra's *You Can't Take It With You* as a fairly direct ancestor also helps to downplay the wartime setting.

Perhaps, though ironically, the real pity is that—whether it deserved it or not—the film was praised so highly by the critics, the *New York Times*'s Bosley Crowther a notable and harshly sour exception. Fessier and Pagano made a promising writer-producer team who had earlier concocted some engaging near-screwball comedies such as *Fired Wife* and *Her Primitive Man*. They obviously controlled and dominated their films, rarely using big or "strong" directors—although Reginald Le-Borg, normally associated with the slightly classier kind of B horror movie rose to the occasion beautifully with *San Diego, I Love You*, and it was easily his best film. But the praise directed at Fessier and Pagano almost immedi-

ately impaired the best element of their work—its easygoing spontaneity. The offbeat elements in *San Diego, I Love You* seem to arise naturally from the plot and characters, but the team's later films *forced* the offbeat and the philosophical. The two were unfortunately prone to repetition, not in the way that Laurel and Hardy would build a gag via anticipation and a *tangential* repetition, but in the assumption that if a gag is funny once, its unvaried repetition throughout the film will be as funny each time. (There are hints of this already in *San Diego, I Love You*, as in the running gag of one of the younger McCooley children constantly kicking the Jon Hall character in the shins to express disapproval of even the smallest infraction of etiquette.)

The flaw was appreciably increased in Fessier and Pagano's later and more expensive musical comedy *That Night With You*, a Susanna Foster–Franchot Tone film. Apart from their highly entertaining western spoof *Frontier Gal* (discussed elsewhere, but also by no means free of the curse of repetition; in fact the same curse of a shin-kicking youngster!), their later work was disappointing. If Keaton's sequence tended (later) to be overrated, as was the famous W. C. Fields episode in *If I Had a Million* (1932), it was still the highlight of the film. Yet Keaton was shamefully wasted by the team in their 1945 follow-up, *That's the Spirit*, which with marked lack of originality reprised Keaton's philosophic bus driver by turning him into a philosophic lunch-wagon attendant. Unfortunately they gave him nothing to do, and nowhere to go.

Apart from its other charms and merits, *San Diego, I Love You* (the title is worked in naturally and effectively by the way, so casually that it is almost thrown away) also has the infallible Edward Everett Horton in a major role—no minor treat in the forties—and pretty Louise Allbritton, perhaps trying just a shade too hard to be another Carole Lombard, although as she had shown us the previous year in *Son of Dracula*, she was really better suited to being another Gloria Holden!

FRONTIER GAL

(UNIVERSAL, 1945)

Directed by Charles Lamont; written and
produced by Michael Fessier and Ernest Pagano.

LEADING PLAYERS:
Yvonne de Carlo, Rod Cameron, Andy Devine,
Fuzzy Knight, Sheldon Leonard, Andrew Tombes,
Beverly Simmons, Jan Wiley, Clara Blandick.

FRONTIER GAL (1945)   Boy meets girl: Rod Cameron and
Yvonne de Carlo.

Although not an important film in itself, *Frontier Gal* is interesting and notable for welding together two increasingly dominant trends in comedy. First, and especially at Universal where *Destry Rides Again* had been such a big hit in 1939, there had been a tendency toward more sex and broader comedy in westerns. *Trail of the Vigilantes* (1940) was light on sex, but strong on both satire and burlesque, giving a cast of ensemble-working comics the opportunity to kid western clichés and introduce slapstick into traditional western action. Though it wasn't a screwball comedy, it could easily have been diverted into one. *Frontier Gal* made up for its shortcomings in that area and might even be termed the definitive battle-of-the-sexes western.

Second, and specifically since *The Awful Truth* and *My Favorite Wife*, screwball comedies had been more and more openly concerned with what Joel McCrea termed "topic A" in *The Palm Beach Story*, namely teasing, comic-suspense sequences aimed at getting the protagonists into bed together before the fade-out. This wasn't the delicate Production Code problem that might be imagined, since in most cases the boy and girl were already married, and bedding before midnight, or whatever the plot contrivance was, merely warded off what was now an unwanted divorce. In *Frontier Gal* the situation is taken to an almost tasteless extreme: the two sequences of connubial passion, though "legal," amount to rape. Not only is it supposed to be funny, but also it presents as acceptable behavior that which had been unthinkable for a western hero since some of the gutsier silents.

Rod Cameron plays a drifter who is looking for the man (Sheldon Leonard) responsible for a crime Cameron has been blamed for. Wandering into a saloon, he strikes up a flirtatious friendship with a saloon singer, Yvonne de Carlo (a role the temperamental Maria Montez had turned down), and apparently carries his lighthearted wooing too far. Falling for him and convinced that he means to marry her, she arranges a wedding ceremony in the saloon—only to find that he has no intention of marrying her, since he's engaged to "a lady" back East. Infuriated and insulted, she saves face by forcing him into a shotgun marriage and then tells him to get out of her life. Equally upset, he whisks her off to a mountain cabin where she fights tooth and nail, but is finally subdued by him. Although the physicality of the sequence is amusing—certainly de Carlo always made a colorful wildcat—the sexual undertone is far from edifying.

This sequence was responsible for the film's being retitled *The Bride Wasn't Willing* in England, partly to make it sound more titillating and to justify the "adult" rating slapped on it

FRONTIER GAL   Bringing up baby can be a problem: (from left) Fuzzy Knight, Andy Devine, Frank Lackteen, Rod Cameron, and Andrew Tombes ponder the protocol of disrobing Beverly Simmons.

FRONTIER GAL   Boy gets girl: Rod Cameron and Yvonne de Carlo.

by the British censors, and partly to sell it as something other than a western, of which there was something of a glut on the market at the time.

The next morning, de Carlo is somewhat mollified, won over by the apparent sincerity of Cameron's lovemaking. But to him, it's the equivalent of a one-night stand, and he plans to move on. When the sheriff's posse rides by, she turns him in, knowing him to be a wanted man.

A few years pass. Cameron has served his time and is now back, still seeking Sheldon Leonard and vengeance. Almost immediately he encounters de Carlo, who now has a small child (Beverly Simmons) in tow. When he asks who the father is and is told that he is, his scornful laughter immediately precipitates physical battle between the two. The rest of the film is fairly predictable: the child is used as a running gag and constantly lands Cameron in fistfights and other problems. He brings his "lady" (Jan Wiley) in from the East, intends to divorce de Carlo, marry the gentle Eastern

FRONTIER GAL   Taming of the Shrew, Western style: Papa spanks Mama while daughter watches approvingly.

lady, and then adopt his own child, since he feels (not without some reason) that a saloon isn't the healthiest environment for her.

De Carlo overhears conversation out of context and assumes that Rod is settling down and loves her as much as she really loves him—and then when she finds what he really has in mind, blows her stack again. All these complications are far less tiresome than they probably sound, because the film never forgets that while it has invaded screwball territory, it is still essentially a western, albeit one with its tongue in its cheek. It is packed with fast action—fights, chases, superbly shot running inserts against excellent scenic backgrounds, all in top-grade Technicolor, and with a humdinger of an action climax that is topped by little Beverly Simmons wandering out onto an unstable log perched high above a waterfall. The film has all the zip and speed of a B western and takes itself no more seriously, yet the production niceties—such as John Fulton's trick effects in the literal cliff-hanging climax—lift it into the category of a nicely relaxed A.

Since Rod Cameron had only recently been promoted from a series of slick Universal B westerns and had presumably led his youthful followers into these greener pastures, they must indeed have been somewhat surprised not only by the audacity of the sex scenes but also by the nonpantomimic violence of the fights, in which a lot of "dirty" combat techniques had been imported from the private-eye films of the same period. And *Duel in the Sun* was just around the corner. Westerns would never be quite as innocent again; but not even in the somewhat vulgar and ungainly *Blazing Saddles* would we ever have again a western that could claim to be an *Awful Truth* of the great outdoors.

Needless to say, the gentlewoman from the East (accompanied by her chaperone/aunt) went back there, finally admitting defeat, the villain got his comeuppance, and hero, heroine, and their daughter settled down happily in the West, although without any clear-cut indication of how they were going to support themselves.

MAD WEDNESDAY (THE SIN OF HAROLD DIDDLEBOCK)
(HOWARD HUGHES/UA-RKO, 1947)

Written and directed by Preston Sturges.

LEADING PLAYERS:
Harold Lloyd, Frances Ramsden, Jimmy Conlin, Raymond Walburn, Edgar Kennedy, Jack Norton, Rudy Vallee, Arline Judge, Franklin Pangborn, Lionel Stander, Margaret Hamilton, Alan Bridge, Robert Greig.

What was planned as not only an almost inspired collaboration between Harold Lloyd and Preston Sturges, but also a major comeback for both of them, succeeded partially on the first count and failed (at least commercially) on the second.

In one sense, Howard Hughes was both villain and savior in the affair. The first version of the film probably suffered from an ego conflict between Lloyd and Sturges. Both were used to being in control; in surviving prints of what must have been the last of many cuts of the original film, under the title of *The Sin of Harold Diddlebock*, some Lloyd scenes run too long, as do some of the stretches of (primarily Lloyd) dialogue. This suggests compromise: that Sturges didn't tamper with the scenes that Lloyd liked, while in return Lloyd wouldn't object to some of the excessive dialogue that Sturges had written for him. Hughes obviously didn't like what emerged, put the film on the shelf for tinkering and recutting, and finally released it (though only briefly, before a subsequent withdrawal) in the early fifties under the title *Mad Wednesday*. Substantially shorter, it was for the most part an improvement. Lloyd's dialogue outbursts were still sufficiently lengthy to be funny and to make their points, but they *had* been judiciously pruned. Most of Rudy Vallee's already small role was gone.

However, in order to get some extra laughs, especially for the fade-out, Hughes had added a talking horse (courtesy of the special effect used in Jerry Fairbanks's *Speaking of Animals* one-reelers at Paramount), which slightly upset the controlled screwball ambience and caused it to spill over into *Hellzapoppin* territory. It wasn't needed, and it gave the critics a wedge to attack Hughes for "ruining" Sturges's potential comeback triumph. Actually, for once Hughes rated applause for an intelligent salvage job; in any case, at that time, the original cut had not surfaced and nobody was in any position to hazard a guess as to its superiority or inferiority to the released version.

The film begins with the closing football-game sequence from Lloyd's silent classic *The Freshman;* Lloyd is carried in triumph from the football field in 1925, and in the very next shot (apparently with the same mud and jersey), into the locker room filmed in 1947, a twenty-two-year jump made possible not just by skilled makeup and camerawork but most of all by Lloyd's incredibly unchanged appearance. Businessman Raymond Walburn, an ardent football fan, waxes enthusiastic over Harold Diddlebock's prowess and tells him he has exactly the kind of get-up-and-go needed in his organization. He gives Harold a job, but immediately rebuffs his outpouring of bright ideas . . . "We have too many of those already," he tells him. "Keep them bottled up."

Harold's progress—or stagnation—is recorded through a series of calendars of American presidents above his desk. The music swells triumphantly to a climax as it reaches Roosevelt's fourth term, then trails off to nothing over a bland picture of Harry Truman. (While this may have been a subtle attempt to link Harold and Harry as small-town boys who made good, it's more likely that the Truman image was deliberately anticlimactic and meant to mirror Harold Diddlebock's failure. Since Truman's real stature emerged somewhat belatedly, this particular gag seems a little unkinder in later years than it did at the time.)

It is 1947, and Harold is still in his little unproductive cubbyhole. He is called to the front office by a still dapper Raymond Walburn, who expresses disappointment in the once dynamic Harold's lack of achievement for the company (though he can no longer remember why Diddlebock was hired in the first place) and gives him a bitter little prefiring pep talk that is almost as funny in its callous way as was his prehiring pep talk a quarter of a century earlier: "Unfortunately, I inherited the business. But you will have a chance to start from the bottom, and your rise will be all the more spectacular!"

Morose, Harold collects his life's savings—not as much as they might have been as he'd invested heavily in the company's stock and lost most of it in the crash of 1929—and before he leaves the premises, pays a visit to Miss Otis (Frances Ramsden) with whom he has secretly been in love for years. Apparently he has also been in love with her older sisters over the years, but always somebody else proposed first, or the Depression made marriage financially impossible, so now, although he knows he has no chance with the last and most beautiful of the Otis girls, he'd like her to have the engagement ring he's always carried for her family, so that when the right man comes along, at least she'll have the ring. It's a tender and touching scene, a complete about-face from the brash/bitter humor of the preceding scene with Walburn, and presents Lloyd with his finest (and perhaps only) serious acting opportunity.

Loaded down with cash and nowhere to go, Harold runs into the second of the film's Preston Sturges stock company—nervous, birdlike Jimmy Conlin, in what was probably his biggest screen role. Conlin takes Harold in hand and introduces him to bartender Edgar Kennedy, who, on hearing that Harold has never taken a drink in his entire life, sees this as "something that brings out the artist in me," and an occasion that is, "what is the word . . . *vestal?*" (since the word that he wanted clearly would not be approved by the Production Code). Over protestations, Harold swallows the drink that Kennedy has so joyfully concocted, believing it to be merely a collection of fruit juices. The effect is instantaneous: he brays like a horse (loudly enough to bring cop Frank Moran in from the street), catches sight of his reflection in a mirror, and concedes that he does look burned-out, and that Walburn was right to fire him. Under the influence of more liquor, and the guidance of Jimmy Conlin, Harold sets out to create a new man. The first step is to acquire a whole new wardrobe at the establishment of Franklin Pangborn (who parries wisecracks from Arline Judge) including a coat notable for "the checks within the checks." Harold also flings a large part of his small fortune in the direction of Lionel Stander, making an absurd bet on a horse that cannot possibly win—and of course does. Montage of more horse racing, high living, gambling, drinking—and an awakening to a hangover the next morning. Only it's not the next morning; somewhere he's lost a whole day, as his sour landlady (Margaret Hamilton) is quick to tell him. (This is one of the sequences that most benefits from editing; the explanatory exchanges between Hamilton and Lloyd in the original version are far too long-winded.)

Hoping to return his wardrobe and perhaps get some of his hard-earned money back, Harold rushes into the street to be greeted by another Sturges regular, Robert Greig. He is driving a hansom cab, which, he informs Harold, the latter bought the day before—along with its horse, and Greig, whose services were paid for well into the future. Dismayed, Harold wonders what else he might have done, since his memory of the events have faded along with the effects of the drink. "Bless you, sir, what *didn't* you do?" responds Greig, rattling off a listing of Harold's remarkable gambling successes, financial windfalls, and incredible generosity. At this point Jimmy Conlin reappears to remind Harold that he also bought a circus—and not only do the animals smell badly, especially the puma, but they are also waiting to be fed. Down to the circus grounds they rush, to find Alan Bridge holding the fort. Bridge used to be almost solely a villain in B westerns, used because he had a mustache, looked like a villain, and had a rasping voice. Sturges recognized that he could be funny if he didn't try to be funny and placed him in a whole series of hilarious cameos as house detectives, train conductors, and Marines, where his sour, underplayed style worked beautifully when fed by Sturges's dia-logue. Here, as Jackie the lion nuzzles him affectionately (and terrorizes Harold), Bridge delivers a magnificent little speech on the eating habits of circus animals, particularly the large ones—lions and elephants in particular. He also points out that circus employees have to eat, too, and that none of those working for the circus that Harold has just bought have been paid in months.

First things first. Harold and Jimmy Conlin pay a visit to the Kitty-Pooh home, a charitable institution, where they hope to get some free food for their lions. But the lady in charge, after delivering a tactful little lecture on ways to keep cats from multiplying, is outraged when Harold asks for two tons of raw liver. (Conlin is even more outraged that Harold didn't at least grab a couple of pounds for themselves.)

Realizing that with his inhibitions unleashed by his introduction to alcohol he had no trouble coming up with solutions, Harold discovers that solutions to his current problems also lie within himself and quickly comes up with one. Everybody loves a circus. Everybody hates bankers. So—a banker should buy affection and goodwill by purchasing his circus and putting on a free show for kids. With Jackie the lion on a leash, and Jimmy Conlin in tow, Harold visits all the leading bankers. This is the funniest sequence of the film, a wonderful succession of gags establishing bankers as unlikable and glorying in being so. Jack Norton is shown rubbing his hands gleefully as he dictates a letter to a widow informing her that he is "reluctantly compelled" to foreclose on her. Robert Dudley, the Wienie King from *The Palm Beach Story*, is unimpressed: "Nobody likes me and I don't like nobody . . ."; Then, near-sighted, but catching a glimpse of Jackie the lion, "What you got there, a dog? I hate dogs!" Using his magnifying glass for a better glimpse of the "dog," he gets a sudden enlarged close-up of the lion, which breaks loose in the resulting confusion, trailing a chain that ultimately ensnares both Harold and Conlin. The lion heads for the window and along the narrow ledges high above Wall Street, dragging his keepers behind them.

The sudden switch from one kind of comedy to another was standard procedure for Sturges, but the return to a comedy-thrill climax of *Safety Last* proportions is unsatisfying, at least to those who remembered Harold Lloyd's original sequences, which looked real because they *were* real (apart from nets, doubles, and safety precautions). The climax of *Mad Wednesday*, though skillfully staged and photographed by Curt Courant, is all studio stuff, back projection and mock-up sets, the camera often in "impossible" midair positions. Moreover, the shrieks of fright from Harold and Conlin remind one of the danger and minimize the comedy content. There are only one or two "straight down" shots of an authentic street far below to lend momentary conviction.

True, in 1947, this kind of comedy was so old as to seem new, and the chances are that the majority of audiences didn't remember Lloyd's original high-and-dizzy thrill set-pieces. It's an amusing climax, and as noisy and frenetic as the rest of the film so that a certain continuity of style is maintained, but it's disappointing Lloyd and atypical Sturges. However, in a narrative sense, the stunt achieves what Harold wanted. The resultant publicity sends bankers, financiers (including Rudy Vallee in the only scene left of his small role), and circus impresarios down to the jail where Harold is incarcerated with incredible offers that will pay all

MAD WEDNESDAY (1947)   Harold Lloyd, Jackie the Lion, and Frances Ramsden.

his debts and leave him independently wealthy . . . a typical Lloyd climax. The publicity also brings out the long-forgotten Miss Otis, who, as they ride home, reminds the forgetful Harold that they were married a couple of days earlier. He is contrite, apologetic, ashamed; of course the marriage will be annulled immediately. But Miss Otis points out that it is far too late for that, and anyway, she loves him and wants to stay married to him. Happily, Harold sinks into her arms—and then explodes into a repetition of his earlier liquor-induced horse bray. "That's what I was doing all day Wednesday!" he boasts, as the horse and cab gallops into an almost Chaplinesque fade-out.

Although the plot of failure into overnight success is typical Harold Lloyd material, it is the unleashed frenzy of the Sturges set pieces and his stock company of character comedians that turn it into a screwball triumph. It may lack the essential boy-girl interplay—in fact it is virtually absent except for two scenes at beginning and end, but in all other aspects it qualifies. Only a modest success when it first

MAD WEDNESDAY   A depressed, in-a-rut Harold Lloyd, fired from the job he has held for a quarter of a century, ponders his future—not knowing that one drink is going to change everything!

229

appeared, it seems funnier on each (infrequent) revival, and it is sad that its future availability seems limited to television and home video, neither of which can feed into it the sense of audience participation, love, and approval that Lloyd comedies always needed.

As a postscript, it is worth noting that *Mad Wednesday* was produced in the same year as Chaplin's *Monsieur Verdoux* and took twenty-five days longer to film. Both represented attempted changes of pace for their stars. Both, for very different reasons, were box-office disasters. Chaplin of course had never really been associated with screwball comedy, though the sequences with Martha Raye in *Monsieur Verdoux* had a near-screwball quality. Typical of so many postwar films, its comedy was brooding and black. It dealt with a mass murderer and found its laughter in murder. Whether or not it directly influenced Sturges cannot be known. His comedies had often had black elements and sour, bitter highlights. But he had never made a truly black comedy. But his next, following Chaplin's film by only a year, would be wholly black and possibly the funniest screwball comedy about murder ever made— *Unfaithfully Yours.*

UNFAITHFULLY YOURS

(20TH CENTURY-FOX, 1948)

Written and directed by Preston Sturges.

LEADING PLAYERS:

Rex Harrison, Linda Darnell, Barbara Lawrence, Rudy Vallee, Kurt Kreuger, Lionel Stander, Edgar Kennedy, Alan Bridge, Julius Tannen, Robert Greig.

Although well reviewed at the time, *Unfaithfully Yours* was not a commercial success, and its failure probably had a lot to do with Sturges's rapid decline in Hollywood's eyes. Today it seems a classic of wit and style, though one with admitted imperfections, and its merits are underlined by the very ordinary (and unnecessary) 1984 Dudley Moore remake by Howard Zieff.

Rex Harrison (in his best, most debonair, and most precise performance, rattling off the superb Sturges dialogue with equally superb timing and emphasis) is cast as a famed British musical conductor, clearly (and there are plenty of clues) if amiably based on Sir Thomas Beecham.

When a friend casually suggests that his wife might have been unfaithful, and then produces a detective's report to back it up, Harrison begins—vaguely—to suspect that there might be something in it, and that his idyllically happy marriage (to Linda Darnell) might be in danger from a liaison with his secretary (Kurt Kreuger). As he conducts that night, the three pieces of music—all highly emotional and dramatic—suggest possible scenarios. In one he plans and executes the perfect murder, slashing his wife with a razor and leaving mechanically faked evidence to implicate his secretary. In the second, he envisions standing nobly aside, uniting wife and lover, making life easier for them with a handsome check. In the third, with wicked bravado, he suggests that fate choose the solution via a game of Russian roulette—which, despite overwhelming self-confidence, he loses!

After the concert, he rushes home to put his plans into effect. Somehow, without the nobility and grandeur of Tchaikovsky behind them, they fail miserably. The attempt to set up the perfect murder (virtually a pantomime sequence, other than for sound effects) falters when what he thought was a recording machine turns out to be a disguised roulette wheel. That rectified, the "so simple it operates itself" recorder baffles his every effort to make it work, dropping records, running at slow speed when it should accelerate, in a wonderful assault on all modern "conveniences" that never work. By the time his wife returns from the concert, the apartment is a shambles of broken chairs, toppled bookcases and tables, and tangled wires. Shifting to the grand gesture of the check, he is defeated there, too. The pen doesn't work, and an upturned bottle of ink stains his checkbook beyond repair. The last resort is the Russian roulette, and that doesn't work either, the totally bemused wife

UNFAITHFULLY YOURS (1948) Rex Harrison as Sir Alfred de Carter (right) with Linda Darnell as his wife and Kurt Kreuger as his secretary.

quite destroying his élan with her benign chatter and the simple remark that she played Russian roulette with her father quite frequently. Exasperatedly expressing his doubts about this, he concludes with, "But I could wish that your mother and father had played it *continuously* before you were born!"

Then a chance remark of the wife's explains the misunderstanding that set the whole pattern of hatred and revenge in motion; husband and wife are reunited without the wife's ever knowing what caused her husband's erratic behavior and, incidentally, because of the seething passion in him that night, his greatest conducting triumph!

The plot is a good one, and one can well envision Joseph Mankiewicz approaching it solely as a witty, sophisticated, nonscrewball dialogue piece, and making it work by virtue of writing and performing. Sturges brings that to it, too, but so much more. His musical knowledge was extensive, and satiric use of music had always been an integral part of his comic technique. Here he has the chance to make

UNFAITHFULLY YOURS   In his imagination, Sir Alfred plans the perfect murder down to the smallest detail.

music, logically, a major component of his comedy. The blackness of some of the humor—there is a manic glee in the abandon with which Harrison slashes his (off-camera) wife to death with a razor, yet the exaggerated physicality of the act matches the film's periodic forays into screwball slapstick. Typical is a sequence in which Harrison attempts to burn the despised report brought by the ubiquitous Alan Bridge as the house detective, and a minor blaze in a wastepaper basket practically destroys the entire apartment, with butler Robert Greig and other Sturges reliables tangled in a maze of firemen's hoses as they try to quench the blaze and succeed mainly in soaking each other.

There are moments of real charm: Edgar Kennedy (as another private detective) and Julius Tannen (as a neighbor, a genial Jewish tailor), are both music lovers who become embroiled in Harrison's predicament and are rewarded with prime seats to his concert. Rudy Vallee, in a sense reprising his role in *The Palm Beach Story*, is married to pert blonde Barbara Lawrence, whose dialogue with him is a never-ending put-down of his shortcomings, which he is always too preoccupied to notice. Vallee makes his initial appearance early in the film when an apparently lost airliner finally touches down, and to the worried, harassed counter attendant he brightly remarks, as he adjusts his pince-nez, "There's one very reassuring thing about planes; they *always* come down!" Possibly Vallee's best scene however is the one in which he casually, slyly, insinuatingly, informs Harrison that he has had Harrison's wife tailed by a private detective, and Harrison retorts with one of the most marvelously vitriolic harangues that Sturges ever created, a mounting fury of insults climaxed by Harrison's hope that he'll never see Vallee again. Largely unmoved by this, Vallee, as he is leaving, says, "Since we have tickets, we'll probably see you at the concert tonight." Harrison's final word is, "You probably will. I'm usually *there* when I conduct."

The film is one of those rarities that one can enjoy on two levels: one, it is hilarious, and two, for the sheer joy of hearing the English language so magnificently manipulated and exploited.

Quite incidentally, because the film was made relatively soon after the end of the war, and because Harrison was British, playing an Englishman, there is an unstressed but rather interesting sensitivity to the British still living under conditions of wartime austerity. The Harrison/Darnell household is one of absolute luxury; she has far more clothes than she possibly needs or wants, purchased solely as an expression of his devotion. At times the dialogue goes out of its way to stress that she, too, regards it as a luxury, and when Harrison's bad temper overtakes him, he frequently makes reference to the fact that just one of her dresses, or one of her meals, would be looked on with envy by her British counterpart. Her defensive retort, justified, gives another opportunity to praise the British housewife, who undoubtedly appreciated the gesture.

In only one respect is *Unfaithfully Yours* flawed. At nearly two hours, it is a long film. Not one second of it is boring; with that cast and dialogue it could not be otherwise. But it takes a long time—nearly a third of the film—for the basic premise to be established. By then one has already had so much wit and so many belly laughs that the more original closing two-thirds don't benefit. This is one case where Sturges the writer should have let Sturges the director step in and either rearrange the pattern of the film or possibly make some structural cuts . . . although it's all so funny that it's difficult to see where. And these days, when wit has almost entirely vanished from the screen, it seems churlish even to suggest that *Unfaithfully Yours* might benefit from just a little less brilliance.

NINE

PEAK, DECLINE, AND FALL

LOVE CRAZY (1941)   William Powell continued to team with
Myrna Loy both in the *Thin Man* films and this return to a
zanier thirties style.

CHRISTMAS IN JULY Franklin Pangborn and Raymond Walburn in superb fettle as executives of the coffee company that accepts, then spurns, and then finally accepts Powell's winning slogan.

CHRISTMAS IN JULY (1940) The forties started off well with Preston Sturges's second directorial hit and his first real comedy; Ellen Drew and Dick Powell as the young folks who suddenly see real money when he wins an advertising contest.

While the forties certainly began at a new high with the inspired comedies of Preston Sturges (and films like his *The Miracle of Morgan's Creek* would have seemed like front-rank classics were they not put in the shade by *The Lady Eve* and *The Palm Beach Story*), the proliferation of genuine screwball product was largely limited to the first two or three years of the decade. The earlier entries ranged from the sophisticated (George Cukor's *Two-Faced Woman* with Garbo, much interfered-with by the Production Code, with some reshooting and reediting to make it morally acceptable) to the raucous (William Keighley's *The Bride Came C.O.D.*, like the Garbo film a 1941 release).

The Bride Came C.O.D. was an especial disappointment, since it promised so much. Despite being yet another *It Happened One Night* derivation, the plot had a great deal of originality. Dear old Eugene Pallette crops up once again as the exasperated father of spoiled heiress Bette Davis. Seeking to scuttle her purely publicity-oriented wedding to Jack Carson, he hires

aviator James Cagney to kidnap her and deliver her to him, unmarried. Cagney's interest is at first purely mercenary—even to the extent of charging for his services C.O.D., to be paid for at so much per pound when Davis is delivered and weighed in. Most of the film takes place in the desert; Carson catches up with them, insists on the marriage's taking place, and Cagney is surprisingly docile about it—not letting on that since they are in a different state, the marriage is not legal. One of the foremost of the later *Taming of the Shrew* updates, the film has Davis and Cagney at each other's throats most of the time, and indulging in aggressively physical humor—comic fisticuffs, Davis falling into a cactus patch, losing her dignity and ultimately her pride wherever possible. However, there's a desperation to the comedy. Both stars are too old for their roles and both seem to admit via their performances that they are slumming, even though they seem to be enjoying it. It was a particularly disappointing climax to Davis's and Cagney's fairly regular sorties into orthodox and near-screwball territory. Cagney in particular, in the late thirties and early forties, had a way of walking—or running—through comedy roles, relying more on energy than subtlety. In *Boy Meets Girl* (1938), a potentially very funny Hollywood

234

THE BRIDE CAME C.O.D. (1941) James Cagney and Bette Davis offered tremendous energy to a traditional screwball echo of *It Happened One Night* that had perhaps been repeated once too often. It didn't work.

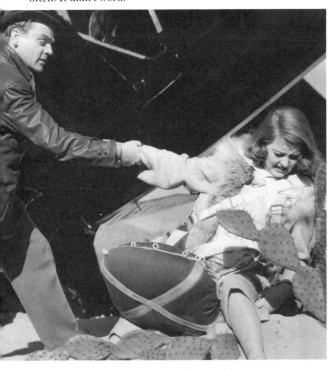

send-up with Cagney and Pat O'Brien lampooning Hecht and MacArthur, Cagney's mugging and fast dialogue delivery were definitely harmful to the film.

Although many of Deanna Durbin's delightful musical comedies of the forties had screwball elements, none of them quite duplicated the quality of her *First Love* (1939), in many ways a kind of *My Man Godfrey* replay felicitously mated with Cinderella motifs. *Nice Girl?* (1941) enjoyed or suffered from the same kind of notoriety as *Two-Faced Woman*, though mainly because critics resented the idea of the wholesome Durbin image being subverted to a mildly risqué one. The film was a casual reworking of *Hot Saturday* (1932) by the same director, William Seiter. Later Durbin films occasionally fell back on screwball's masquerade formula: Deanna is suspected of being a dead millionaire's mistress, is unable to convince anyone otherwise, and resigns herself to making the best of the situation, usually to laudable ends—such as finding a home for Chinese war orphans in *The Amazing Mrs. Holliday* (1943). Mostly though, the Durbin films like *It*

Started With Eve in 1941 (with some, at the time, unrecognized satirizing of *Citizen Kane*) were too charming, sophisticated, and sentimental, to say nothing of being devoted to the obligatory musical interludes, to be characterized as screwball.

A notable near-exception was *Lady on a Train* in 1945 (directed by her husband-to-be, Charles David), which had perhaps a shade too many irons entertainingly in the fire to be limited to a screwball categorization, although all the elements were there. Deanna and David Bruce made an engaging parallel to Nick and Nora Charles, albeit Bruce was a reluctant partner for most of the film; Edward Everett Horton and Allen Jenkins kept the tangential insanity nicely on the move; and the crazy family this time was a menacing one, headed by Elizabeth Patterson, Dan Duryea, and Ralph Bellamy, with the murderer hidden somewhere among them. As a screwball-comedy murder mystery its closest relation was James Whale's *Remember Last Night?* of ten years earlier, but 1945 was the height of film noir, and such noir elements as Elwood Bredell's cinematography and Miklos Rozsa's musical score helped to throw the purely comedic qualities pleasantly and unpredictably off-balance.

WHISTLING IN THE DARK (1941) Conrad Veidt, superb as the villain, Red Skelton as radio sleuth The Fox, and Ann Rutherford as his girl, in the first and best of three screwball comedy-thrillers, followed by *Whistling in Dixie* and *Whistling in Brooklyn*.

The war obviously invaded stories that, a few years earlier, would have been carefree escapades. *Once Upon a Honeymoon* (1942) had Cary Grant and Ginger Rogers as a wonderfully compatible team. Rogers, however, was married to the urbane Walter Slezak, always a delightful "other man" or comic heavy. But here he's a Nazi and has to be disposed of to pave the way for a patriotic and happy union between the two stars. Nazi or not, Slezak is so enjoyable in his role that his too casual death (its melodrama played down by being turned into a deliberately artificial sight gag) leaves a somewhat bad taste. So does a sequence in which Rogers poses as a Jewess so that her servant may escape Nazi persecution. Expectedly, Rogers is "detained," and her subsequent outrage at the inconvenience, and her insistence that she, as an American citizen, should not be treated that way, seem almost to suggest that the tragedy is awkward but understandable for those who happen to be Jewish. Overlong and uneven in its mixture of drama, comedy, and occasional *misfire* comedy, *Once Upon a Honeymoon* is nevertheless one of the more interesting comedies to be born out of America's sudden immersion into World War II.

The same year's *The Talk of the Town*, a George Stevens film costarring Cary Grant, Ronald Colman, and Jean Arthur, likewise took a more serious turn than it might have a year or two earlier—though it did permit Grant (as an innocent on the run, accused of murder) and Colman (as a Supreme Court judge) to bear the delightful names of Leopold Dilg and Michael Lightcap respectively. Not always sure of what it is trying to say, but at least saying it with charm, aplomb, and acting expertise, it is not your basic screwball comedy, but easily could have been. It is all these "nearly" and "could have been" comedies around the beginning of the war that began to slow and finally turn the screwball tide by the end of the forties. It is appropriate that it was Preston Sturges at least who closed off the cycle with *Unfaithfully Yours*, a classic, followed by *The Beautiful Blonde From Bashful Bend*, a western satire that starred Betty Grable but, more importantly, *featured* Rudy Vallee, Hugh Herbert, Margaret Hamilton, and

Alan Bridge. Though a disappointing film, it's a lot funnier than it's usually given credit for.

What happened from the fifties on is outside the scope of this book, though somewhat hinted at in the introductory chapter. Rare, full-scale attempts at reviving bona fide screwball comedy (Howard Hawks's *Monkey Business*, Peter Bogdanovich's *What's Up, Doc?*) were at most spasmodically successful. A Cary Grant vehicle of 1953, *Dream Wife*, at the time seemed like an oasis of sophistication in a barren comedy desert; today it seems merely silly and labored, though not unentertaining. Before the advent of CinemaScope and the full-scale competition of television, some of the best early-fifties comedy writing could be found in the sophisticated scripts of films that were not essentially comedies: *All About Eve* for example, or *Five Fingers*—both of them from Joseph Mankiewicz.

If any one genre has replaced or perhaps supplemented the screwball comedy in the eighties and nineties, it is the parody film— *Airplane, Top Gun, Hot Shots,* the *Naked Gun* movies. These films get their laughs from parody and outrageous sight gags. *Airplane*, the first, was by far the best and most original—not

TWO FACED WOMAN (1941)   Garbo went sexy in this, her last film, mauled by the censors, partially reshot, and unfairly savaged by critics. Despite its compromises, it remains a very funny comedy.

TWO FACED WOMAN   The ubiquitous Melvyn Douglas, Constance Bennett (who came close to stealing the film from Garbo), and Robert Sterling.

MURDER, HE SAYS   MacMurray at the mercy of a murderous family, only *some* of whom are shown here: (from left) Porter Hall, Marjorie Main, Helen Walker, Peter Whitney, and Jean Wallace.

MURDER, HE SAYS (1945)   Fred MacMurray as a salesman investigating the disappearance of fellow salesmen in hillbilly country, and Helen Walker, in a black screwball comedy obviously patterned after *Arsenic and Old Lace*.

least in that it was satirizing a *specific* film, rather than hoping that a scattershot approach of lampooning everything in sight would work.

Considering the boundaries of such a genre, the laugh content of such films has been surprisingly high—the first time around. *Airplane* apart, they are not films that (like the classic screwballs of the thirties) repay repeat viewings.

More and more, contemporary comedies

THE RUNAROUND (1946)   Ella Raines and Rod Cameron (with Broderick Crawford as a third star) in a unique blend of cross-country chase and tongue-in-cheek private eye satire.

EASY TO WED (1946)   Van Johnson and Lucille Ball in a creditable remake of the thirties classic *Libeled Lady*.

CLUNY BROWN (1946)   By the mid-forties Ernst Lubitsch had turned his back on orthodox screwball comedy; *Cluny Brown* was generally genteel, but occasionally the screwball qualities would peep through thanks to situations, characters, and dialogue. Jennifer Jones in the title role as the housemaid who yearned to be a plumber, meets with household staffers Queenie Leonard, Ernest Cossart, and Sara Allgood.

THE BIG HANGOVER (1950)   One of the more underrated fifties screwball comedies: Van Johnson as a war veteran who was trapped in a cellar of liquor, and now gets drunk at the merest suggestion of its smell; and Elizabeth Taylor as the society girl who takes him in tow.

SITTING PRETTY (1946)   The same year at the same studio, one of the big, zany hits was *Sitting Pretty*, launching Clifton Webb (left) on a comedy career as Mr. Belvedere, here with nominal stars Robert Young and Maureen O'Hara.

SITTING PRETTY   Mr. Belvedere provides a no-nonsense lesson in baby sitting.

SOME LIKE IT HOT (1959)   Billy Wilder abandons wit for screwball farce, disappointing the purists among his fans, but creating one of his biggest hits, with Jack Lemmon and Tony Curtis masquerading as members of an all-girl orchestra.

WE'RE NOT MARRIED (1954)   Jane Darwell, "married" couple Ginger Rogers and Fred Allen, and Victor Moore, the justice of the peace who wasn't one when he performed the ceremony.

seem to rely for their inspiration on the screwball comedies of the thirties-along with the hope that their audiences are too young to recognize the pillaging. A mid-1993 release, *The Night We Never Met*, is a more than coincidental rehash of a charming though low-key 1933 comedy, *Rafter Romance*. Too gentle to be a genuine screwball entry, it was directed by William Seiter and starred Ginger Rogers and Norman Foster—the trio who had collaborated the same year on *Professional Sweetheart*, a zany blast at radio advertising. *Rafter Romance* dealt with two impoverished young people, one of whom works at night, the other in the day, who rent (and share) the same apartment. They meet independently and fall in love. Although not exactly a subgenre, it was a theme used with many variations, first during the Depression, and then during the housing and accommodation shortages during World War II.

And Roger Ebert, starting off his review of *Three of Hearts* (released in April of 1993), remarked:

> *Three of Hearts* would have made a terrific 1930s screwball comedy, except that the subject matter would have caused apoplexy

KISS ME STUPID (1964) Critics found this new Billy Wilder comedy tasteless; possibly it was, but it had a curious kind of charm, too. Here are the three leads: Ray Walston (who replaced Peter Sellers), Dean Martin, and Kim Novak.

among the movie censors of the era. It's about a lesbian whose bisexual girlfriend walks out on her—and about how she hires a male escort to seduce and abandon the girlfriend, who will then presumably hate men so much she'll come home.

Just the thing for Carole Lombard, William Powell, and Gail Patrick; but is there a good part in it all for Eugene Pallette?

But these are problems to be faced by somebody—way in the future—writing a history of the descendants of screwball comedy from the sixties on! One of the major problems such a film historian will have to face however is not what to write about, but how to find interesting stills to illustrate his tome.

Time was that the eight-by-ten black-and-white still (backed up by eleven-by-fourteen color stills and title cards) was *the* major advertising accessory. Still manufacture was a work of art, and the studios provided ample time and facilities for photographers to shoot during filming or in photo shoots afterward. Many stills from dramatic films such as *Sunrise* and *All Quiet on the Western Front* were masterpieces of lighting and composition, quite transcending their relationship to a given film. The purpose of the still was to attract customers. Westerns showed stills of action, horror films scenes of menace, and comedies tried to create stills that captured the spirit of the film *and* were funny.

Even the humblest B western was issued with a set of at least twenty-five good stills. These were displayed outside the theater, while the lobby would contain further racks containing stills promoting films appearing over the next few weeks (to say nothing of posters, lobby cards, inserts, and other attention-getters). Enterprising exhibitors would also use these stills for elaborate tie-ins and window displays in their town.

Today the still is virtually unused in advertising. Films are sold via television and radio campaigns, and via newspaper advertising. Theaters no longer use still racks outside to attract passersby, and certainly not inside where any available space is usually devoted to the moneymaking candy concession. (Euro-

GOODBYE CHARLIE (1964)   In a good year for bad taste, this screwball comedy about death and reincarnation was a far cry from the whimsy of *Here Comes Mr. Jordan* in 1941. A notorious womanizer is murdered and is reincarated as a sexy and libidinous Debbie Reynolds(!), confronting Walter Matthau.

SEX AND THE SINGLE GIRL (1965)   Censorship taboos were blurring, and screwball comedies could deal with sex far more openly now–though nobody guessed in 1965 how those restrictions would soon virtually disappear altogether: bed on left, Natalie Wood in center, Tony Curtis and drinks on right.

pean theaters still retain some of the old-time showmanship, and one *can* find stills outside movie houses in France, Germany, and Switzerland.) The sole use for the still today is to plug a star or a film in a newspaper, hopefully with a review or an interview. To that end the still is usually devoted to a large star head, or an obviously posed action or comedy shot—which, since it is often the only one available, is used ad infinitum until its repetition becomes boring.

Glancing through literally a couple of hundred stills from *The Lady Eve,* one is impressed by the number that actually tell the story of the film, by those that concentrate on comedy highlights (Henry Fonda's pratfalls for example), a further group that spotlights each and every character comedian in the film, always caught in a typical bit of business, and a group of admittedly posed two-shots of Fonda and Stanwyck, which nevertheless sell, attractively and accurately, the glamour, excitement, romance, and comedy of their teaming. Not one

still seems to exist that can make *Death Becomes Her* or *Kiss Me Goodbye* seem worth an innocent moviegoer's taking a chance on seeing. Admittedly, they were not very good comedies, but they *did* have selling angles.

And there were many poor comedies in the thirties, too, where a good set of stills probably made all the difference in attendance figures. Perhaps there's no such thing as the casual moviegoer anymore. Movies make their big money after they've left theaters and hit television . . . and still later, the home video market. The still display outside the theater may well be meaningless today; but it's a pity to see such a major and enjoyable aspect of the old moviegoing experience disappear so totally. On the other hand, the kind of movies that made that experience so enjoyable have disappeared, too. A twenty-first century without still displays is probably no harder to bear than a twenty-first century without Preston Sturges and Eugene Pallette.

THE LOVED ONE (1965)   A good point at which to halt this brief post-forties survey. One of the great (if one of the grossest!) cinematic comedy highlights of all time was rotund Ayllene Gibbons's almost sexual delight at the King Crab commercial on television, and the eating orgy that followed with Robert Morse.

THE SCREWBALL FAMILY

A final nod and farewell to some of the stars and character players who have been the mothers, fathers, sons, daughters, family retainers, and friends since screwball comedy began.

Billie Burke, scatterbrained matriarch; Mrs. Topper, too

Walter Connolly, definitive father to madcap heiresses, equally definitive editor

Edward Arnold and Jean Arthur, father/daughter on occasion, opponents on others

Rosalind Russell and Brian Aherne, a second-string Powell-Loy

Charles Winninger, father to Deanna Durbin, Joel McCrea, and others

S. Z. Sakall, excitable Hungarian gentleman's gentlemen to millionaires, and befuddled, kindly uncles

Melvyn Douglas, leading man to just about every leading lady in Hollywood

John Hubbard, smooth farceur, at his screwball best in *Turnabout*

Frank Jenks, wisecracking cops his specialty

Robert Warwick, an old-timer who became a Preston Sturges regular, leading light of the Ale and Quail Club

Charles Butterworth, timid best-friend,
spurned millionaire

Alan Mowbray, millionaire, other man,
ham actor, butler—screwball comedy
would have been lost without him

247

Robert Benchley, boring best friend, lecherous neighbor, well-meaning father

Harry Davenport, occasionally one of the upper crust, usually a sympathetic underling

Raymond Walburn, another Sturges regular: classic blowhard
and blusterer

Rudy Vallee, a bland crooner whom
Sturges turned into a great comedian
(given a great script!)

Charlie Ruggles, equally at home as a debonair or a roustabout

George Chandler, who carved a career out of being thoroughly unlikable at all times; at his best as the husband in *Roxie Hart*

250

Herman Bing, unique accented continental: waiter, private detective, sucker, a passion player who shared a great scene with Barrymore in *20th Century*

Edward Everett Horton, dithering best friend, frequently misunderstood: a major asset for Lubitsch

Lionel Stander, gravel-voiced cynic, used too little in screwball comedy

Cass Daley and Percy Kilbride, useful second bananas, as here in *Crazy House*

Jody Gilbert, the mountain of flesh who made life difficult for Shemp Howard in *Hellzapoppin*, W.C. Fields in *Never Give a Sucker an Even Break*, and here with Red Skelton and rascal in *The Yellow Cab Man*

ORDER NOW!
Citadel Film, Television and Music Books

If you like this book, you'll love the other titles in the award-winning Citadel Film Series, as well as our television and movie books.

From James Stewart to Moe Howard and The Three Stooges, Woody Allen to John Wayne, The Citadel Film Series is America's largest and oldest film book library. With more than 150 titles--and more on the way!--Citadel Film Books make perfect gifts for a loved one, a friend, or best of all, yourself!

A complete listing of the Citadel Film Series appears below. If you know what books you want, why not order now? It's easy! **Just call 1-800-447-BOOK and have your MasterCard or Visa ready. (Tell the operator code #1534)**

STARS
Alan Ladd
Arnold Schwarzenegger
Barbra Streisand: First Decade
Barbra Streisand: Second
  Decade
The Barbra Streisand Scrapbook
Bela Lugosi
Bette Davis
The Bowery Boys
Brigitte Bardot
Buster Keaton
Carole Lombard
Cary Grant
Charlie Chaplin
Clark Gable
Clint Eastwood
Curly
Dustin Hoffman
Edward G. Robinson
Elizabeth Taylor
Elvis Presley
The Elvis Scrapbook
Errol Flynn
Frank Sinatra
Gary Cooper
Gene Kelly
Gina Lollobrigida
Gloria Swanson
Gregory Peck
Greta Garbo
Henry Fonda
Humphrey Bogart
Ingrid Bergman
Jack Lemmon
Jack Nicholson
James Cagney
James Dean: Behind the Scene
Jane Fonda
Jeanette MacDonald & Nelson
  Eddy
Joan Crawford
John Wayne Films
John Wayne Reference Book
John Wayne Scrapbook

Judy Garland
Katharine Hepburn
Kirk Douglas
Laurel & Hardy
Lauren Bacall
Laurence Olivier
Mae West
Marilyn Monroe
Marlene Dietrich
Marlon Brando
Marx Brothers
Moe Howard & the Three
  Stooges
Norma Shearer
Olivia de Havilland
Orson Welles
Paul Newman
Peter Lorre
Rita Hayworth
Robert De Niro
Robert Redford
Sean Connery
Sexbomb: Jayne Mansfield
Shirley MacLaine
Shirley Temple
The Sinatra Scrapbook
Spencer Tracy
Steve McQueen
Three Stooges Scrapbook
Warren Beatty
W.C. Fields
William Holden
William Powell
A Wonderful Life: James Stewart
DIRECTORS
Alfred Hitchcock
Cecil B. DeMille
Federico Fellini
Frank Capra
John Huston
Steven Spielberg
Woody Allen
GENRE
Black Hollywood, Vol. 1 & 2

Classic Foreign Films: From
  1960 to Today
Classic Gangster Films
Classic Science Fiction Films
Classics of the Horror Film
Classic TV Westerns
Cult Horror Films
Divine Images: Jesus on Screen
Early Classics of Foreign Film
Great Baseball Films
Great French Films
Great German Films
Great Italian Films
Great Science Fiction Films
The Great War Films
Harry Warren & the Hollywood
  Musical
Hispanic Hollywood
Hollywood Bedlam: Screwball
  Comedies
The Hollywood Western
The Incredible World of 007
The Jewish Image in American
  Film
The Lavender Screen: The Gay
  and Lesbian Films
Martial Arts Movies
Merchant Ivory Films
The Modern Horror Film
More Classics of the Horror Film
Movie Psychos & Madmen
Our Huckleberry Friend: Johnny
  Mercer
Second Feature: "B" Films
They Sang! They Danced! They
  Romanced!
Thrillers
The West That Never Was
Words and Shadows: Literature
  on the Screen
DECADE
Classics of the Silent Screen
Films of the Twenties
Films of the Thirties

More Films of the 30's
Films of the Forties
Films of the Fifties
Lost Films of the 50's
Films of the Sixties
Films of the Seventies
Films of the Eighties
SPECIAL INTEREST
America on the Rerun
Bugsy (Illustrated screenplay)
The "Cheers" Trivia Book
The Citadel Treasury of Famous
  Movie Lines
Comic Support
Cutting Room Floor: Scenes
  Which Never Made It
Favorite Families of TV
Film Flubs
Film Flubs: The Sequel
Filmmaking on the Fringe
First Films
Frankly, My Dear: Great
  Movie Lines About Women
Gilligan, Maynard & Me
Hollywood Cheesecake
Howard Hughes in Hollywood
More Character People
The Nightmare Never Ends:
  Freddy Krueger & A Nightmare
  on Elm Street
The Northern Exposure Book
The Official Andy Griffith Show
  Scrapbook
100 Best Films of the Century
The 1001 Toughest TV Trivia
  Questions of All Time
The Quantum Leap Book
Sex in Films
Sex In the Movies
Sherlock Holmes
Son of Film Flubs
Who Is That?: Familiar Faces and
  Forgotten Names
"You Ain't Heard Nothin' Yet!"

For a free full-color Entertainment Books brochure including the Citadel Film Series in depth and more, call 1-800-447-BOOK; or send your name and address to Citadel Film Books, Dept. 1534, 120 Enterprise Ave., Secaucus, NJ 07094.